Between Islam and the State

Between Islam and the State

The Politics of Engagement

BERNA TURAM

Stanford University Press
Stanford, California 2007

Stanford University Press
Stanford, California

Library of Congress Cataloging-in-Publication Data
Turam, Berna.
    Between Islam and the state : the politics of engagement / Berna Turam.
        p. cm.
    Includes bibliographical references and index.
    ISBN-13: 978-0-8047-5500-9 (cloth : alk. paper)
    ISBN-13: 978-0-8047-5501-6 (pbk. : alk. paper)
    1. Turkey—Politics and government—1980–   2. Islam and politics—Turkey.
3. Islam and state—Turkey.   4. Nationalism—Turkey.   5. Democracy—Turkey.
I. Title.
DR603.T77   2007
322'.109561—dc22   2006023065

Typeset by BookMatters in 10.5/12.5 Bembo

Contents

To Sevim, Batur, Esra, and James

Acknowledgments

This work originated in 1997 as a field study in Istanbul, my hometown. Since then, it has gradually expanded to Ankara, Almati, Kazakhstan, and North America as a multi-sited ethnography. Many people, organizations and academic institutions have hosted and supported this study at different stages.

The first and smaller version was written in the form of a dissertation project in my most beloved city, Montreal, surrounded by the most supportive intellectual community, my friends and colleagues at McGill University. While the amazing café culture, delicious food and good life in Montreal made the writing of the first versions a real pleasure, the academic support I received was of a unique sort. Most of all, I am grateful to John A. Hall, my mentor, adviser and great friend, for the freedom of ideas, the space and the excellent direction he provided for my work and writing. He never stopped encouraging and motivating me. He always believed that this work was going to become a book, even when I almost lost my courage during long years of revisions. My special thanks goes to Suzanne Staggenborg, Charles Lindholm and Elisabeth Özdalga, whose critiques and comments have always been most helpful.

I appreciate the openness, transparency and cooperation of the Gülen movement, qualities that enabled me to get access to every sphere of the movement. I thank the leader and the followers of the movement for their genuine understanding for my wish to remain distant and critical. I appreciate their cooperation especially because there is an explosion of studies that promote and praise the movement inside and outside of Turkey. I owe special thanks to the movement organizations Gazeteciler Yazarlar Vakfı (Journalists and Writers Foundation) and Istanbul Ilim re Kültür Vakfı (Istanbul Foundation for Science and Culture) in Istanbul, Türk-Kazak Eğitim Vakfı (Kazak-Turk Education Foundation) in Almati and numerous schools, mosques, universities, classrooms, dormitories and prayer groups in Turkey, Kazakstan and the United States, all of which kindly accepted and facilitated my participation. I am also indebted to my friends Selin Sancar, Hande and Ahmet Bitlis for helping me get initial access to people and sites in the movement and the party, and to Sezai Bayar for helping me enter the AKP government in Ankara and interview political leaders and Ministers.

Yeşim Bayar, my wonderful friend and colleague, supported me at every stage of this work and never left me alone in the long, isolating years of writing. She read first and last drafts of several chapters and shared her precious comments. Over the years I became indebted to many colleagues. I thank Joel Migdal, whose line of scholarship this study follows, and Reşat Kasaba, Karen Pfeiffer, Charles Taylor, Said Arjomand, Haldun Gülalp, Metin Heper, Ulf Hedetoft, Mario Diani, Richard Wood, Frank Holmquist, Margaret Cerrulo, Jutta Sperling, Murat Tezcür, Filiz Başkan and Devrim Yavuz for reading and commenting on various drafts of this work. I also thank Fred Weaver and Aaron Berman, my colleagues at Hampshire College, for their support for the scholarship. Hampshire College also offered me the most engaged student body. I especially thank Zoe Joly for her copyediting and all my students, whose challenging questions have made me think further. My friends and colleagues Annalisa Salonious, Jeff Cormier and Chris Hydal helped improve the language at different stages. Many others, but especially Barış Gümüs-Dowes and Aslı Baykal, have given me inspiration by sharing my excitement and preoccupation with this project, and Leyla Neyzi, Ayşe Gül Altinay, and Esra Özyürek have generously shared their experience and knowledge of academic and scholarly issues.

Some of the arguments appeared first in an article in the *British Journal of Sociology*, and a part of the analysis from chapter 4 was published by *Nation and Nationalism*. I thank these journals for permitting the use of some material in the book. The argument benefited to a great degree from many presentations at ASA and MESA conferences and talks, including the ones at Harvard University, the Rockefeller Foundation in Bellagio, Indiana University, Georgetown University, Five-Colleges Middle East Studies Center in Amherst, Queen's University and Dalhousie University in Canada, Aalborg University in Denmark and Tel Aviv University in Israel.

Different parts of the multi-sited ethnography have been funded by various organizations. I am thankful for the generous funding from SPIRIT Institute at Aalborg University in Denmark, McGill University in Canada and Hampshire College at Amherst, Massachusetts. I am also indebted to Taha Parla for allowing me to use the library of Bosphorus University in Istanbul, and Cemal Kafadar for opening the doors of Harvard University's libraries to me. Having access was a luxury of the most unique kind for my writing.

The reviewers and editors of Stanford University Press have turned a potentially exhausting review and editing process into an actual enjoyment. I can never thank Kate Wahl and the reviewers enough for their time and constructive critique they offered to me. Kate displayed the utmost punctuality and efficiency at every stage of the publication process. And the meticulous copyediting of Mike Mollett made a potentially annoying process of reviewing the edit a pleasure for me.

Since 2001, the revisions and expansion of this work have constituted the largest part of my life. Most of all, I thank my family in Istanbul, who have kindly tolerated my long-term seclusions and periodic disinterest in everyday life. They have filled my life with unconditional love when I needed it most during those long days of writing. I am grateful to my parents, Sevim and Batur, my first teachers of freedom, who equipped me with skills of questioning boundaries free of any imposition and indoctrination. I thank my sister, Esra, for being my closest friend and supporter, someone who has always shared her wisdom at the end of the phone line regardless of the time of the day or night. Special thanks go to Semra, Hasan, Nesrin and Solmaz, who came to visit me in my study and work places across the world; Melis, who followed me to Montreal to study with me; and finally my grandmother Nadide, the only practicing Muslim in my family and probably the original source of my curiosity about the faithful.

I could not have finished this work without the regular jogging, film watching and wining and dining with my husband, James B. Whitney. His academic impetus and rigor have kept me in self-discipline even when I have tended to lose it from time to time. I can never thank him enough for his patience in having my life on hold during the completion of the book.

Between Islam and the State

Introduction

DURING THE NATO SUMMIT in Istanbul in June 2004, downtown city life was incapacitated, and most offices were closed due to the blocked traffic. The shutdown—conducted by the Turkish military and the police backed up by American air forces—was primarily a safety precaution against the perceived threat of what was being called "global Islamic terror." My neighborhood in Istanbul, Teşvikiye, where most of my family lives, was less than a mile from the NATO summit meeting. During those days, I spent a good deal of time watching the American aircraft and chatting with local people who crowded the Euro-cafés of Teşvikiye. The usual small talk on fashion, leisure and Istanbul life seemed to be replaced by heated discussions of Turkey's potential membership in the European Union and which role the Islamic party in government was to play in that process.

During the summit meeting, Tayyip Erdoğan, the pro-Islamic Prime Minister of Turkey, and the President of the United States, George Bush, shook hands and spoke on friendly terms. Bush looked at the picture on the wall of the founding father of the secular Turkish Republic, Mustafa Kemal Atatürk, and commented: "Very elegant man." Dressed similar to Atatürk in a Western-style two-piece suit, Erdoğan replied: "He is *our* leader." During the summit, the neighborhood hosted political leaders from across the world and local actors in close proximity, debating and negotiating the future of Turkish society and polity. What was Turkey's role going to be in the world order? As a Muslim majority state with an authoritarian secular state tradition and a procedurally functional yet illiberal democracy, which direction would Turkey go? How was one to make sense of the current pro-Islamic government that, as the secular founders of Turkey did eight decades ago, was engaging Western democracies rather than the Middle East?

Upon the fall of the Soviet Union, Islam began to be singled out as the new source of fear in world politics. However, contrary to the expansion of political Islam as an anti-Western force in countries from Afghanistan to Iran, Islamic social forces in Turkey began opening up to the West in the mid-1980s, and became recognized internationally throughout the 1990s. In the new millennium, they have appeared as supporters of both democratic reform and Turkey's entrance into the European Union (EU). After more than two decades of global expansion of political Islam, was the staunchly secular Turkish state democratizing under a pro-Islamic government?

The Turkish transition attracts particular attention from Western powers, which hope that Turkey will provide a model for democracy in the rest of the Muslim world. Bush praised Turkey during the summit for the example it has set on how to be a Muslim democracy and apply the rule of law. However, his praise provoked a reaction among secular Turkish patriots, who did not feel comfortable with—or were even insulted by—the label of "Muslim" attached to their democracy.[1] Why would Turkey be characterized as a Muslim democracy, they questioned, if the United States, with a largely religious society, was not referred to as a Christian democracy?

The NATO summit was clearly a reminder of a developing dialogue between the West and the pro-Islamic Turkish groups. Have perhaps Western audiences more readily acknowledged the pro-democratic and reform-oriented agendas of the Turkish Islamists than the secular Turks have? A closer look at Turkish society suggests that this view misses the other half of the story. Little attention has been paid to an increasing number of secular Turkish citizens who have been developing more accepting and even sympathetic attitudes towards Turkish Islamic actors.[2]

The Islam-inspired Justice and Development Party (Adalet ve Kalkınma Partisi, AKP) came to power by fair and free elections in the staunchly secular Turkish Republic in November 2002. At the time of the victory, the leader-to-be of the party, Erdoğan, was banned from politics temporarily. A speech that he had delivered during his term as the mayor of Istanbul was believed to pose a threat to the secular state. On 12 April 1998, Erdoğan was found guilty of attempting to mobilize people for an Islamic state.[3] When his sentence ended a few months after the victory of the AKP, he was invited to come back to the Party and became the Prime Minister of Turkey on 13 March 2003.

Two years after he came to power, Erdoğan's name came to be associated with reform, democracy and dialogue with the West rather than Islamism.[4] When I referred to Erdoğan as an Islamic leader in moderate secular circles in Istanbul, I was corrected: "Why are you labeling him as an Islamist? Is it just because his wife covers her head? Erdoğan is not an *Islamist*. He is *our* Prime Minister."[5] His Islamic identity was often denied while his modern and cosmopolitan characteristics were proudly high-lighted.[6] I was surprised by these comments, because the very same people had been consumed with anxiety in 1994 when Erdoğan had won the local municipal elections in Istanbul. Later, in 1996, the fear of the secular Turks had deepened and turned into hopeless pessimism when the Islamic Refah (Welfare) party won the elections and came to power in a coalition government. The majority of the secular actors feared that "Turkey was becoming another Iran," until the party was banned by the Turkish state in 1998. Despite (or rather, because of) this deep-rooted prejudice against Islam, there was little or no "curiosity about the long-range influence of an Islamic 'voice' in Turkey," but rather a denial that Erdoğan was a product of this voice.[7]

Since the late 1990s, Islam seems to have gone a long way from being perceived as the main threat to Turkey's secular heritage to being regarded as one of the forces of reform and democracy. What has changed the minds of many secular citizens about Islamic actors in such a short time? Were they losing their collective memory? Chains of emails have been circulated by patriots in order to remind the masses of what happened in Iran and what Erdoğan said and did until a few years ago. Clearly, nobody could have forgotten Erdoğan's background in political Islam and the fact that until recently he objected to Turkey's entrance into the European Union. Was he not also regarded as an opponent, or rather betrayer, of the Republic and *laicism* (state control of religion), one of the main pillars of the Turkish Republic? Obviously, the controversy was not due to the short memory of the Turkish society. What, then, was at stake?

During my short visits in the Summer and Winter of 2005, the debates over the AKP government were continuing. Yet those expressing their discontent were no longer substantiated by a strong secular opposition. Secular citizens did not disappear, but their strong opposition weakened. Fewer of them were complaining about the Party or Islam in general. As the subject of discontent changed frequently from one controversial moral issue to the other, at the time of my next visit it was about Erdoğan's new policy against alcohol. In some smaller cities, the AKP forced bars and restaurants that serve alcohol to move from city centers to the outskirts. A few opponents of the Party insisted on the freedom to consume alcohol in every corner. Other opponents were still thinking of Iran with fear and were concerned that the party's negative attitudes against alcohol were just another sign that the "future of children was jeopardized by moral conservatism of Islamists." Surprisingly, however, in every visit to Turkey, I found an increasing number of educated people, professors, intellectuals, artists and businesspeople from secular circles appreciating the AKP's success in liberal economic and institutional reforms. A well-respected secular professor, known for his liberal views and life style, commented to me: "While some narrow-minded people are still busy obsessing with the details such as bars and liquor, the AKP speeded fast in economic growth and political reform. We are a society stuck in details ignoring major breakthroughs."[8]

Clearly, it was *not* only Erdoğan and the Islamic followers who have changed in this short period from their confrontational *Islamist* position to a moderate reform-oriented pro-*Islamic* mode.[9] On the contrary, the attitudes of a growing number of secular actors towards Islam have also been moderating from intolerant forms of laicism to moderate secularism since late 1990s. This change has been particularly hard and painful to acknowledge for the majority of Kemalists, who were the supporters of official ideology, laicism in particular. Committed to preserving not only the state's control over Islam but also state domination over society in general, Kemalists have predominantly (mis)perceived this transition as a defeat of secularism by a pervasive Islamization.

Popular Misconceptions and Prophecies of a Clash

One of the main pillars of the "Republican project," the making of a Westernized, secularized and modern nation and its state, was laicism.[10] This overarching grand project had not only pushed religion to the private sphere but also repressed and marginalized Islamic actors since the early 1920s. The secular Republic was consolidated out of the remnants of an Islamic Empire, in which the rulers gained legitimacy from religion.[11] Unlike in the Persian Qajar Empire, where religion and state were independent of each other, religion was a part of the state in the Ottoman Empire. After the decay of the Empire, the establishment of the secular Turkish nation-state relied heavily on the integration of religion into the state machinery. This task was accomplished mainly through the formation of Diyanet İşleri Müdürlüğü (Directorate for Religious Affairs). However, the question of religion has proved much more complicated throughout the history of the Republic than the founding fathers had envisioned.[12] The Republic has displayed ongoing swings of the pendulum between repression and toleration of Islam.[13] Each time Islamic social forces gained power and were thought to pose a threat to the secular state, the Turkish military, the staunchest protector of laicism in Turkey, intervened in the political process through a coup d'etat.

My ethnographic research started when the military intervened in politics again in February of 1997. Typically, the state put an end to the toleration that Islamic social forces had enjoyed since the mid-1980s and banned the Islamic party Refah, which was argued to threaten the secular tradition, in 1998. Religious associations, sects and centers were being monitored and sporadically attacked by the police.

My research started with numerous informal conversations with both Islamic and secular actors from a large spectrum. For several months, I free-floated among these groups until the focus of the research was narrowed to a specific topic. The most common question I received from the secular individuals was, "So, what did you find out about the Islamists? What are they hiding? What is their secret agenda?" Not only did the secular actors distrust the Islamic actors but they also disliked their life styles and headscarves. However, the secular actors have also increasingly fallen into conflict among themselves in their views of, and attitudes towards, Islamic movements. The late 1990s seemed to be an era of ongoing disagreement and discontent. Like every transition period, it was unsettling and troubling for all social actors.

Soon, I collected a good number of stories of despair and fear. As genuine as these views and feelings of Islamic and secular actors were, they were mainly myths of clash and confrontation, which my research eventually discredited. Neither of these groups may cherish this book, as it does not share either the predominant perceptions of a clash or the festive perceptions of diversity and multiculturalism in Turkey. In contrast to what is in vogue in current scholarship, this book is about the demise of confrontation in the Turkish context. It reveals the limits of disagreement and the boundaries of diversity. It tells the story of a rising agreement, cooperation and a growing sense of belonging between the secular state and Islamic actors.

Several myths of the clash between the Turkish state and society have circulated since the 1980s and clearly predated Huntington's prophecies of clash between civilizations. The first dominant view, which I refer to as the "oppression prophecy," was that the Turkish state was so *inherently* authoritarian and illiberal that it was doomed to repress and eventually obliterate Islamic movements. "No opposition was strong enough to challenge or even *survive* the Turkish state's repression." The advocates of this prophecy about the "strong state and weak society" understandably reached this conclusion by looking back at the Republican history and the state repression of social actors, Islamists and ethnic minorities in particular. The victory of the AKP has largely challenged this prophecy since 2002.

The second view, which I call the "threat prophecy," has made the opposite claim. Accordingly, the rise of Islam and the victory of Refah in 1996 showed that Islam was a real threat in Turkey.[14] Allegedly, Islamic groups were so powerful that they would gradually penetrate political institutions and undermine the Republican project in order to "conquer" the secular state (*devleti ele geçirmek*). The people most concerned about this "strong society and weak state" thesis were a large group of threatened secularists in late 1990s, who were fearfully anticipating the decay of Atatürkism and the defeat of official secularism. Their numbers also shrunk dramatically at about the turn of the millennium due to the persistence of the secular regime under the pro-Islamic government.

Paradoxically, these seemingly opposite views converged in their conclusion with Huntington's thesis of the clash of civilizations. In the first scenario, the secular institutions would wipe out the Islamic social forces. In the second one, Islamists would conquer and defeat secular institutions and the state. As simplistic as these prophecies of state-society interaction may seem, they played a great role in maintaining Turkey in the league of the so-called "gray zone" or "sustained transition" countries along with Egypt, and even akin to failed "political openings" together with Iran. Like other prophecies, the aforementioned views suffered from partisanship and a lack of analytical distance. More importantly, they suffered from the absence of empirical sensitivity to contemporary patterns of social change. This ethnographic study challenges these views, in which the secular state is juxtaposed against Islamic social forces in explaining social change.

Due to the highly politicized nature of the debate on Islam and democracy both in and out of Turkey, it is often assumed or even expected that the author, like most other citizens of the Republic, takes sides in the opposition between Islamism and secularism. It has not been an uncommon practice to assess scholarship in the field according to the ideological side it takes rather than for its scholarly contribution to the understanding of a phenomenon beyond ideology.[15] Contrary to this unspoken expectation, this study is not motivated by a commitment to the defense of any group or ideology. It does not seek to support either the secularist Kemalist or Islamist point of view. Hence, the absence of advocacy is likely to render this book unappealing to ideologically motivated audiences, Islamist or secularist. The disengagement is caused not only by the author's analytical distance from both but also by a critical analysis of both—rather than one—of these camps. More importantly, the lack of advocacy is not merely a matter of choice, strategy or methodology. The evidence provided by this work renders the rhetoric of advocacy redundant by empirically revealing the demise of the confrontation and emergence of cooperation between Islam and the secular state in the Turkish context.

Few scholarly works have moved beyond the dichotomy between authoritarian states and good Muslim societies.[16] Even fewer have criticized the predominant representation of Islamic social forces as con-frontational and oppositional to the states.[17] There are, of course, good rea-sons for the wide appeal of this dichotomy between state and society in the Turkish context. For a long period, Turkish society was characterized by the gap between the center and the periphery.[18] The unbridgeable dis-tance between the dominant state and over-defiant Muslim masses was seen largely as an effect of the absence of institutions that were supposed to link the state and society.[19] Similarly, the Westernized political elite had no sympathy for the periphery and mistrusted the Muslim masses. Although the center-periphery gap gradually diminished, the distance between the Westernized Kemalist elite and the marginalized masses has persisted for a longer time.

Recently, Islamic actors have become more vocal in their demand for more recognition for faith-based and morally conservative ways of life, which have been looked down upon by the Westernized elite. Until Islamic actors started to contest the accepted norms, the secularist elite *claimed* to have a monopoly over national education, markets, corpora-tions, the media, civil society, nationalism (even patriotism), and politics in general (and gender and ethnic politics in particular). The secularists' claim reigned until moderate Islamic actors accumulated social, economic and intellectual power, and emerged as an alternative pro-Western and secu-larization-friendly social force.

The shifting relations between the new Islamic actors and the Turkish state are very important, partly because they inform us about the demise of a gap between the state and society. Interestingly, this transformation has preceded and even facilitated institutional reform by, I argue, creating *alter-native* linkages and affinities between the state and Islamic actors. This book documents the everyday manifestations of this transformation. It is not a process of "fusion" of the state and Islam. Put differently, it is not about unification between them, whether in the form of Islamization of the state or the defeat of Islamism by secularism. Nor does this study illus-trate a process that blends Islamism and secularism. In contrast, this is a modest attempt to capture and analyze the contemporary everyday set-tings that have allowed Islamic actors and the state to interact and reshape each other. The study has no pretension of providing a historically or ethnographically exhaustive account of these meeting points. Rather, it provides an in-depth analysis of the shifting dynamics between Islamic ways of life and the state's conduct.

The literature has not yet sufficiently acknowledged this current trans-formation of the interaction between the state and Islamic actors in Turkey. A few ethnographies have pointed to an emerging *convergence* between

Islamists and secularists, while focusing mainly on the diversity of Islamic voices.[20] There is a shortage of historical approaches that account for the background of what Mardin refers to as the "setting where secularism and Islam interpenetrate."[21] Instead, many studies have pitted Islam against the state in the Turkish context and have regarded confrontation as a force of democratization.[22] The emphasis has remained on the ways in which Islamic actors struggle with, confront and seek to replace the state's functions, whether politically, culturally, discursively or through alternative ways of life.[23] The juxtaposition of Islam against the secular state has been reinforced further by the representation of Atatürkism as an ideology of the Westernized elite that has either excluded or failed to appeal to Islamists. This was the case for most of the Republican history in Turkey. However, contemporary social research has not yet fully acknowledged the parallel transformations of Islamism and Atatürkism—or the mutually changing views of Islamic and secular actors.

As a result, emergent non-confrontational forms of interaction and cooperation between the state and Islam have gone largely unnoticed.[24] Similarly, while the focus has remained on oppositional forces, which challenge authoritarian regimes, the agency of the non-defiant social actors has been almost completely neglected. The Middle Eastern context has reinforced these prevalent tendencies in the literature. Not only has Islamic action been largely associated with insurgence but also authoritarianism in the Middle East has been seen as curable only by the confrontational forces.[25] As a result, the non-resisting Islamic actors, who have come to terms with several codes of conduct of the secular nation-states, were denied both power and agency. Regardless of the large variety of non-defiant actors, all fell under the broad category of the "co-opted"— if not the "oppressed, repressed and silenced"—without a second thought being given to the consequences of their non-confrontational action.

The aim of this book is to examine the matter from a different perspective. Rather than portraying the Islamists' resentment towards and struggle with the Republic, this work captures the emergence of Islamic agency at a certain historical moment, a moment of transition when it starts to reach out to, engage, negotiate and even associate with the state. I specifically explore the sources and outcomes of this changing energy between Islam and the most secular state of the Muslim world. This dynamic has often been misinterpreted as a new statism of Islamic social forces. Instead of denying Islam its agency in this process, I explore the contemporary specifics of what Mardin calls the "primacy of the state in the Islamic voice."[26] Moreover, a particular interest of this study is how shifting dynamics of state-Islam interaction transforms the bitterest expressions of state laicism into much more tolerant forms of secularism.[27] Put differently, changing attitudes of the state as a social actor is a major concentration of this work.

Considering the hostile separation of Islam and the state in the early Republic, the worldwide interest that the AKP's victory attracted should not be surprising. Was this victory informing a new page in Turkish history? In fact, the conditions that prepared the rising popularity of the AKP and the state's accommodation of it have been maturing outside traditional institutional channels, state policies, party politics and deliberate forms of political mobilization. In order to explore the broader scope of contemporary dynamics, this study looks beyond the actions and agendas of political leaders and the party agendas and delves into the heart of everyday life.

The Scope

This ethnography follows the everyday encounters between the state and Islamic actors. Here, the state is seen as a multi-layered social organization made up of branches, officials, offices and diverse agendas.[28] By treating the state as an everyday actor, I aim to overcome the prevalent split in the literature that sets in opposition not only cultural processes against political ones but also civil society against the state. Moreover, the civil society literature itself has also differentiated social actors and associations from political parties, by assigning them different roles. Unlike these approaches, this study bridges these separate yet interacting realms of culture and politics, as well as social movements and political institutions.

Recently, the AKP has almost come to be seen as the icon for reform and democracy, not only in Turkey but also in the Muslim world. However, contrary to what has been often presented in the literature, the party is not metamorphous, that is, it is neither an object without a history nor a simple break from the past. By tracing the shifting state-Islam interaction within the last decade from local, everyday life to the macro-institutional level, this study reveals a largely neglected continuity between state and non-state actors. I pay attention to the convergence between the Islamic actors outside and inside the government. Specifically, I trace state-Islam interaction in everyday sites, from those in the largest and most influential Islamic movement, the Gülen movement, to those in the AKP government. The political ethnography explores how the social movement's network and activities have translated into political terms and political dynamics.

The Gülen movement emerged out of the fragmentation of another

Islamic movement, Nur, in the 1980s and expanded internationally across the continents throughout 1990s.[29] The exact size of the movement is not easy to guess. In addition to a fast-growing Diaspora across the world, it is estimated that there are approximately six million followers of the Gülen movement within the national boundaries of Turkey. The movement, unlike Islamic sects, does not have formal membership. On the contrary, the fuzzy boundaries of this diffuse movement attract a diverse constituency. Affiliations range from the devout and benefactors, who are unconditionally in service, to distant admirers and sympathizers. The inner kernel is often referred to as *cemaat* (Gemeinschaft), while the loosely connected outer layers of the movement are seen as a *cemiyet* (Gesellschaft). Similarly, the AKP government (2002–?) attracts a larger base from both Islamic and secular circles. Interestingly, there are an unknown number of secular Turks who either refused to vote at all in 2002 or voted for the AKP without admitting it publicly.[30]

Except for their wide appeal across the old Islamic-secular divide, however, the continuity between the movement and the party is *not* of a direct or cooperative kind. Unlike the close relation between diffuse social movements and well-organized parties, such as that embodied by the environmental movement, the Gülen movement and the AKP are indeed disconnected. In fact, the leader of the Gülen movement, Fethullah Gülen, has neither approved of the previous Islamic parties nor agreed with the previous Islamist leader, Erbakan. The followers of the Gülen movement refused to vote for Islamic parties, including Refah, and preferred the center-right conservative parties to Islamic ones. This picture changed dramatically in 2002 when the AKP ran for elections. Upon the AKP's declaration of its break from Refah and its radical Islamist faction, Milli Görüş (National View), most of the followers of the Gülen Party voted for the AKP.[31] Still, the Gülen movement and the AKP have remained organizationally independent and disconnected in their activities.

The parallel that this study draws between the social movement and the party in power is not due to overlapping memberships, either. Put differently, the members of the party and the followers of the movement are generally not the same people.[32] Although they have both attracted followers across class boundaries, there has been a major difference between them in their appeal to different groups. The movement mainly appealed to people who had bourgeois aspirations for upward social mobility, while the party relied largely on the votes from the urban poor, residents of shantytowns and economically lower status neighborhoods.[33] Where, then, is the parallel that this study draws between these distinct Islamic groups?

What made the Gülen movement and the AKP the subject of study among many other Islam-oriented groups and parties is an organic continuity between them.[34] Both have displayed similar cooperative attitudes, as opposed to confrontational ones, towards the secular Turkish Republic. This shift in state-Islam interaction is the key to explaining a much broader transformation in Turkey. Hence, my interest in this study in the sources and outcomes of non-confrontational Islamic activities has made the movement and the political party obvious subjects. Only a few studies in the literature have linked organizations in the realm of civil society with political parties in the Middle East by tracing the continuity between them.[35] Even then, these studies have pointed to the continuity of opposition between the associations and parties to the authoritarian regimes. In contrast, this work focuses on the continuity between the Gülen movement and the AKP in terms of the absence of confrontation and the power of non-defiant forces.

The Book

This study is an ethnography on how Islamic actors and the state have transformed each other within the last decade.[36] It reveals the dynamics of the shifting relationship between the Turkish Islamic actors and the secular state from confrontation to cooperation. As a sharp contrast to their historically confrontational relationship, I explore the sources, nature and outcomes of emergent *engagements* between Islam and the state. *Engagements* refer to a continuum of interplay between Islamic actors and state actors, ranging from contestation and negotiation to accommodation, cooperation and alliance.

Each chapter analyzes a different kind of interaction between Islam and the state. Concretely, the new Islamic actors *contest* with the secular state in the area of education (chapter 3) and moral ways of life (chapter 6). They *negotiate* the boundaries between public and private lives, and thereby the nature of secularism (chapter 2). They *cooperate* with the state in promoting Turkic ethnic politics in Central Asia (chapter 4) as well in promoting institutional reform and Turkey's membership in the European Union (chapter 6). They also *ally* with the secular male elite in gender politics (chapter 5). It is imperative to note that all of these diverse patterns exclude clash and confrontation with the state.

Needless to say, none of these patterns of interaction can be captured in a pure form in practice but are found only intermixed with other forms of engagement in a given everyday setting. For example, even when Islamic actors cooperate with the state in ethnic or gender politics, they still do not cease to negotiate over their own Islamic agenda. Whether it

is pronounced explicitly or not, their primary agenda remains the revitalization of faith, and acquisition of legitimacy for faith-based lives in the
secular institutional milieu of Turkey.

THE OUTLINE

Chapter 1 introduces the Islamic actors of engagement who are the
main subjects of this study. By discussing their relevance and importance
to the Turkish transition, the chapter situates their activities, networks and
organizations into the larger debate on Islam, civil society, state transformation and democratization.

Chapter 2 explains how the disputed boundaries between the state and
Islam have gradually transformed into sites of engagement through the
history of the Republic. I illustrate this macro shift through a micro-level
analysis of the readjustment that Islamic actors undertake in public and
private realms. Subsequently, I show how public activities of Islam have
provided the platforms of engagement with the state, while the private
Islamic sphere has expanded and transformed faith-based practices into
more legitimate activities.

Chapter 3 starts by analyzing the confrontation between the Gülen
movement and a consortium of secularist civil society organizations. At
one level, by revealing the secularists' war against the movement, I show
the extent to which both associations and public debates can divide and
polarize, rather than integrate, the society. At another level, I discuss how
the legal scrutiny of the Gülen schools through the court system opened
the way for symbolic negotiations between the state and the movement.
More importantly, I illustrate how state actors contradicted each other in
their attitudes toward the movement, while the Islamic followers responded differently to the state's various claims over the schools.

Chapter 4 follows the sites of engagement to Kazakhstan of the post-
Soviet Central Asia, where the movement has concentrated its activities
since the mid-1990s. I reveal the emergent Islamic sensibilities for national
and ethnic identity. On the one hand, I illustrate how national loyalties
currently help to facilitate the movement's cooperation with the officials
of both the Turkish and Kazak states. On the other hand, I highlight how
the homogenizing tendency of Turkic ethnic politics contradicts the claim
of the movement to develop a pluralist civil society as it promotes ethnic
unity latent in both Islamic and secular nationalism in Turkey.

Chapter 5 compares the significance placed upon gender reform by the
early Republican male elite with the position of the contemporary Islamic
male actors. I reveal the overlap between their seemingly progressive gender discourse, which aims to incorporate women into the public sphere

without actually intending to empower them. The findings demonstrate how the similar views of gender reform create a male bond between the Islamic and secular elites, thus facilitating further cooperation. While highlighting another dark side of state-Islam cooperation in sustaining patriarchy, the chapter also notes that Islamic women may take advantage of public participation as a means for further emancipation, as the secular women had done in Turkey.

Finally, chapter 6 traces the engagement from the everyday sites of the movement to the pro-Islamic party in the government. The continuities show that the AKP's significance lies not in its invention of engagement with the state but in its "institutionalization" of it. I illustrate the AKP's leading role in undertaking economic and political reform. I argue that the politics of engagement resulted in the formation of a limited consensus between the Islamic actors, the Turkish state and the international actors, especially the EU.

The conclusion explicates the nature of this minimum agreement on the source of political authority, which, in turn, enables the toleration of less fundamental disagreements between Islamic and secular actors on such issues of morality and ethics. I conclude by discussing whether the emergence of accord between Islam and the state may foster political pluralism by facilitating negotiation between the state and society.

CHAPTER 1

The Politics of Engagement:
First Encounters with the Non-defiant

IN 1997 AS THE TURKISH state was enforcing more rigid rules such as the headscarf ban on Islamists, I met with three students involved in Islamic activism in the Beyazıt campus of Istanbul University. The university had a long history of ideological confrontation between the left and right in 1970s, and continued to host opposition between Islamist students and supporters of state's laicism in the late 1990s.[1] Each of the three students was active in a different Islamic group: the Refah party (which was in power at that time), the Gülen movement, and the smaller Yeni Asya group.[2] Because the increasing diversity of Islamic groups had been attracting a lot of attention since the mid-1980s, my initial goal was to explore the ways in which this diversity and the related public debate may have been contributing to or undermining civil society and democracy. The students did not know each other before this meeting. Still, I did not need to ask questions that day, as they immediately engaged in a burning debate, which soon turned into a battle.

Aysel, a history major, was a student representative of Refah. As a self-defined "radical" and "fundamentalist," she was devastated by the headscarf ban in the university. She attacked Ali, from the Gülen movement, the followers of which were mostly obeying the headscarf ban: "How could you participate in a group that preaches passivity and conformism to a system that has undermined Islam for so long? There is so much to revolt against, and you guys just preach "dialogue." How superficial! Wake up! We must fight for our cause to "live true Islam.""

In sharp contrast to Aysel, Ali was very difficult to antagonize and maintained his poised attitude during several hours of accusations. He was in charge of supervising a student house, Işık Evi (House of Light),[3] of the

Gülen movement. He listened with patience, without reacting or inter-
rupting. When she was finally finished accusing him of betraying Islamist
agendas, he smiled and talked very calmly:

Fighting would not help. Which revolution had a happy ending in history? All we
need is patience, mutual respect and understanding. If we could finally start lis-
tening, we might actually convince each other. Who will listen to you if you
attack and offend the people who disagree with you, as you are doing now. . . .
Besides, the Gülen movement is closer to what you call the "fundamentals" of
Islam. We believe in tolerance and peaceful ways of negotiation, and definitely not
in confrontation and blood.

Ahmet from Yeni Asya was disappointed with both Aysel and Ali: "It is
easier to talk when you have so much money or political power. You both
stand close to a corrupted system, whether it is through the corporate
world of the Gülen movement, or the political power of the Refah government." According to him, Ali and Aysel were hypocrites who were
enchanted by material rewards. He thought they were "reinforcing the
system," instead of challenging it. They were "playing the game by the
state's rules," he said, "at the expense of the 'true Islam.'" The dilemmas of
these three Islamic students eventually became one of the main preoccu-
pations of this research.

Were Islamic social forces becoming a mere reflection of the authoritarian state, as Ahmet insisted?[4] Or were the confrontational practices of
Islamic groups that Aysel advocated transforming the state by undermining its image?[5] Although I have benefited immensely from the latter approach, the evidence provided by this work suggests a slightly different
take on the issue. This is a story, as promoted by Ali, of non-confrontational
interactions between the Islamic actors and the state. Moreover, this is also
a story of how these non-confrontational practices have transformed the
practices and images of not only Islam but also the state. Specifically, to the
extent that they ceased confronting each other's hostile *image* and came to
terms with its *practices*, both parties started developing skills to engage and
shape each other in mundane everyday life.

Who Are the Islamic Actors of Engagement?

Having observed several disputes that were similar to the conflict
between Ali, Aysel and Ahmet, my initial research interest in the much-
celebrated concept of "diversity" and its presumed association with civil
society declined fast. Contrary to public opinion, mistrust was not a characteristic defining only the relations between the Islamists and secularists.

Diverse Islamic groups also became fragmented and ceased to cooperate with one another. Increasing state repression and contradictory responses by the Islamic groups turned some of these groups into isolated, and even hostile, units. The divide was most unbridgeable between the followers of the two largest groups, Refah and the Gülen movement. Similar to the leaders of these groups, Erbakan and Fethullah Gülen, the followers of each group disliked and mistrusted the other.[6]

As I was free-floating among Islamic groups, a rather unusual dynamic between the Gülen movement and the Republic began to catch my attention. I became increasingly interested and drawn into in the emerging non-confrontational patterns of interaction between Islam and the state. These patterns sporadically presented themselves in my field sites when I was least expecting them. While the resentment of other Islamic groups and parties was peaking because of the state's repression in the late 1990s,[7] the followers of the Gülen movement were articulating wide-ranging loyalties to their country, the nation and *its* Republic, and even the military. This new dynamic was surprising and difficult to make sense of. Salwa Ismail critically notes a misleading tendency in the literature. The rise of Islamic revival has often been associated with a crisis, in which "the state fails to meet rising expectations [and] Islamist opposition emerges as the expression of social discontent."[8] In the midst of all the discontent from both Islamic and secular circles, the Gülen movement stood out because it was clearly deviating from this generalization. Motivated by its affinities to the state, the movement was mobilizing to make more space for the faithful individual within the boundaries of the secular Republic.

The Gülen movement is the largest and most influential Islamic group in Turkey and the most widely recognized one internationally.[9] Because of its fast-growing financial resources (since the mid-1980s) and the expansion of its networks and schools abroad (since the mid-1990s), it has rapidly become "the richest and most important offshoot of the Nur movement."[10] Like other successors of the Nur movement,[11] the Gülen movement's major *dava* (goal, issue) is to revitalize faith. Followers strongly believe that faith has declined or almost become "lost" in the rigidly secular sociopolitical milieu of the Republic. Unlike other Nur groups, however, the Gülen movement has successfully negotiated the boundaries between religion and the staunchly secular Turkish state in various realms of social life. The movement has had several layers of leverage supporting its success.

The main outlet, education—high schools, universities and dormitories—and the secondary outlet, trade and business networks, both expanded first to Central Asia in the mid-1990s and gradually across the globe. The movement's international expansion has largely been accommodated by the host states.[12] In the newly independent Muslim-Turkic majority states of Central Asia, the movement has prioritized ethnic politics, revitalizing the "forgotten Turkic roots." In the United States, on the other hand, it has undertaken extensive interfaith activities. Along with attending to the current American agenda, the followers have concentrated on religious identity politics, reconciling conflicts in the post-9/11 period, working on a dialogue between people from different religious denominations.[13] Thus, the locus of the movement's activities in America has been to reduce or eliminate sources of major conflict and achieve harmony and dialogue. In all these secular states, the followers have cooperated with the host states in undertaking these context-specific activities while mainly continuing to pursue their broader goal of reviving faith.

Similar to the Gülen movement, which has differed from other Islamic groups by internationalizing its nationalist Islamic mission, the AKP government has become a globally recognized model of a "Muslim democracy" in the new millennium. These Turkish Islamic actors have had a strong ideal of service, not only to the community but also to the country (*vatan*) and nation (*millet*). The nationalism of these Islamic actors has reinforced their international undertakings. Parallel to the conflict-diffusing attitudes of the Gülen movement, "the AKP avoids strong ideological commitments and open conflict and adapts its positions to the expectations of other political leaders."[14] At a time when most Islamic action reminds most Western observers of terror, both the Gülen movement and the AKP have been generally recognized in the West, particularly the United States, as moderate and pro-democratic forces.

The Gülen movement and the AKP are strong advocates of economic liberalism and prosperity. The movement has taken full advantage of a growing economy and has expanded its investments through corporations, private schools and media outlets, and the AKP has stabilized a previously fluctuating economy and has rapidly passed reform bills. The growing economic and political power of these Islamic actors may have created an elitist image, which represents the "polished" urban Islamic social forces of high socioeconomic status. It is true that, unlike in Iran, Islamic activism in Turkey does not come from a strong tradition of Islamic leftism.[15] However, Islamic action in Turkey is far from an elite activity. This misunderstanding originates from two misconceptions.

First, the Gülen movement has been extremely successful in fostering upward social mobility. It has attracted cross-class constituents who aspire to the attainment of middle-class ethics and bourgeois life styles through education. The constituents include a large body of bright and promising students from lower economic status, students whose education depends on the funding from the movement's foundations and individual benefactors. With the exception of wealthy benefactors of the Gülen movement, who mainly finance schools and students, most of the followers serve in movement activities, education in particular, voluntarily or for very low salaries. When I asked intellectuals, writers, teachers and the businesspeople in the Gülen movement how they would describe their background and socioeconomic status, they often said that they were "the children of Anatolia" (*Anadolu çocuğu*), which stands for folk people as opposed to the urban elite. Sencer Bey, a leading intellectual and writer, smiled and told me: "My parents are farmers in Trakya [Thrace]. I was raised in a small village and worked as a shepherd until I was twelve." Another intellectual, Bilal Bey, said that his father was a postman who looked after his mother and four brothers and sisters. He was the only one of the siblings who continued his studies after elementary school, "thanks to the movement's support." His statement about the movement confirmed my own observations. He said that most of the people in the movement come from similar backgrounds in small towns and villages of Anatolia. This explains why the movement's teachers reach out to, and enthusiastically serve, the youth in the remotest parts of not only Turkey but also the world, in places such as Siberia.

Second, the misconception also arises from the fact that the movement's major associations and foundations are based in large cities and urban centers. In reality, however, the movement's networks and activities are diffuse. They are scattered not only throughout small towns in Anatolia but also across the world. I accidentally came across these networks far from major cities, not only in Turkey but also in European countries such as Denmark. Similarly, upon my arrival in Amherst, Massachusetts, the followers had heard about "the new Turkish faculty member" in town, and invited me to their get-together. Both inside and outside of Turkey, the networks of the movement and the "*Risale* readings"[16] extend to neighborhoods that range from lower to higher socioeconomic status.[17] The dispersed quality of these networks does not affect their efficiency and effectiveness.

Similar to the Gülen movement, the AKP has flourished on the basis of extensive and efficient networking. Although the party has relied heavily on the votes of the urban poor, its economic policies and political agendas have attracted and pleased people from across class boundaries, including middle-class and upper-middle-class constituents. This trend has been criticized widely as a betrayal of the poverty-ridden base of the party.

Making Sense of the Engagements

Originally, I observed engagements between Islam and the Turkish state as they surfaced on a small scale in the dispersed sites of the Gülen movement. Since then, I have traced the expansion of the sites of engagements from the local to the national and to the international realm outside the Turkish borders. The last decade has witnessed the gradual expansion of engagements from the level of everyday life to the macro-institutional level of the government.

The first signs of engagement surfaced when mostly educated, socially conscious and faithful Muslims, whose parents and grandparents defined themselves as loyal citizens through the values *imposed* by the early Republic, started to seek ways to revitalize faith in everyday life. The parents of these newly engaged Islamic actors lived according to the secular Republic's uncompromising principles toward Islam. They either kept their religious activities hidden underground or accepted privatization and marginalization of religion.[18] Contrary to their Republican parents' passive or active acceptance of Muslimhood as a private matter of life,[19] more and more social actors have wished to practice and express religion freely in their everyday lives, including in their public self-presentation, such as the way they dress.

However, although they were in disagreement with the rigidity of authoritarian laicism, they were convinced by, and supportive of, several other values and characteristics of the Republic.[20] They strongly *associated* with the nation, and voluntarily participated in the democratic electoral procedures as strongly as any other secular citizen did. In that sense, the new Islamic actors probably felt more like the children of a secular nation-state than their Muslim forefathers had in the early period of the Turkish Republic. Clearly, the Turkish state was not the only secular state, which had an impact on shaping the nature of Islamic action.[21] However, it was by far the most authoritatively secular one, controlling religion in every sphere of life.[22]

With the state's increasing tolerance of Islam in the 1980s, largely encouraged by the Prime Minister at that time, Turgut Özal, Islamic actors finally started to step forward and seek legitimacy in a way their parents did not and could not. In a fast-growing free market economy and civil society, they found economic, social and political conditions favorable for the articulation of their needs and interests. They formed their own associations, media outlets—including television stations, radio stations and newspapers—as well as corporations and hospitals. Perhaps most importantly, they dedicated themselves to raising faithful and "morally superior" future generations, who would also be internationally competitive in science, business and technology. The Gülen movement opened schools and universities inside and outside of Turkey, while other Islamic actors persisted in forming and joining successive Islamist parties each time their existing parties were banned by the Turkish state. Still others formed prayer groups, religious organizations and foundations. Turkey, like other authoritarian states in the Middle East, has seen Islamic networks and activities mushroom.[23]

Although the level of Islamic activism rose when the state loosened its control over religion in the 1980s, the engagements of Islamic actors with the state surfaced in the late 1990s, when the state repression peaked again. Yet they remained rather timid and uneven until around the turn of the millennium. The politics of engagement have gained momentum and have started to permeate the political culture at large, and become institutionalized *only when* the confrontation between the Turkish state and Islam has finally declined in the new millennium. Islamic actors and the state became actual bargaining and even cooperating *partners* on issues like education, ethnic politics and gender politics *only after* they began to recognize each other's autonomous sphere of action. The decline of the ideological clash between official secularism and Islamism marked the beginning of more democratic forms of negotiation between various branches of the state and Islamic actors.[24] This tells us two important things. First, the engagements have clearly been the product of a long historical process, including, but not limited to, the tolerant 1980s. Second, the fact that they surfaced in the midst of rigid state control suggests that the engagements are directed to an illiberal authoritarian state. The Gülen movement began to engage the state when it was distrusting and temporarily disowning Islam.

The *hostile* separation between Islam and the Republic, a characteristic of laicism, came under critique and questioning. At the same time, however, the basic idea of separation between religion and political sovereignty referred to generically as secularism has increasingly become accepted by the new Islamic actors. Needless to say, Turkish Islamic actors have put Gellner's famous claim that Islam was inherently "secularization-resistant" into question.[25] They appeared to be resistant only to certain ways of interaction between religion and the state, the ones that were aggressive and confrontational. This reminds us that different patterns of secularization have to be understood in their own right.[26]

Despite the gradual demise of sheer hostility between Islam and the state, the broader question remains: have Islamic movements and associations been contributing to or undermining civil society and democracy? A fast-growing literature on Islam has split into two polarized camps. One has taken a rather promotional edge and became a festive celebration of the perfect fit between Islam and "elastic" definitions of pluralism, civil society and democracy.[27] In the wake of 9/11, the other has waged a war against Islam, condemning it in every form, not just fundamentalist.[28] As mentioned before, the Islamists and Kemalists in Turkey participated fully in the war between these universally polarized camps.

Despite the unproductive extremes of the debate, civil society has also been constructively redefined in the Muslim context.[29] Three major strengths of civil society in the Muslim context were highlighted: the scope of local (grassroots and communal) networks, the vitality of the public sphere and the power of social capital (interpersonal ties, reciprocity, trust relations). Not surprisingly, the Turkish Islamic actors have become major players in all of these realms of activities.

Have the Islamic actors in Turkey been friends or enemies of civil society and democracy? This study does not pretend to have an easy answer for this question. It also does not strive to provide "consistent" evidence that supports the claims of one of the aforementioned camps. In contrast, it illustrates and analyzes paradoxical evidence. Diverse Islamic practices and organizations have had both liberating and restricting tendencies along with civil and uncivil outcomes. Clearly, civil society does not embrace each and every act "outside" and "against" the authoritarian state.[30] "Not all social associations are part of civil society; some organizations contribute to its growth and others do not."[31] Organizations that demand *unconditional* commitment to group agendas and collective interests may easily violate individual liberties and harm civil society.[32]

I argue that both outcomes of Islamic action, whether they advance or undermine civil society, are primarily shaped by the shifting dynamics of state-Islam interaction, an issue largely neglected in the debates on civil society and Islam.[33] This claim, in turn, requires a narrower definition of civil society in the Middle East, which brings the understudied illiberal and authoritarian states back into the heart of the debate.[34]

DISTINGUISHING CIVIL SOCIETY
FROM PROJECT-BASED UNDERTAKINGS

For a better understanding of Islamic activities, networks and organizations, I asked Sedat Bey from the Gülen movement for a term that could cover the scope of the movement's Islamic endeavors. Sedat Bey is a prominent intellectual who played a pivotal role in the formulation of the Gülen movement's motto "Dialogue between Civilizations." He did not immediately answer my question. After thinking for a few days, he called me at home in Istanbul and said: "We work on *civil society projects* such as opening schools, the research center called Akademi, publication houses and foundations, such as the Journalists and Writers Foundation. These are 'civil' undertakings that are organized by diverse individuals *regardless* of their religious orientation. . . .You should call us a 'civil society organization.'"

When the followers brought up civil society in my interviews, I asked them what made the movement a part of civil society. They mostly stated that the movement's associations, organizations and all activities were transparent, accountable and visible both to the public and the state. Some followers emphasized that the movement's schools were scientific rather than religious and that the teaching in these schools was largely conducted in English "rather than in Arabic." Overall, the civil society that the followers referred to consisted of a multitude of *small-scale projects* connected through dispersed yet efficient networks across the globe.[35] These international networks of schools, companies, media outlets, hospitals and associations reconcile faith with education, business, science, and Western technology.

Not only the followers of the Gülen movement but other Islamic actors in Turkey have also looked up to these Islamic activities as projects of civil society. In its reform-oriented undertakings, the AKP has also aimed at strengthening civil society vis-à-vis the state.[36] Civil society has become a motto for Islamic reformers across the Muslim world who push for project-based change. Similarly, Mohammad Khatami in Iran extensively used and misused the term *civil society* to mobilize support for his projects and agendas.[37]

Not surprisingly, scholars have also represented the Islamic revival as either the sum of small-scale projects or a universal scheme. It was often seen as a systematic and coherent plan presumably aiming to connect the *Umma* (Muslim community of believers).[38] Similarly in Turkey, Islamization has largely been regarded as a "pragmatic project of civilization," an "effort to build Islamic ways of life" that was organized around a political project to set the moral standards of society.[39] Subsequently, the emphasis on the project-based aspect of the Islamic revival has created a major concern about pluralism in the minds of secular citizens. Could this project possibly accommodate cultural and moral pluralism?[40] From this perspective, pluralism has been seen as the main test for these projects. Unless the projects passed this test, they apparently could not "contribute to the democratization of the state apparatus."[41]

However, a closer look reveals that the sharp focus on the deliberate project-based aspects of Islamic action obscures its unintentional and unplanned consequences. The Islamic networks of both the Gülen movement and of the AKP have facilitated democratization *not deliberately* through their presumably pro-democratic projects but mostly *accidentally*.

The fact that the Islamic political and moral projects are *diverse* does not correlate with their *pluralistic* attitudes within each project.[42] Yet, ironically, democratization occurs despite the homogenizing agendas and goals of Islamic action. The *planned* short-term projects of Islamization have been superseded by their *unintended* long-term outcomes of engagements with the secular state.[43] Put differently, Islamic activities have had an indirect impact on transforming the state, especially when they were not really aiming for it.[44]

In order to capture the transformation of Islamic social forces and the state, we need to see beyond the idea of Islam as a project. The grand design of the Republic has been transformed into a new and previously *unforeseen* direction, as new forms of state-Islam interaction have had a transformative effect on the main pillars of the Republic. This kind of dynamic, which has linked Islamic actors to the state, has been scarce in most Muslim contexts in the Middle East.[45]

DISTINGUISHING CIVIL SOCIETY
FROM THE PUBLIC SPHERE

Both in the premodern and modern contexts, the public sphere has offered the most attractive places to look for diversity and public debate in Islam.[46] The difference in the recent revival of Islam from the Islamic past was that its entrance to the public sphere (and stepping out of the private sphere assigned to it by secular regimes) was celebrated as the development of civil society and democracy.[47] As many scholars have suggested, Islamic activism in Turkey and elsewhere has been diverse, and it has either expanded or strengthened the public sphere further.[48]

Yet the new Islamic actors in Turkey and elsewhere have worked towards making more space for faith, not only in public but also in private and political realms.[49] When the followers of the Gülen movement opened science schools and taught a secular curriculum, for example, they made sure that boarding was obligatory. This was their access to the private lives of the students, through which they socialized them not only into Islamic ways of life but also into discipline. The private sphere has not only included extracurricular activities in schools, but most of the charity work and fund-raising have also taken place in the private lives of social actors. Despite the multi-sited nature of Islamic revival, the deep interest in public Islam has rendered civil society and the public sphere as almost interchangeable terms in the Islamic context.[50]

During my fieldwork, I found that the appeal of public sites has obscured our understanding of broader processes such as democratization, which cannot be limited to one sphere of social life while being missing in other realms. The probing of private sites, from which I might have easily been distracted by the predominance of the Islamic public sites, revealed an important trend. I found that Islam has gone public by mingling with secular idioms and a variety of practices. The Gülen schools had "Atatürk corners," in which Atatürk's statues, pictures, sayings and other symbols of the secular Republic, such as the flag, were exhibited. At the same time, however, I found an explicit contrast between the liberating, pluralist and tolerant tendencies of Islamic public sites and the pious uniformity and rigid morality in the domestic and communal sites of the movement. Similarly, the tolerant pro-democratic discourses and reform-oriented actions of the AKP clearly have contradicted what happens within the party itself.[51] Paradoxically, "the homogenous inside" of Islamic groups has had less space for disagreement and differences than "the diverse outside." Not surprisingly, the former was left understudied, whereas the latter attracted most of the attention.[52]

At first, public sites and projects of the Gülen movement and the AKP may seem to be obvious forces of democratization. However, the ways in which actual projects are pursued beyond these public sites of display often contradict the highly valued discourses of toleration and pluralism. For instance, the seemingly progressive gender politics that the Islamic public sites promote has a dramatically different color in the private lives of the Islamic actors.

This study illustrates that the success of Turkish Islamic actors lies in their potential capacity to reconcile these explicit tensions, not only between the public and private spheres but also between the state and Islam. Islamic activities in the domestic realm have been separate from the public sphere yet are no longer in opposition to the secular state. Concretely, there were no Atatürk corners in the Islamic actors' homes, but the actors were also not hostile or fearful of the secular heritage, as Islamists in the 1960s and 1970s were.

Only a few recent ethnographies have explored the continuities and discontinuities between public and private realms and the state in the Turkish context.[53] However, even fewer studies have explored the connections between the public sphere and broader transformations in history.[54] There is clearly no inherent link between the public sphere and democratization. Similarly, public religions are not inherent propellants of liberal democracies. In order to contribute to a broader transformation towards a liberal democracy, the public sites must be not only independent from the state[55] but also in contact with political institutions and the state.[56] How were the Islamic actors in Turkey, who have voluntarily differentiated their activities in the public and private spheres, able to create alternative pathways to reach out to and negotiate with political institutions and the state?

DISTINGUISHING CIVIL SOCIETY FROM SOCIAL CAPITAL

Similar to religious actors elsewhere,[57] Turkish Islamic actors have been remarkably resourceful and efficient in their local networks and participation.[58] They have been particularly praised for the strength of their face-to-face relations based on trust and interpersonal skills of interaction, referred to broadly as "social capital."[59] Tocqueville's America in the nineteenth century has provided a reliable model for civil society, in which religion served as a force of cooperation, an "infinite art to fix a common goal."[60] Yet Tocqueville praises religion in nineteenth-century America, not simply for reinforcing local organizational skills but for the role it played in interacting with the institutions of liberal democracy.[61] However, unlike Tocqueville himself, most recent studies of social capital have failed to pay attention to the role of political rule and the state in shaping the nature of local participation.[62]

If social capital and associational life was a propellant of democracy, as Putnam argues,[63] how do we explain the persistence of autocracies and dictatorships in the Middle East, where social capital is argued to have been abundant?[64] Could informal Islamic associations and networks possibly fill the vacuum left by inefficient political organizations and authoritarian states in the Middle East?[65] Okan Bey, of Gazeteciler ve Yazarlar Vakfi (Journalists and Writers Foundation) of the Gülen movement, said:

We serve our people, not just the Gülen Community, but also our nation in all spheres of life ranging from education to health. We are mobilized purely by self-organized and autonomous acts of the people. We do not ask for anything but the state's accommodation of our activities. If this is not civic initiative, then what is?

As Okan Bey emphasized, the Gülen movement is indeed economically and organizationally independent of the state.[66] However, the organizational capacities of Islamic networks should not be interpreted as major sources of broader transitions from authoritarian rule. The nature of local Islamic activities is widely shaped by the nature of their links, or, often by the absence thereof, to the states in the Middle East. Okan Bey continued:

Challenging the state means "we can do better than you". Nobody is claiming that our civic initiative can replace the state. You cannot compare apples and oranges. Everybody fulfills their own duties. . . . Confrontation with the state is motivated by greed for power and self-interest. You can see examples of this in neighboring Muslim countries. This is contradictory to the principles of Islam.

The followers share Fethullah Gülen's views on the state. Fethullah Gülen is in favor of a strong state that "protects" one's honor, dignity, property and religion.[67] Paradoxically, although he is the leader of a social movement with rich sources for social capital, he does not give much credit to the interactions among non-state actors to maintain stability and progress. He believes that religious groups and sects would fall into deep conflict that would lead to chaos in the absence of a legitimate state. His dislike and fear of social disorder underlies his preference for a responsible state that citizens can trust. This aspect of his approach to the state has been widely misunderstood as his and the followers' total agreement with the state on every issue. As I will discuss in chapters 3 and 6, neither the Gülen movement nor the AKP agrees on everything with the state, but instead of confronting it the followers create alternative patterns to negotiate their own terms and demands.[68]

Engagement: From Horizontal to Vertical?

The politics of engagement refers to the process by which horizontal activities organized among Islamic actors have provided the platforms of *vertical* commitments between Islam and the state. Across the Muslim world, Islamic groups and movements failed to "muster enough support to gain power through revolutionary means, but are also blocked by governments from transforming their societies through elections or persuasion."[69] Unlike the majority of Islamists elsewhere, the new Islamic actors in Turkey have actually come to the forefront of a transition from an authoritarian Republic to a liberal democracy. The followers of the Gülen movement stated consistently in my interviews that they wished "to revive Islam under secular democratic political institutions, not in the mosque or a theocracy." Clearly, they were cognizant of the fact that their faith-reviving activities in education, business or media required a more responsive and tolerant state that would accommodate rather than crack down on Islamic action.

As Turkish Islamic actors have started to search for ways of articulating their discomfort with the intolerant faces of the Republic, they have come to *proactively* reflect upon and critically rethink the Republic. I asked Hilmi Bey, a spokesperson from the Journalists and Writers Foundation, why the movement would not fight back and contest the state's authoritarian acts against Islam. As he smiled and remained silent, I probed further: "Change requires challenge," I said. "Says who?" asked Hilmi Bey. "Challenge does not often result in constructive change. On the contrary, it divides, estranges people . . . and cuts the bridges of dialogue and undermines the

potential for negotiation. If you think reform can be attained by mere confrontation, you are wrong. We think independently, but work collectively!"

This constructive attitude differentiated these new actors from Islamists
of the 1970s, who were mobilized by Erbakan against the secular state. The
new Islamic actors have engaged the state more powerfully than most of
the secular actors have ever done in Turkey. This is how they have become
instrumental in a larger transformation from authoritarian rule.

By linking civil society to the state, Skocpol argues, civic groups in
nineteenth- and early-twentieth-century America were not merely local
but highly political.[70] Many were linked to translocal organizations,
national leaders and formal organizations that were influencing state policies. Unlike in the West, however, the nature of the links between social
forces, associations and the states in the Middle East has remained largely
understudied.[71] As a result, there has been a remarkable split in the literature between festive theories of vital civil societies and pessimistic
accounts of the failed attempts of democratization in the Middle East.
Instead of complementing each other, cultural accounts of Muslim societies and political accounts of institutions and the states have remained
largely disconnected. They even grew at the expense of each other in the
Middle Eastern context.[72] This highly problematic divide in the literature
blurs the close connection between the transformation of social forces and
the states in non-Western contexts.[73] What remains to be further studied
are the manifestations of these broader transitions in the everyday life of
ordinary social actors. Until the renewed ethnographic interest in the state
as a research site, little attention was paid to the manifestation of formal
political institutions and states as social actors in everyday life in Turkey.[74]

Were civil societies really growing while authoritarian states, regimes
and rulers were persisting in the Middle East and, if so, how? Were civil
societies flourishing as a result of the deliberate actions of social actors, as
it has been widely argued, at the expense of authoritarian states and rulers
and, if so, how? The main challenge for the Middle East has been the
difficulty of transferring the resourceful horizontal networks formed
among social actors to the vertical interaction between society and the
state.[75] Conventional political channels between the state and people have
often failed, or have been totally absent in Middle Eastern states. Despite
its functional procedural democracy and free and fair elections, Turkey was
not a real exception to this dark picture. The ban of Islamic parties in
power as well as periodic military interventions sporadically illustrated the
fragile nature of democratic institutions.

The politics of engagement explains the emergence of *alternative* vertical channels, which *link* rather than divide or antagonize Islamic actors

and the state.[76] More importantly, this study shows that these alternative linkages preceded and facilitated institutional reform and the consolidation of a liberal democracy in Turkey. Accordingly, the analysis of engagements requires a narrower definition of civil society, which incorporates the availability and nature of avenues of interaction between the state and Islam.[77]

Civil society is neither the sum of networks, projects and public sites nor a collection of settings and designated places. It may entail, embrace and nourish any of these, but it cannot be reduced to any one of them. Civil society manifests itself in the overall "quality of social life."[78] It is empowered by the achievement of neither homogeneity nor diversity but by the development of skills, ways and legitimate frames of both agreement and disagreement.[79] The analysis of the politics of engagement suggests that civil society is the fine balance between contestation and cooperation that connects independent social actors and an autonomous state. Clearly, this balance cannot be constrained to a specific venue or arena of social life while it is lacking in others. This explains why authoritarian states in the Middle East have selectively accommodated Islamic public spheres, social capital and strong local participation by Islamists but not strong civil societies.

Civil society yearns for liberal democracy.[80] It cannot be fully comfortable, and remains weak and fragile, until it attains a liberal democracy. It does definitely struggle to exist at different capacities and scopes in undemocratic and autocratic regimes in the Middle East.[81] However, unlike local horizontal networking, which can expand in the private or communal sphere under authoritarian rule, the effective and strong existence of civil society depends primarily on its interaction with a responsive state.[82] Hence, the flourishing of a strong civil society (distinct from the public sphere, local participation and social capital) cannot be envisioned without the transition from authoritarian rule to liberal democracies in the Middle East.[83]

POLITICS OF ENGAGEMENT MUST NOT BE REDUCED TO POLITICAL INCLUSION

Authoritarian states of the Middle East have largely integrated Islamic social forces throughout the 1990s and put an end to the radical and revolutionary spirit of Islamism.[84] While incorporation of Islam has clearly not led to democratization in the region, the wide-ranging practices of states and rulers suppressing Islamists have often undermined and postponed transition from authoritarian rule.[85] Islamic social forces were either co-opted, as in the case of Egypt, or their revolutionary spirit was repressed and routinized, as in the case of Iran.[86] Interestingly, however, the integration of Islamic social forces into the secular Turkish Republic has rendered Islamic actors one of the negotiating partners of the terms of democratization. How and why has the integration of Islam brought about such different outcomes?

Political scientists have distinguished Turkey from other Muslim majority states for its routinized procedural, though illiberal, democracy, that is, the functional competitive multi-party system.[87] They have made a strong case for the "democratization of the political system" as the key to the moderation of Islamic social forces.[88] Similarly, a comprehensive secularization of law, including the civil code, has been highlighted as the major force of compatibility between Islam and democracy.[89] Other approaches from political science have explained the distinct trajectory of Turkey by strategic convergences between the Islamist and secularist political elites in Turkey.[90] Although the political system and political integration has been the focus of social research on Turkey, not much has been said on the quotidian extra-institutional ties between the Turkish state and Islamic actors.

As conventional political channels have continued to fail in accommodating the rise of Islamic social forces in Turkey,[91] the centrality of alternative channels that link social actors with the state have become evident. While political inclusion through the conventional institutional channels actually played a major role in containing opposition and moderating Islamic social forces, this explanation falls short of explaining the recent centrality of Islamic forces in transition. Why have the historically marginalized Islamic actors engaged the state more effectively than many non-religious secular forces, which were fully incorporated by the Republic?

Moreover, conventional approaches to political processes have also decoupled the AKP's clear positioning within the formal political sphere from the presumably "apolitical" nature of the Gülen movement.[92] Whether the Gülen movement was seen as a friend or enemy of civil society, its place outside the political field was often taken for granted. This view assumes that the political realm consists of only the state organizations and the political elite.[93] The in-depth ethnography of this study selectively focuses on Islamic action that is separate from the state but that interacts, shapes and also becomes transformed by it. From this perspective, the Gülen movement and the AKP have had a lot to share. Similar to followers of the AKP, which was formed much later than the movement, the followers of the Gülen movement have simply had a lot to gain from any political reform and EU membership that would curb the state's authoritarianism.

It is important to note, however, that neither the leading figures of the

Gülen movement nor those of the AKP have had the goal of reducing the state's power or delegitimizing it, as is often suggested.[94] To the contrary, they have recognized and understood the nature of state power perhaps better than many non-religious social actors. What Islamic actors have yearned for is the decline of a specific kind of power, the despotic powers of the Turkish state, which had repressed and marginalized Islam in the past.[95] After all, would not the new Islamic actors benefit more from a powerful yet responsive and accommodating state than the secular Turkish majority of the country would?

The terms of liberal democracy were *originally* negotiated in everyday life as a space where Islamic actors and state actors learned how to accommodate and cooperate with each other. In these sites of engagement, previously marginalized Islamic social forces have created ties and linkages to the state, connections that have provided an alternative to the periodically failing institutional channels. These alternative ties are imperative for democratization, not only in Turkey but also in other parts of the Middle East. During the transition period, these linkages may temporarily become more helpful than the conventional institutional channels of political inclusion. Indeed, for a long time, political inclusion through a competitive multi-party system benefited selectively the secular Turks while marginalizing Islamic actors and ethnic minorities. Inclusion depended on the condition that social actors were fully committed to, and did not question, the main pillars of official ideology.[96] Unlike the politics of inclusion, the politics of engagement was not bound by this condition. On the contrary, it flourished among the marginalized.

So, are the Islamic actors the new democrats of Turkey, as it has been widely argued?[97] The politics of engagement suggest neither that the Islamic actors are democrats nor that Islam in Turkey is liberal. As a matter of fact, anti-democratic forces can also engage, and even cooperate with, states, as the fascists of Europe did during the Second World War. Zubaida correctly argues that "few Islamists are principled democrats, [so] they are *not unlike* the great majority of political activists of all persuasions" in the Middle East region.[98] Can the Turkish transition be completely entrusted to these "Muslim democrats," as they call themselves? Can the transition rely completely on Islamic mobilizational skills in creating a strong civil society and consolidating a liberal democratic state?

Although Islam, like any other religion, is not an intrinsic spur to liberal democracy, Islamic social forces may *temporarily* stand close to or even collaborate with democrats under certain conditions. Islam-oriented social forces already have become major players in the transformations in the Middle East by *occasionally* allying with the pro-democratic forces.[99] The main goal of this study is to identify the specific historical and sociopolit-ical conditions and cultural venues that enabled Turkish Islamic actors to cooperate with pro-democratic forces in negotiating the terms of liberal democracy with the Turkish state.

National Loyalties and International Undertakings

"States are not distinct from the rest of the social life," argues Michael Mann.[100] Hence, it is highly problematic "to locate freedom and morality in society, not the state." In sharp contrast to his view, authoritarian states and Muslim majority societies in the Middle East have often been decou-pled in both practice and analysis. Have Islamist actors in the Middle East really been radically different from the state actors in authoritarian states? Similarly, have not Turkish Islamic actors been influenced to a certain extent by the overarching design of the Republic? As they come to advo-cate freedom of faith-based ways of life and religious association, have they not inherited any characteristics from the nation-state? One of the goals of this study is to illustrate the resemblance of the attitudes, agendas and rhetoric between state actors and Islamic actors. These similarities, which surface consistently in the sites of engagement, by no means deny or cancel out the differences and distinctions between Islamic social forces and the state. On the contrary, by legitimizing the differences, they facili-tate negotiation between Islam and the state.

A striking characteristic of Islamic actors in Turkey is the efficiency and success they have achieved within the framework of the most staunchly secular state in the Middle East.[101] Although this was the result of a tur-bulent process of learning, a sense of familiarity has gradually developed out of continual interaction within the boundaries of the Republican project. Even when the walls between the state and Islam were rather uncompromising and hostile to Islamic social forces, the availability of meeting points in everyday life has sporadically familiarized the Islamic actors and the state in the long run. Familiarization is a peculiar process of continuous query. Its implications are paradoxical. On the one hand, familiarity facilitates and nurtures a feeling of belonging, whether in the imagined or face-to-face form. On the other hand, it also endows one with the capacity to criticize and the wish to dissociate oneself from the familiar. The predominant focus on the former, the national belonging aspect of state-society interaction, has often ignored or underestimated the urge and capacity of nationalist social actors to mold and transform their own nations and states.

In contrast to strategic and tactical alliances, the feelings of belonging inform us of a sensibility between Islamic actors and the state. Concretely, they notify us about "elective affinities," a new kind of chemistry, between them.[102] Although nationalism of Turkish Islamic actors and other forms of religious nationalisms elsewhere have a long history,[103] the elective affinities between the Turkish state and Islamic actors are a relatively new phenomenon. This is the outcome of an organic process of interaction between them within the bounds of an institutionally well-defined frame, the Republic. Hence, it should not be mistaken as either co-option of Islam by the state or dissimulation (*takiye*) of Islamic actors. Unlike policies and pacts, affinities are not planned or strategic, and are, therefore, more difficult to note and acknowledge.[104]

Engagements between Islam and the state are largely an effect of emergent feelings of belonging to the "nation and its state."[105] They link national belonging and loyalties to the nation-state.[106] Interestingly, this dynamic can best be captured in the international sites of Islamic action. It is manifested more explicitly outside the national borders, such as in Gülen schools across the world and in Erdoğan's progressive speeches in North America. Tracing the sites of engagement, this ethnography follows the adherents of the Gülen movement to Almati, the largest city in Kazakhstan, where the activities of the movement have been concentrated. In Almati, I found that the followers were heavily involved in ethnic politics, aiming not only to revitalize faith but also to disseminate Turkish Muslim ways of life to the Central Asian Muslims. Affinities between the state and Islam surfaced both in practice and rhetoric. They were manifest in the cooperation between the Islamic actors and state officials in Almati (chapter 4). Affinities also arise in rhetoric, such as in the overlapping gender discourses of Islamic and state actors (chapter 5). This book illustrates how these affinities have emerged, flourished and come to overshadow deep conflicts by facilitating bargaining between Islamic actors and the state.

The international activities of Islamic actors are primarily based on their commitments for the "nation," not above or beyond it.[107] When I asked the followers of the Gülen movement why they organize interfaith activities in the United States, their answers were in agreement: "We would like to show the world and the United States that 'Turkish Islam' is peaceful and pro-democratic." In this sense, the international exposure of Turkish Islamic actors challenges a growing literature on the transnationalization of Islam.[108] Once translated into an international context, the Islamic actors reformulate what constitutes a nation in cooperation with state actors.[109] This new *collective* effort has had a smooth transformative effect on the main characteristics of the Republic. As a result, the Republican project becomes an everyday process, rather than a fixed abstract plan. It is constantly being transformed through street-level negotiations between the state officials and Islamic actors in the international arena.[110] This edge of the study, in turn, sheds light on both the dark and bright faces, as well as secular and religious forms, of nationalism in relation to civil society. Similarly, I explore the positive and negative implications of the affinities and cooperation between Islamic actors and the Turkish state for the future of liberal democracy in Turkey.

CHAPTER 2

From Fences That Divide to Boundaries
That Link the State and Islam

DURING A CONVERSATION over a cup of tea with a teacher in one of the Gülen movement's schools in Turkey, I asked him if they were teaching Islam in these schools. He said:

I am a mathematics teacher. . . . I believe that is why they wanted me to teach in this highly competitive school. Well, of course, I am also a faithful believer and live according to the principles of Islam . . . like many of us who are in the service of the movement. . . . However, this would not qualify me to teach Islam. . . . But to answer your question, there is no space in our classrooms for Islamic teaching. We are science schools. The place for worshipping is the home or mosque, not the classroom.

My conversations with the devout teachers made me question if we were witnessing one of the most glorious victories of secularization in the Muslim world. Did privatization actually win in Turkey, pushing religion behind the walls that the Turkish state had originally set?[1] But did not Islamic actors go public after 1980 and become popular in public and political realms? How did they accomplish this without really confronting and threatening the secular order in Turkey? Before joining the festive celebration of public religions, we need to explore further the *kinds* of diversity and homogeneity they foster.[2]

Ethnographic evidence discussed in this chapter suggests that the traditionally hostile fences between Islam and the Turkish state have gradually been replaced by hospitable boundaries that *link* the state and Islamic actors. Although the apparent function of the fences was supposed to divide religion and the state, originally they actually served as guards of the state. They enabled the state to take precautions against Islam, to control it, to enter and invade its sphere when it was deemed to be necessary.

This hostile dynamic at the fences has recently changed into one with a much more neighborly tone. Here, it is useful to remember Migdal's remark that boundaries designate more than "lines of dividing spaces as represented on the maps. . . . Boundaries signify the point at which the way things are done changes, at which 'we' end and 'they' begin."[3] As boundaries have become friendly markers of autonomous spheres of both the Islamic actors and the state, they have begun to *tune* Islam and the state. They have become the sites in which Islamic actors and the state adjust to each other's different ways of doing things.

As Mardin brilliantly argues, the ability of Islam to operate within the framework of the state was not a "present day development" but a result of a longer process. The breadth of this historical process cannot be covered by the scope of this chapter.[4] Instead, this chapter provides a brief overview of the historical background, which made the recent engagements possible. After a long history of tense encounters between Islam and the state, loosened state control in the post-1980 period facilitated Islamic actors' voluntary rearrangement of their everyday life. The long-lived fear of secularists has been that Islamists would demolish the boundaries that separate the state and the mosque. In fact, Turkish Islamic actors have readily compartmentalized public and private faces of Islam in pragmatic but creative ways. To the extent the Turkish state has accommodated the Islamic actors' reorganization of their lives, the actors have reshaped the nature and the actions of the state toward Islam. The details of this dynamic are manifested at the "micro-boundaries," the ad hoc miniature markers of territory between Islam and the state in everyday life. At these micro-boundaries, numerous Islamic actors interact constantly with the state as a social actor, which has operated on the basis of an overarching Republican project. These spontaneous encounters are particularly important for our understanding of the trajectory of the Turkish transition.

Roots of Tension between the State and Religion

Not only Islam but all modern-day religions are located between the public and private realms and the political field.[5] Although this strategic location of religion is originally determined by the founding fathers of the nation-states, the actions of religious actors do continually reshape the original design of the state. "No single integrated set of rules, whether encoded in state law or sanctified as religious scriptures, [remains uncontested] for guiding people's lives."[6]

The contestation between state and religion pre-dates the formation of the secular Turkish Republic. The tensions originated in the nineteenth century in the Ottoman Empire. Contrary to the separation of the church from the state in medieval Christianity, Islam was a central part of the Empire. Although the ruler was the highest political authority, he needed the support of *Ulama* (the learned men of Islam), to ensure his sovereignty and the state's legitimacy.[7] This scenario changed in the nineteenth century when the Ottoman state encountered the rise of the West, an encounter that was "bound to lead to some modernization in the conception and organization of government."[8] State-induced change was a novelty in the Muslim world. "Islamic societies and their theoreticians had a tendency to see the *state as an extension of the religious community*, existing for the protection of the community."[9] In the case of the Ottoman state, the emphasis on the "life of the community" shifted to "the life of the state" long before the formation of the Turkish nation-state.

The state legacy became one of the most striking characteristics that distinguished the Ottoman Empire from the rest of the Muslim world. A centralized legal-rational tradition was accomplished in the Empire as new ideas of the rule of law and lawmaking were initiated during the early reform period, referred to as the Tanzimat (1839–1876).[10] As the earliest constitutional document in any Muslim country, the Tanzimat Charter[11] opened the first formal breach between the temporal and religious.[12] As religion became a bureaucratized department of the state, state-led reforms led to a dual system, split between religion and various spheres, including administration, law and education.[13]

As a result of top-down reform and Westernization, Ottomans did not experience a smooth and clear separation between religion and the state but a split between Islamic traditionalists and Westernist secularists. The Young Ottomans, reactionary conservatives, attacked the authoritarianism and superficiality of Westernizing policies.[14] They called for a synthesis between progress and the Islamic state by insisting on basing modern constitutionalism upon the tradition of Islam.[15] Challenging the young Ottomans' idea of political unity based on Islamic tradition, the Young Turks called for a secular conception of unity based on "rationality." The swinging pendulum between Islamization and Westernization swung again towards the reform attempts of the Young Turks.[16] The Turkish masses acted politically and not religiously for the first time when the constitutional regime (Meşrutiyet) was restored in 1908.[17]

The founding fathers of the Turkish nation-state were not simply reactionaries who positioned themselves against the Imperial past and Islam; they also had strong roots in the Young Turk movement and carried along certain aspects of the Ottoman legacy. This gave Atatürk a considerable advantage in comparison with other Westernist founding fathers such as

Reza Shah of Iran. Several tenets of modernization, such as bureaucracy and communication and "a secular judicial system (except for the family law)," were already initiated by the end of the Ottoman Empire.[18] However, despite the fact that the followers of Atatürk, the Kemalists, matured out of the Young Turks' ideas and controversies, the consolidation of the Turkish Republic in 1923 changed the relations between religion and state dramatically.

Although state-led reform and a centralized rational-legal tradition continued in the Republic, there was a clear rupture between the Empire and the nation-state in terms of the institutionalization of state-Islam interaction. While the bifurcation between religion and politics led to disagreement in almost every sphere of life in the Empire, the authoritarian imposition of laicism in the Republic silenced the disagreement and dissent of the religious masses.

The Birth of the Overarching Republican Framework

The main challenge of nation building was to unify a highly heterogeneous society divided across the lines of ethnicity, religion, class and cultural life style. As Kasaba argues, the authoritarian attitudes of the Republic split the state and society in the early years of the Republic by repressing, alienating and marginalizing social forces that resisted the grand design of the secular Republic.[19] Although the majority of the population came out of the war of liberation too exhausted to resist the imposition of a new order, some—such as wealthy families, who controlled economic networks in the southeast and the religious orders and movements, the Nur movement and Said Nursi in particular—still resisted and opposed Atatürk's dictatorial rule.[20]

However, while most projects of state formation in the Middle East were accompanied by the aloofness, if not cruel, images of the ruler,[21] Atatürk strategically avoided an unbridgeable hierarchy, or distance, between the ruled and the ruler. He established the idea of the "oneness of chief and nation" (*şef-millet birliği*), the "unity" of the state and the society.[22] Indeed, this seemingly populist notion of the inseparability of the ruler and the nation facilitated his claim for absolute powers and legitimacy. Accordingly, there could be no conflict of interest between him and his people, as the leader convincingly claimed to *know* the collective good and to be unconditionally committed to achieving it.[23] "The chief-nation identification was not only a myth of political legitimacy and a subjective psychology of the charismatic leader, it was also a *sociological circumstance*, a collective psychology of crisis periods, a societal state of mind."[24]

Not only in the Middle East but elsewhere, there is a clear disparity between the image and practices of the state.[25] The image of Atatürk's nation and state appears in *perfect harmony* embodied in the overarching framework.[26] This framework, often referred to as Kemalism, was a non-systematic, pragmatic collection of codes of conduct and rules of life that penetrated and forcefully transformed all spheres of life, including clothing, alphabet and measurement.[27] Only a minority elite group accepted Atatürk's reforms initially, while the masses were largely reluctant. Yet Atatürk effectively denied the vocabulary and possibility of difference and opposition.[28] Political and social dissent was blocked throughout the 1930s and 1940s, that is, until the multi-party regimes were introduced.

Although the commitment to republicanism and a secular conception of the rule of law constituted the cornerstone of the Republican project, nationalism became the most successful pillar of Kemalism.[29] Atatürk stated, "Sovereignty belong[ed] to the nation. It [could not] be segmented or divided. Not even an inch of it [could] be spared."[30] To the extent that the source of political sovereignty was the nation, that is, the rule of people as opposed to God, it was secular. One of the long-lived successes of the Republic was the eloquent intermingling of secularism with national sentiments of the people. In the long run, strong national loyalties have kept the discontents of secularism within the bounds of the Republic.

Authoritarian Secularism: Divided beneath the "Unity"?

Despite intolerance for any kind of opposition to his rule, Atatürk treated the religious sensibilities of the Muslim people with strategy and caution. Although he eliminated any potential Islamic political dissent in the secular Republic, he did not attack the Muslim faith. After population exchanges and the elimination of the Armenians, the majority of the remaining population was Muslim. Atatürk believed that "the modern state would be shored up by *civic religion*" and used it as another force to glue the nation together.[31] In sharp contrast to the Shah's estrangement of the clergy by his anti-religious arbitrary rule, Atatürk often used religious idioms in his discourse and refrained from anti-religious attitudes and discourses.[32] Delaying the abolition of the Caliphate for four years, he waited for the right moment to initiate reform in the sphere of religion.[33] Instead of denying religion, he emphasized the incompatibility of the nation–state with the idea of a unified Muslim community, *Umma*. Hence, any argument that pits the Republic against the Muslim faith misses the contingent relationship between them.[34]

However, Atatürk's understanding of laicism encompassed more than a mere differentiation between state and religion. He aimed at a broader societal and cultural rationalization.[35] In order to "rationalize" the public sphere, he eliminated symbols of religion from it and relegated religion to the private sphere. Moreover, by establishing the Directorate of Religious Affairs as an organization subordinate to the state, he placed religion under the control of the state.[36] Starting from this early Republican period, Turkish history has been an experiment in *integrating* Islam into the secular institutional milieu rather than totally abolishing it or merely separating from it. Until the 1950s, this process repressed and silenced Islamic social forces and eliminated religious freedoms.

Although the fear of freedom in public spaces can be traced back to the Ottoman Empire,[37] the effectiveness of the Republic in controlling it was rather new. As the state's intolerance for religion in the public realm increased, the boundaries of Islamic activity in the private sphere expanded to accommodate the organization of secret Islamic movements.[38] Said Nursi, who was trained by the Nakşibendi sect, became the leader of the most prominent of the Islamist movements, the Nur movement. Initially, he was close to the Young Turks. He supported nation building and opposed the ethnic resurgence by Şeyh Şaid. Even though he participated in the new parliament, his relationship to the Young Turks remained largely inconsistent and mostly rough. He soon became alienated from both the Republic and politics.[39] He advocated a "return to Islam," a move that contradicted the principles of the authoritarian state. As a result of successive lawsuits, he spent the rest of his life in exile, and his followers, the Nurcus, were stigmatized as an Islamist threat to the Republic. Mardin's inspirational study *Religion and Social Change in Modern Turkey* portrays Said Nursi as an Islamic figure who tried very hard to come to terms with the Westernist and modernist faces of the Turkish Republic. However, despite his nationalist inclinations, Nursi did not have readily available the opportunities and platforms to reach out to and interact with the Turkish state during his lifetime (1876–1960).

As the secrecy of Nur activity during the early period of the Republic demonstrates, the private sphere was also not a free realm or a comfort zone for Islamic activity. Privatization of religion in the early Republic required that religious practice and faith be confined to the boundaries of the personal as opposed to the collective. Collective religious practice and the sharing of the religious text, ideas or even the faith became suspected and stigmatized. Subsequently, Islamic activities in the private realm, unless confined to the individual, gradually came to be seen as subversive. Numerous sects, Islamic orders and religious associations were closed down and went underground, where they survived as secret societies. The leaders of religious sects were punished, imprisoned, killed or kept under strict surveillance. The expanded realm of the private also became illegitimate from the state's perspective if it hosted any kind of Islamic collective activity.

The consolidation of the boundaries between the state and religion was overall a deliberate and central part of nation building. Due to the authoritarian images of the Middle Eastern states, these boundaries may seem impenetrable by social forces.[40] States' tendency to invade, repress or co-opt Islamic social forces in the Middle East may have given the wrong impression, that the realms of states and society *permeate* each other.[41] However, in the everyday life of social actors, these realms remain distinctly separate. As a result of continual interactions, the boundaries between the state and Islam may move, transfigure, become temporarily abolished, as in the case of the Iranian Revolution, and be reinstalled by military forces, as in the case of Algeria. Depending on their nature and infrastructural capacities, states have different ways of penetrating social life to different degrees and with various levels of success.[42] No matter how boundaries between states and social forces alter (and become rigid, blurry, leaking or moving), the fact that they exist in one form or another indicates that states and societies must be treated as analytically and ontologically separate entities.[43] This becomes more evident when the shifting linkages between Islam and the state are traced historically.

Failed Initial Attempts at Political Pluralism: Multi-party Politics

Although he repressed dissent and undermined prospects of a civil society, Atatürk "left the political institutions—national assembly, the party—sufficiently alone to allow them to develop a solid identity. Unlike the Shah in Iran, he allowed the regime to be institutionalized to the extent that it could continue without major disruption after his death."[44] While the omnipresent image of the state has eventually become the major obstacle to the consolidation of liberal democracy in Turkey, the durability of formal political institutions has helped to contain opposition and disagreement within a democratic polity.[45] This outcome distinguished Turkey from other cases of authoritarian modernization and top-down secularization in the Middle East.

Unlike the dynastic rule of the Westernist Shahs in Iran, Atatürk's authoritarian rule (1923–1938) was followed by the adoption and institutionalization of competitive multi-party politics in 1946. In contrast to most of the elections held in the region, which are conducted by undemocratic means or unfair procedures, the introduction of the multi-party system into Turkish politics set the stage for free and fair elections.[46] Throughout Republican history, the success of pluralist politics has often been tested by its tolerance for Islam and has periodically been ruptured by state repression and military coups. Although the competitive political system has always been restored rapidly, military domination over politics has harmed civil and political liberties in the long run.

Once Atatürk's single-party rule by the Republican People's Party (CHP, *Cumhuriyet Halk partisi*) was changed to allow for opposition parties, the Democrat Party (DP) gained popularity and won the elections in 1950. The DP's main accomplishment was its integration of marginalized social forces into the system. Along with the party's economic policies in the 1950s and 1960s favoring provincial and rural areas, its more tolerant attitude toward religion soothed the discontent of alienated religious masses.[47] The Nur movement was accommodated in this period, as Said Nursi's sentence was cancelled temporarily. As Kasaba argues, the 1950s can be seen as the first time attempts were made to bridge state and dissenting social forces.[48] In that sense, the DP can be compared to the AKP's attempts for reform. Similar to the AKP's policies, the DP's ethnic and international policies were in line with the Kemalist establishment, and the party remained pro-Western. During its rule, Turkey became a member of the North Atlantic Treaty Organization (NATO) and the Organization for Economic Cooperation and Development (OECD).

Despite the DP's loyalty to the Republic, however, its critical attitudes came to be seen as a threat to Atatürk's legacy and turned officials against the party. As the DP's inclusiveness and tolerance started to decline, its popularity decreased, not only among the rural masses but also among the intellectuals in the large cities. The political opening in the 1950s was interrupted by the military coup in 1960, which resulted in the executions of the Prime Minister and several other leaders of the party.

The political opening was clearly a failed attempt at political pluralism and liberal democracy. However, it opened the way for long-term "organizational space" for the Islamic social forces, space that has eventually contained and moderated dissent within the system.[49] More importantly, despite the failure of the conventional political channels, the 1950s and 1960s introduced new meeting points between Islamic actors and the Turkish Republic. The gap between the elite and the people decreased due to broader diffuse changes outside the institutional realm. The new media particularly, and especially the introduction of television, helped the spread of the Islamic voice.[50]

The Illiberal Democracy and Its Discontents

State repression and intolerance played a major role in promoting the growth of Islamism as a political ideology in Turkey. In order to impose its principles, the Turkish state "relied on a dedicated generation of teachers and bureaucrats who spread across the country and served as the bearers and implementers of modern ideals".[51] Most of the current followers of the Gülen movement, who had lived in small towns of Anatolia before the 1970s, were previously adherents of the Nur movement. Life stories of elder followers of the Gülen movement show the extent to which the overarching design of the Republic gradually reached out to the remotest towns of Anatolia. Throughout their lives, they encountered hostility, not only from the authoritarian state but also from a society and their families that denied them recognition for their Islamic identity. One of these former Nurcus, Ayşe, who became a contemporary follower of Gülen, recalled those days with sorrow:

From the moment I was introduced to a group of Nurcu women who secretly were gathering to read *Risales*, my whole worldview began to change radically. It was the beginning of a new journey to a deeper inner-life for me. . . . Unfortunately my inner spiritual development had to remain hidden. . . . There was no way that I could share it with any of my friends or family members. The majority of people in our town were Kemalists, who associated with "Atatürk's party," the CHP. As we were living in one of those little towns of Anatolia where almost everybody knew each other, our *Risale* readings had to continue with incredible secrecy for years. Can you imagine that reading an Islamic publication was the biggest crime? Set aside forming religious associations, we were scared to be caught reading Islamic books. Like the other women in town, my mother was a traditional Muslim woman who wore a little, symbolic headscarf just for her respect for tradition—rather than for her "educated faith." In time, my life became a torture and a hypocrisy, tearing me apart between my forced secular appearance in public and my growing devotion to God. . . . I lived in agony and pain for years until I had the courage to start wearing a bigger scarf and admit my true feelings and faith. . . . And then I became a shame for all my family.

The rule of fear governed the Nurcus' lives for a long time. After moving from town to town in Anatolia and participating in *Risale* readings in different secret groups, Ayşe eventually met her husband, who had gone through similar humiliating experiences. The couple's close friendship with Fethullah Gülen and his family flourished in Erzurum. She still recalls "the warmth and distinguished quality of Islamic life" she felt in the household in which Hocaefendi[52] was raised. Currently, the couple lives in Istanbul, where their Islamic orientation and active participation in the

Gülen Community are no longer a threat to their security. To the contrary, they are a highly respected couple, both in the Gülen Community and in society. Ayşe is a housewife who is highly involved in charity organizations of the movement. Her husband is an internationally recognized Professor of Islamic studies. They are also often invited to other countries, where Ayşe's husband teaches or gives lectures as a visiting scholar.

In my interviews with them, both separately and together, they recalled memories of their "fugitive past," and "the pain of hiding the most intimate parts of their self-identity." Then they thanked God that they had found a space and recognition for their faith in contemporary society. Ayşe said: "It feels like our past was another century, but in fact that was only a few decades ago. It is only because of God's justice that we reached to today's peace and freedom."

Another follower, Mualla, told me her story of how she was marginalized when she decided to wear a bigger headscarf after her exposure to *Risales*. She was encouraged to read the *Risales* by her brother, who was a medical student in Ankara at the time. The most aggressive reaction to her radical decision to join the *Risale* readings came from her secularist Kemalist parents, who were also voting for the CHP. She recalled:

Our parents were wondering what kind of a mistake they made in raising us, and how they could straighten us up, their disloyal children, betrayers of the Atatürk's reforms. Indeed, Islamism was the strongest stigma at that time. My situation was definitely more difficult than my brother's. He was at least away from home in Ankara, the capital city. He was a part of a circle of Islam-oriented medical science students, who were sharing Nur teachings and philosophy. I was confined to my little town and the local fans of Atatürk. . . . With my new *tesettür* (veil), I became one of those marginalized women. This is how my husband, a wholehearted follower of Said Nursi, noticed me as a "properly covered" woman [she smiles]. . . . It was so rare and unacceptable that we were just a few people who easily noticed each other. . . . Very different from today's reality, where you see women like me everywhere. It took us years to gain public recognition. . . . It took years of conflict and embarrassment to feel comfortable with who we are, how we feel and what we think.

Risale networks all over Anatolia were organized secretly but very efficiently beyond the visible sites of the public sphere. Although the readings were conducted in secrecy, it was easy for insiders to locate and join these groups in every town through the tight-knit underground networks. "The most obvious way to be connected was to stop by a bookstore and ask for *Risale* volumes. The person at the bookstore would often know the Nurcus in town and whisper their location," said an older man from the Gülen movement. Another woman, Zeynep, told me similar stories with regard to the reactions against the spread of the Nur movement: "When I decided to marry my husband I was secretly told that he was participating in the Nur activities. I was so scared, because, by that time, all we knew was that they were *dinci* (people associated with religious bigotry) who would get organized for illegal, anti-state purposes. For me, there was no difference between a witch or magician and a Nurcu until I got to know my husband closer and was initiated to read the *Risales*."

All my informants who were a part of the Nur movement before the late 1970s had a hard time understanding why they were hated and ostracized because of their Islamic faith, which, according to them, was a source of good morals and civic virtue. One major reason why religious associations were suspected in secular societies is the ascriptive status of membership in these associations.[53] However, a closer look at the followers' lives shows that their affiliation with both the Nur and the Gülen movements was by no means inherited from their families. In other words, rather than being born into these networks, most of the Islamic actors that I interviewed had voluntarily joined them, often against the will and approval of their secular families and at the cost of hatred by their neighbors and the society at large.[54]

Under authoritarian political rule, social networks and local participation fragment rather than integrate the society.[55] By undermining trust, both within and between social actors and the state, authoritarianism may also place social groups in the service of non-democratic goals, and turn them against each other.[56] It is not surprising, then, that the Turkish society was polarized into extremist left-wing and right-wing ideologies and violent struggle in the 1970s.

As a counterpart of rigid state laicism, radical Islamism made its first formal political appearance in Turkey in 1969. Necmeddin Erbakan (1926–), who was a mechanical engineer, formed successive political parties mobilizing political Islam.[57] Milli Nizam (the National Order Party) was formed in 1970 and closed down by the military coup in 1971. Similarly, Milli Selamet (the National Salvation Party) that was formed in 1972 was terminated by the 1980 coup. In 1983, Erbakan founded his last Islamic party, Refah, and became the Prime Minister in 1996 in a coalition government formed by Refah and Doğru Yol (True Path). Refah not only opposed Turkey's membership in the EU but also hosted a radical Islamist faction, referred to as Milli Görüş (National View).[58] The party leadership failed to moderate the party, as its main position remained against the secular state.[59] As the chairman of these successively banned Islamist parties, including Refah, he challenged the secular state tradition by his advocacy of an Islamic state. After the closure of Refah in 1998, he was banned from politics. Nevertheless, he acted as a mentor and informal adviser to the Fazilet (Virtue) and Saadet (Felicity) parties, the mass appeal of which remained marginal.

The initial radicalism of Islam in Turkey was partly shaped by the rigid laicism of the Republic and partly by the personality of Erbakan. In my interview with Süleyman Demirel, a center-right contemporary of Erbakan, I asked him about his views on Islamism in Turkey.[60] During his long years of leadership as Prime Minister, and later as the President of Turkey, he showed considerable tolerance, sympathy and recognition to Islamic groups, but never to Erbakan and his parties. He said, jokingly: "Erbakan's Islamic appeal remained always marginal in Turkey. Has he ever got to stay in power? Not that I can remember. And also, where is he right now?"[61] Demirel emphasized that Turkey was a secular Republic, where the principle of separation of Islam and politics has always been non-negotiable. Erbakan's confrontation with the secular foundations of the Republic, until his ban from politics in 1996, has been associated with his shortsightedness.

However, despite the seemingly stormy past, the accounts that oppose Islam and the state in Turkey misunderstand the nature and extent of the disagreement. As Heper correctly argues, "from 1969 to the present, religiously oriented political cadres in Turkey have increasingly adapted themselves to the secular and democratic system."[62] The rocky encounters between secular and Islamic actors were enveloped by relatively strong political institutions of a functioning competitive electoral democracy. Moreover, they were embedded in a widely shared frame of belonging, the national culture. Multi-party politics contained Islamic dissent within the political institutional framework. Even when there was not enough space in the public sphere for the expression of Islamic symbols and identities, low-key Islamic party politics provided Islamist actors with a limited voice. Radical Islamists remained a marginal group.[63] Islamic parties did not appeal to large masses until the 1990s. The existence of a strong center-right and its appeal for conservative Muslim voters has also limited the popularity of Islamic parties for a long time.

Despite their fragility due to periodic interruptions by the military, the formal institutional channels that were available differentiated the Turkish case from that of other Middle Eastern countries, where street protests have remained as the most common, if not the only, option. These channels have prevented insurrection from becoming a historical pattern of Islamic action in Turkey. Consequently, exiting the system by overthrowing it has never been an attractive option for Turkish Islamic social forces, as it was in Iran.

Post-1980: Public Islam and Its Limits

The military coup in 1980 not only ended the ideological confrontation but also demolished individual and political freedoms. Paradoxically, in sharp contrast to the anti-democratic enforcements of the coup, the post-1980 period witnessed a remarkable turn in state-society relations. The Turkish society and politics have gone through multi-layered transformations in the post-1980 period. "A relaxation of the secularist stances of the state during Turgut Özal's leadership has led to the admission that Islam too is an essential component of Turkish national identity."[64] Prime Minister Özal's efforts (1983–1991) to reconcile neoliberalism, the free market and increasing tolerance for Islam definitely contributed to the expansion of the public sphere in multiple directions.[65] In sharp contrast to the leftist overtone of Islam in Iran (led by Shariati), Islamism in Turkey developed in tune with, and along with, an expanding free market in this period. In the early 1980s, the military rule also supported tolerance for religion in its fight against the ideological extremes of the 1970s, communism in particular.[66] While Islamic associations mushroomed at a dramatic pace, secularist associations also mobilized widespread support for Republican sentiments. Associational life expanded horizontally—and this time legitimately in the public sphere.[67] Loosened state control led to a dramatic reexamination of the persistence and rigidity of Kemalism as an official ideology, which came to be accused of creating a barrier to liberties and liberal democracy. The most vocal critique of the rigidity of Kemalism came from the non-religious Westernized, educated, urban elite, mostly intellectuals and businesspeople, who came to be referred as "Second Republicans."

Beyond an increasingly vivid public sphere, the 1990s also witnessed the rising popularity of Islamic politics in Turkey. The Refah party displayed an exemplary grassroots mobilization by reaching out, recruiting and serving people across the lines of class, occupation, gender and age. However, the victory of Refah, led by Erbakan, in the local elections in 1994 and in national elections in 1996 sparked widespread public fear and suspicion by the state and secularists. This was partly caused by historically rooted mistrust between Islam and the state and partly by the radical faction, inspired by Erbakan's anti-system attitudes, that called for an Islamic state. Due to the limits of the state's tolerance for public Islam, the effectiveness of Islamic networking and grassroots participation also met its limits. Regarded as a threat to secular tradition, Refah was banned in 1998, and its successor Fazilet (Virtue) was banned in 2001. In sharp contrast to the Islamic party's armed reaction against the military intervention in Algeria, religiously oriented masses in Turkey did conform to the state's ban.

Fethullah Gülen and the New World Order

As Charles Tilly successfully argues, modern political regimes could not survive without incorporating the "trust networks" that had previously existed as clandestine groups.[68] Western democracies found themselves in a situation in which they had to "de-democratize" if these networks extracted their resources from society and the polity. The transition of the illiberal Turkish Republic into a liberal democracy has required an effort to largely integrate the Islamic networks, which were previously pushed underground.

As Islamic groups were mushrooming in the 1980s, the already apparent cleavages in the Nur movement were transformed into fragmentations.[69] In one of my earliest interviews with the Nurcus, a writer of the movement told me that "the major disagreement is not on the content and/or meaning of the Kuran, the *Risales* or any other religious text. It is simply about life, power, money and politics. . . . Unfortunately, this is the last thing Nurcus want to hear."[70]

Along with national and global changes, the contemporary Gülen movement differentiated itself from the Nur movement in numerous ways.[71] One of the followers who often visited the leader told me that "although Hocaefendi is deeply influenced by the *Risales*, he also reminds us that Said Nursi never demanded that people should agree with all of his views at all times and places."

Social movements cannot be understood independently of the broader context and structural changes that they are embedded in. When I asked Fethullah Gülen to name the people who influenced his worldview most, he said that he adopted ideas from a wide range of scholars, both from the Islamic and Western worlds, but did not agree fully with any of them. As he made references to both Islamic and Western thinkers, he also mentioned Atatürk's views, especially with regard to nationalism.

Fethullah Gülen was born in 1941 in Erzurum, one of the cities in the eastern Anatolian part of Turkey. Because his mother taught Islam to the children of the village, he was highly educated on the Kuran even in his early childhood.[72] His father was a *vaiz* (Islamic preacher). Some of the followers who knew his parents told me that the depth of their Islamic knowledge, virtue and personal charm were impressive. They observed to me that Gülen's household was hosting leading religious men of those times and offering dinners where Islam was celebrated, discussed and appreciated.[73] During a time when Islamic public activity was strictly prohibited, these private gatherings connected the leader-to-be with many Islamic role models and their ideas.

Fethullah Gülen started *namaz* (prayer five times a day), when he was four. After attending elementary school for two and a half years, he was already alienated and intimated by secularist teachers, who were irritated by his *namaz* in school. Due to the inconvenience of religious practice, he did not continue formal education when the family moved to another town. Instead, he learned to read Ottoman and Arabic from his father and had private tutoring from distinguished mentors, the Hoca. At that time, Said Nursi was a very preeminent religious figure in Turkey. In his first meeting with Said Nursi's students,[74] Fethullah Gülen was enchanted by them and soon joined the movement.[75]

Fethullah Gülen lived and worked in several towns and cities in Turkey. However, most of my informants' stories about the Gülen movement started in Izmir-Kestanepazarı, where Fethullah Gülen was teaching Islam in a Kuran school. The Community around Gülen started to emerge in Izmir in the late 1970s, which was long before the fragmentations in the Nur Community became evident. His preaching started to not only have mass appeal but also to attract prominent national political leaders such as Turgut Özal. Özal was flying from Ankara to Izmir regularly to listen to Hocaefendi, and when he became the Prime Minister in 1983, his increasing incentives for export played an important role in empowering the Anatolian industrialists who constituted a major segment of the growing Gülen movement. The financial and intellectual centers of the movement, including the media outlets, companies and foundations, moved to Istanbul in the early 1980s.

While its forefathers, the Nurcus, experienced severe repression by an authoritarian secular state, the Gülen movement has flourished in the midst of a growing civil society and transition politics in the post 1980-period. As one of my key informants said, "Nurcus encountered and struggled with both the hostility of the Republic and materialism of the West. Today, we see such an opposition irrelevant, as we are active, effective and welcome in a growing market, both inside and outside Turkey."[76]

Paradoxically, the impetus for joining the world market comes from the leader, Fethullah Gülen, whose life and worldview display a consistent asceticism.[77] His "worldly asceticism" keeps him away from material attractions in his personal life. Instead, he insists on a remarkably humble life style and simplicity.[78] He spends most of his time secluded in his room praying and contemplating. At the same time, however, he has also been a strong advocate of commerce and wealth production. Under the political leadership of Özal and religious leadership of Gülen, the followers have been encouraged to accomplish not only cultural but also economic ties with Central Asia. The new Anatolian industrialists who expanded their business to these places are grateful to Fethullah Gülen for his ideas.

Clearly, the larger milieu that the Gülen movement relates to is a radically different kind of Republican project than the one the Nur movement was exposed to up until the 1980s. While a central issue for the followers of Said Nursi was to understand and adapt modernity per se in the 1940s and 1950s, the Gülen movement is comfortably in tune with Western modernity and up-to-date with the latest international trends. Its major *dava* (issue or goal) is the spread of Turkish Muslim ways of life within and outside of the Turkish Republic. They see this goal as part of an expansion of civil society and democracy that is more tolerant to Islamic ways of life.

Unlike Said Nursi, Fethullah Gülen relates to and addresses a Republican project that has gradually come under *re*construction by diverse social and political actors. This is neither a smooth nor a finished process of transition. Both the leader and the movement occasionally come under attack from secularist groups and different branches of the state.

In March 1999, Fethullah Gülen moved to the United States for medical treatment of an ailment. Since then, he has resided in seclusion in a house in northern Pennsylvania surrounded by the houses of the few followers who accompany him there.[79] He rarely leaves the house and spends most of his time reading. As a nationalist, he expresses deep sorrow and nostalgia due to his homesickness.[80] As his guests told me during my visit, he said once sadly that as all his *eş dost* (friends) were in Turkey, he was living far from them in company of *çoluk-çocuk* (young people) of the age of his grandchildren. Although he is legally permitted, he has not returned to the country at the time this book goes to press. When I asked him why he has stayed in the United States, he answered that he did not wish to create another disruption and deep conflict in Turkey.[81]

Fethullah Gülen genuinely despises confrontation and conflict and admires moderation and harmony. Despite ongoing contestations and sporadic attacks against the movement, Fethullah Gülen has not changed his idea about the importance of *"toplum-devlet işbirliği"* (cooperation between the state and the society).[82] He believes that social problems should be dealt with and coped with through cooperation between the state and the society. He sees this cooperation as the basis for progress towards a pure (*temiz*) and moral society. I asked why he insists on advocating non-confrontation and not recommending any form of vocal critique. When I brought up secularists' attacks on the movement, he smiled and repeated his worldview of non-confrontation: "One must open arms to the people even if they come with a knife. *Only* then, you have a chance to change their opinion."When he left after our conversation, his followers told me one of his favorite jokes.

Two mothers-in-law (*kaynana*) in a small village used to fight across the river by saying the meanest words and throwing stones at each other. This continued until one of them gets sick one day. This time, she sends her daughter-in-law and instructs her to swear twice for every insult she hears from the other side. The daughter-in-law goes to the river, meets with the other woman, and does not reply to any of her assaults from across the river. Being left without any response, the woman at the other side of the river increasingly becomes infuriated and "cracks" (*çatlamak*). The daughter-in-law goes back home. When her mother-in-law hears what happened, she starts attacking the daughter-in-law. As the latter refuses to reply, the mother-in-law also cracks from anger.

The Gülen movement has clearly diluted the conflict and gained recognition from the Republic without fighting for it. The leader avoided confrontation without denying the followers' major needs or demands from the state. His view of social and political change is clear: "Regardless of the conditions, the legitimacy [of the state] must not be damaged. . . . Anti-democratic interventions never worked, as we already experienced in Turkey. . . . Problems have to be solved within the system."[83]

He disapproves of both sectarianism and ideological confrontation. Similarly, the followers are in a remarkable consensus on moderation in all aspects of life. They share their leader's dislike of factionalism and ideological extremism, a dislike that came up frequently in my interviews with them: "Islamist, secularist, feminist, leftist . . . I am not any of them, and that is why I find comfort with Gülen's philosophy and insight. Enough with pushing people into camps! We do not want these imposed polarizations anymore."

In line with Fethullah Gülen's views, the movement not only denounces collective representations and labels but also avoids erecting stout boundaries of its own. The movement's fuzzy boundaries facilitate free access and exit. People from diverse backgrounds affiliate to different degrees with the movement. These affiliations range from sympathizers and admirers to benefactors/beneficiaries and the people who are unconditionally in the service of the movement. Pragmatism is a central characteristic of Gülen's associational world, which facilitates the welcoming and incorporation of supporters from diverse backgrounds. A businessman who is a benefactor of several students in the movement's schools told me:

I am not religious. I hardly have time to contemplate metaphysics or spirituality. But I care for good education, scientific and technological progress. This is why I appreciate the Gülen Community. They generate funds for poor bright students who do not have the opportunity to go to a good school. . . . Personally, I am really tired of the cleavage between Islamists and secularists. I do not see why there should be a split between the secular and Islamic businessmen associations, TÜSIAD [Türk Sanayici ve Isadamları Dernegi (Association of Turkish Businessmen)] and MÜSIAD [Müstakil Sanayici ve Isadamları Dernegi (Association of Muslim Businessmen)].

Similar to the AKP's break from Refah, the dissociation of Gülen from the Nur movement suggests that Turkey is witnessing a transformation from radicalism to moderation. There is an explicit shift from Islamic politics to secular-friendly forms of Islam, and from parochial ties to the Muslim community to national and international commitments.

Between the Zones of Comfort and Discomfort

When I visited the movement's research center, Akademi, in Çamlıca-Istanbul, it was still a project in process.[84] I met with Ihsan Bey, who was in charge of the center. When I explained to him my research on Islamic movements, his immediate response was rather interesting: "So, how am I supposed to be related with this subject matter? We are not organizing *Risale* readings here. It is about science and knowledge." I was puzzled. He was an Islamic scholar who had studied theology and had also been a Nur student. He was Fethullah Gülen's close friend and a leading figure in the Islamic movement. Ihsan Bey explained that religiosity was not primary to most of the movement's organizations, activities and projects. He said, "Religion is a subtitle in our undertakings."

Due to the popularity of the movement, it has been under continual public scrutiny. Hence, public life has had to be thought of and fashioned carefully. Ihsan Bey was skillful in impression management, to use Goffman's term. He was intimately involved in working on the self-presentation of the movement in public life. He told me how hard he had to work on "Hocaefendi's image," his clothing and his public appearance. He had a very hard time convincing Fethullah Gülen to become used to Western clothing, that is, the suit, after many years of wearing religious forms of clothing. He said: "He really resisted strongly being a public figure in this sense. He was a man of a deep inner world and preferred to be left alone there. . . . But soon he found himself in front of the masses." In addition to Ihsan Bey's efforts, the movement has also worked with a professional advertising company, which has organized public relations and the public images of the movement.

"What kind of an Islamic movement would make religion a subtitle?" I asked. He answered: "The one that is a part of civil society and works on developing it." Islam and civil society had for a long time been regarded as a "contradiction in terms" in the Republican context.[85] This stood in sharp contrast to the countries such as the United States that are based on the idea of compatibility between religion, freedom, civil society and democracy. Due to the Republican discomfort, there has been an unspoken self-reflexivity and self-consciousness among the followers of the Gülen movement. This awareness surfaces either in some form of passive uneasiness in the lives of followers or proactive rearrangement of everyday life.

Cognizant of the heavy historical baggage of Islamism in the secular Turkey, the movement has engineered a progressive, tolerant and thereby pluralist image by highlighting its focus on science, knowledge, education (mostly in English) and international commerce. The public self-presentation has been achieved at the cost of under-representing the Islamic face, faith and faith-based activities in the public sphere.[86] Here, one issue is of great importance to our understanding of the movement. Although image making is a conscious act of adaptation, the feeling of discomfort is often a non-deliberate and emotional response rather than a rational one. It reflects the followers' aspiration for recognition and for visibility as legitimate social actors in the secular context of Turkey.

The self-presentation is the outcome of long-term individuation of the movement through its interaction within the larger institutional milieu. Despite this shared belonging and connectedness with the national, however, the fact that the movement stands *separately* from both other Islamic groups and the secular Republic creates a good deal of discomfort in the lives of followers.

CONDITIONS OF "SHARING" A PUBLIC SPACE

As the movement was not located in a single location, neighborhood, city or country, I participated in the widely spread private and public sites where the followers lived, socialized, ate, studied, worked and mobilized in organizations. However, on one occasion, I invited a few young women to my neighborhood, Teşvikiye. This part of Istanbul is filled with Western-style cafés, restaurants, beauty salons and boutiques, which reflect primarily the life styles of the secular actors. Although the neighborhood has a highly secular outlook, it is considered liberal enough to accommodate diverse social groups ranging from jet-set society to bohemian artists, intellectuals, writers, students and human rights activists. There are also a few students' houses of the movement, Işık evleri, that are shared by several students of the Gülen movement in the neighborhood. When I met with a few female followers of the Gülen movement and started to walk towards a café, the immediate symbolic interaction was smooth. My guests seemed to feel comfortable.

Soon, one of the female followers, Fatma, stated that she "did not feel comfortable walking in a group of covered women" on the street. She said, "We must be looking as if we are *Islamists ready for taking action* rather than ready for afternoon tea. We should have met in a café instead of walking all together." I asked if she received any negative vibes or looks from people on the street. She said, "Well, we share the same streets, same public space, you know. . . . I would be fine if I were alone, but I feel uncomfortable in public when I realize that we may attract too much attention as a group of *Islamist-looking* people. . . . We simply look different than everybody else around us." Fatma's discomfort was clearly caused by not fitting the predominant outlook of the public space. This was a clear difference from the private and communal realm of her life, where I had met with her several times in Üsküdar. It is important to note, however, that when she was crossing the boundary between the zones of her self-comfort and discomfort, she only became self-conscious. She and her friends did not express any resentment or desire to change the way things were organized between these two zones. On the contrary, she was willing to adjust the difference between home and street by diluting a potential conflict and distracting attention as much as possible. The incident helped me to gain a deeper understanding of the public sites of the movement. After observing many similar instances, I realized that conflict-avoidance and readiness to adjust was not simply a strategy or a result of training but was also, and mainly, an emotional response of the Islamic actors.

In one of my meetings with some of the male followers, I brought up similar incidences of discomfort experienced mostly by covered female followers. Talal Bey, who was in charge of public relations, told me: "What is so strange about this? People avoid eating garlic in public places in order to be considerate to others, don't they? Public life is based on civilized consideration of other people's needs and freedoms."

AT THE "WINDOW SITES":
THE DISPLAYS OF PUBLIC ISLAM

Classic accounts have regarded the public sphere as a *shared* realm that escapes not only state control but also religious censorship of the society.[87] More recent approaches have highlighted the *antagonistic* nature of the public sphere, where social actors and informal associations challenge the formal political institutions and states.[88] The fast-growing public exposure of the Gülen movement cannot be explained by either of these views of the public sphere. First, these sites produce not confrontation but cooperation. Second, they do not avoid or escape from state monitoring but overtly invite its gaze. The movement engineers "window sites" (*vitrin*) in the public realm. By "window sites," I refer to the movement's numerous public events inside and outside of Turkey that ensure transparency and accountability, both to the public and the state. Not surprisingly, they are very hospitable to the media channels and the researchers who wish to study them. Moreover, like the schools of the movement, these sites invite and welcome a wide range of visitors, including state and military officials. The purpose of these sites is to exhibit the movement's civic goals, pro-democratic undertakings and increasing appeal of the movement. Despite their wide dispersion across the globe, the window sites are a perfect example of efficient collective action. They are more organized than they appear.[89]

The movement entered the public sphere with a strong motto for toleration, referred to as the "Dialogue between Civilizations." The public sites have been fashioned accordingly to appeal to diverse groups and to accommodate individual and group differences. The ultimate goal was passing the long-due test of pluralism. This goal has been remarkably facilitated by the fuzzy boundaries of the movement in the public realm. Blurry boundaries not only intertwine Muslim and secular symbols, identities and practices but also facilitate free access and exit for diverse constituents. The diversity of associational life proactively encourages toleration between the old enemies, the Islamists and secularists. It also mobilizes cooperation across the lines of class, gender and religious and political orientation, attracting even Jewish businesspeople. These are the sites where you may see an Imam next to a Jewish businessperson discussing a new school project in one of the African countries. The public sites and associations accommodate people with very different degrees, and types of, affiliation. In addition to devout followers, I met individuals ranging from curious celebrities, such as pop singers and film actors, to benefactors, such as businessmen and public intellectuals.

In some window sites, a considerable amount of charity is collected from a wide range of sources. The public events encourage the masses to contribute to educational projects, to finance schools and to help students to study and pay for their living expenses. Charity and fund-raising events, which are often by invitation, aim to accumulate more funding through endowment. Other window sites also bring Turkish and foreign scholars from different religious orientations together and encourage the discussion of laicism, democracy, religion and other topics. Followers and sympathizers in North America transfer funds from foundations in order to provide interfaith activities and dinners.[90] The funds are also used to build mosques where Muslim religious practice is taught to people who are either interested in Islam or converting to it. Hence, the public sites of the Gülen movement in North America are even more pluralistic than the ones in Turkey, especially in terms of the participants' religion, nationality and ethnicity.

The public sites qualify as civic associations by creating a public spirit of tolerance and cooperation.[91] They have promoted Turkey's specific goals, such as membership in the European Union and alliance with the United States, as prerequisites for opening to Western democracies across the world. Except for the strikingly Western look, the movement's public sites display a pattern that is hardly unique in the Muslim context. In many respects, they resemble Islam-motivated "civic engagement" in other Muslim countries, promoting similar—although not identical—goals in the public sphere, such as pluralism and tolerance.[92]

However, what distinguishes the Gülen movement from similar Islamic projects in the Middle East is the *unintended* outcomes of these public activities. Ironically, these Islamic sites display more loyalty to the secular republic and Atatürk in Turkey than several other secular organizations do. The movement displays a secularized outlook at the associational level. Most of the Gülen schools inside and outside of Turkey have Atatürk corners. Many public events reiterate famous quotes from Atatürk. As one of the leading figures of the movement stated: "I may be religious, but our companies, schools and other associations are not." Similarly, one does not need to wear a headscarf in the public sites of the movement. Considering the heterogeneity of constituents these sites attract, this is not at all surprising. As Fethullah Gülen emphasized clearly, faith (*iman*) could not be reduced to such politicized Islamic symbols as the headscarf. He preached that these "details" should not prevent or discourage one from having faith in modern times.

What, then, was the unintentional, unplanned consequence of these planned beneficiary activities and project-based civil society action? These window sites have provided platforms for dialogue with both the Turkish state and the West. They have facilitated mutual recognition between the state and Islam. They have mobilized a wide range of social actors to address and actively take part in the rethinking and debating of the basic principles of the Republic. Most importantly, by mobilizing and accommodating engagements with the "grand design" of the founding fathers, they have provided alternative channels of communication with the state. Hence, they have contributed to the proliferation of civil society, not just by purposely creating horizontal networks and civic projects but also by

unintentionally creating vertical ties to the state. State actors, even including high-ranking military officials in Turkey, either visit these sites—the
events and schools—or observe them through the media and public
debates.

The window sites and the public events they host change from country to country. Their goals and agendas seem to be in complete accord
with the national culture of the host country and adapted to its broader
associational life in general. While most sites in Turkey accommodate public discussions on laicism, the window sites in the United States consist
predominantly of interfaith and faith-provoking activities and seminars on
dialogue between civilizations. Not surprisingly, the latter nurture a
peaceful atmosphere between various religious traditions and groups—
especially Christianity, Islam and Judaism—as a solution to the global terror most feared by the United States. When I asked the followers in service in Massachusetts what the purpose of the movement's activities in the
United States was, they answered: "We want to show the Americans and
the American state that Turkish Muslims aim at peace in the world, and
democracy at home. We must clarify our distinction from terrorist organizations before it is too late."[93]

Similarly, in Central Asia, the window sites concentrate on the organization of cultural events that glorify the heroic past of the Muslim Turks.
A striking example of displays of belonging takes place in window sites
when the movement displays the success of the schools in the Turkic
Central Asian countries in Turkey. They show videotapes of the Kazak,
Kirghiz and Turkmen kids singing the Turkish anthem. This creates an
emotionally charged atmosphere, which often leads to tears and ecstatic
applause in the audience.

The goals of the extremely visible and highly advertised activities in the
window sites differ across the world. However, regardless of the nature of
the "civil society project" at hand, these sites provide the platforms for the
participants to engage the broader political and institutional frame of the
nation-states.

INVISIBLE BOUNDARIES BETWEEN FRONT AND BACK
STAGES: LIMITS OF TOLERATION

During my travels between various sites, I realized that the window
sites differed from the followers' undertakings in the private realm. This is
how I gradually discovered different levels of front and back stages in the
movement. The back stages were more intimate places in people's homes
and dorms, where informal get-togethers among circles of friends and,
most importantly, community undertakings took place. I gained access to

the back stages of the movement very slowly as the informants began to trust me. Slowly, as they opened up, an entirely pious and moralizing world opened its doors to me, a world that was dramatically different from the secular face of the window sites.

Because the back stages were relatively less affected by the image-making and project-based undertakings, they often lacked the commonly shared discourses of dialogue and tolerance that the window sites promoted.[94] More importantly, the tributes to Atatürk and the display of Atatürk's corners and symbols did not translate to the private sphere either.[95] Hence, while window sites of associational life facilitated engagements with the state, the private realm of domestic and communal life mobilized extensive faith-based undertakings and moral ways of life. It is important to note that the transparency of the window sites definitely contributed to the increasing acceptability and legitimacy of the private lives of the devout.

A good example of a back stage would be women's *Risale* readings, which brought female followers together for various kinds of sociability in the domestic space. In contrast to the mixing of men and women in the public sites, activities in the private and communal sites displayed consistent gender segregation. Women's *Risale* readings consisted of reading, interpreting and teaching of the text among the female followers, during which they also chatted, had tea and ate. Moreover, unlike the free access to window site activities, these readings were taking place in the female followers' homes, where access was naturally limited to the insiders and acquaintances. New participants could be incorporated through other women in the groups and had to be invited by the hosts. Numerous women's groups gathered weekly in many neighborhoods across Turkey as well as in many cities across the world. Spirituality, faith-based emotionality and religiosity were the basic characteristics of these gatherings, in which the devout shared their inner world and faith. These get-togethers were clearly not seeking pluralistic constituents but aimed at strengthening the communal ties.[96]

I participated in various women's *Risale* reading groups regularly. Unlike in the public sites, I was soon encouraged by the women participants to wear a headscarf and to start practicing *namaz*. Indeed, at one point I was given a fancy handmade headscarf as a gift "from the heart of the women" of the reading group. This was a striking difference from the window sites, where a woman does not need to cover her head, practice religion or be part of any religious activity. I slowly learned that in the back stages, the "power of suggestion" (but not force) and the hold of the pious community (even though not an ascriptive one) were stronger than individual inclinations. Although entrance was by individual choice, once one was *in* he or she was expected to meld into the group. After a while, I could clearly discern the boundaries that distinguished public and private activities in the movement. The differences also affected the role I was playing in the followers' lives. While I was recognized as a designated "participant observer" and a sociologist in the front stages (window sites), in the back stages (more private domestic and communal sites) I was seen less as a sociologist and more as a follower-to-be in the eyes of the adherents. In contrast to the successfully engineered lightness of being in the front stages, I could feel the tangible requirements and heaviness of being "inside."

THE PRIVATE SPHERE: UNIFORMITY
AND ITS ILLIBERAL TENDENCIES

Şerif Mardin, the prominent sociologist, noted in his classic study of the Nur movement that the boundaries of the private sphere expanded in Turkey to accommodate religious activities that had been banned or marginalized in the public and political spheres for a long time.[97] When we follow the Nur movement to its successor Gülen movement in the post-1980 period, we see that the increasing visibility of Islam in the public realm has not coincided with a shrinking of the private sphere of Islamic activities.

In the public sphere, the meaning of freedom refers to individual freedom to be different, to be able to disagree and to experiment. In the private sphere of Islamic actors' lives, freedom is regarded as the free exercise of religion and morality without having to downplay the central role of religion in one's life. The novelty and attraction of this kind of freedom becomes obvious when we recall that this was not tolerated by the state until recently.

The inner core consists of altruistic followers who are unconditionally in service (*hizmet*) of the Community inside and outside the national borders.[98] They voluntarily serve the "common good" in the name of God but also for their love and loyalty to the Community's leader. *Hizmet* is a broad term encompassing a wide range of activities of service and work done for the Community movement. In the realm of education, *hizmet* includes the work of teachers, mentors and staff in schools. Some followers have paid jobs in the movement's organizations or schools inside and outside of Turkey, and some do it as unpaid voluntary work and charity.[99] The strength and efficiency of *hizmet* have been regarded very highly as the cornerstone of networking for Islamic action in Turkey. However, as communal service, valued often as "social capital," is a common characteristic in most Islamic movements in the region, it definitely does not explain the success of the Gülen movement and the AKP in becoming participants in broader democratization.

The main characteristic of everyday life among those in the inner core is communal order and discipline. There is no obligation to join and remain in the inner core or to be in service. However, if one chooses to be a part of it, there is not much negotiation over the ruling principles of life and morality. It is an all-encompassing package deal that cannot be chosen halfway. The uniform rule-bound piety in the private sites provides an ambiguous contrast to the tolerant discourses in the public sites. The pious private sites impose rigid restrictions on individual liberties. Depending on the context, the control of the devout may include even the arrangement of intimate issues such as marriage, friendships and hygiene by the Gülen Community. The Community also imposes traditional gender roles and explicit gender segregation and inequality, restrictions that do not apply to the associational sites. For instance, marriage with more than one woman is unseen and unheard of in the window sites, but there are few instances of polygamy within the Community. These cases are recognized and accommodated by the followers and leadership of the movement. Liberal values promoted in the window sites, such as tolerance for individual freedom, are replaced by the rule-observing moral life of the inner core. The communalistic overtone of these private sites is clearly distinct from the public life of the Community, where contract-based and impersonal ties reinforce respect for individualism. Why, then, have the states accommodated the movement, despite this striking discrepancy between front and back stages?

Reconciling the Tension between In and Out: The School Sites

The schools provided me with the most illuminating piece of evidence to help understand how the tension between the private and public life is reconciled in the movement. While curricular activity in the classroom was secular and scientific, extracurricular activities in the dormitories socialized the students into Turkish Muslim ways of life. Put differently, the movement reconciled pious ways of life and secular institutional milieus through the departmentalization of scientific teaching in the classroom (perceived as public) and pious and moral life styles in dormitories (perceived as private). Such pragmatic departmentalization can also be observed in many other areas of activity of the movement, such as business, trade and health and media outlets.

Ironically, there was nothing private about the dormitories. Private lives were more communally shared than in the ostensibly shared public sites.[100]

Here, the meaning of "private" needs to be redefined as not only domestic, pertaining to the person and/or household, but also, primarily, communal and therefore implying the privacy of the Community. Whether it is domestic or communal, it remains outside the realm of window sites. As I continued my journey towards more private lives of the staff and students, another paradox surfaced. The everyday lives of the insiders revealed that insiders accepted restrictions while at the same time agreeing to tolerate the freedoms in the public sites, especially for the outsiders. Indeed, the insiders genuinely tolerated individual liberties in associational life. However, their toleration is conditional. The more remote the affiliation of constituents to the inner core, the more tolerance was shown to them. As many informants agreed, the highest level of tolerance and openness was offered to potential newcomers. This is why and how the solidarity and commitment in the inner core of the Community, a Gemeinschaft (*cemaat*), enables the mobilization of a larger, diffuse and loosely organized network of public associational life, a Gesellschaft (*cemiyet*).

Shared morality and pious ways of life are spread particularly through obligatory boarding schools and summer camps, that is, in dormitories and Işık Evleri.[101] The educational projects and extracurricular activities do not leave private space for individual experimentation. Schools and a program of moral education are major ways to recruit followers for *hizmet*, whereas public events and the business world are the windows of the Community to the "outside."

The schools and dormitories were not reserved for, or chosen only by, the followers and their children. Students from different backgrounds attend the Gülen schools for different reasons. Some non-religious factors that render Gülen schools attractive for parents are high standards of safety, morality, cleanliness; the use of technology; the high quality of teaching; and the availability of guidance.[102] These qualities appeal to conservative families from rural areas who wish to send their children to safe and good schools in the city. *Ağabeys* and *ablas* (advising brothers and sisters)[103] fulfill their *hizmet* as voluntary mentors. They help students academically as they also supervise their lives. Once the students begin living in dormitories or Işık Evleri, they soon find themselves surrounded with the Community and its absorbing world. There are varying degrees of control over what the students do, learn and read; what they wear, eat and drink; and with whom they associate. The movement also organizes summer camps for religious training and intense worshipping. The camp schedules are inflexible, and students' lives are structured rigidly.

It is important to note that the discontinuities between public and private are largely a matter of different manifestations of the Islamic way of life as experienced by Islamic actors, rather than spatial boundaries that separate people into two realms or groups. Put differently, the Islamic actors constantly cross these boundaries, which link rather than separate their multiple affiliations, belongings and practices. Although the inner core tends to curb individual freedoms, Islamic actors' increasing freedom of mobility between private, public and political realms leads to an emerging self-questioning. Self-reflection is more common among Islamic women and among youth who reflect upon the discomforts that originate from crossing boundaries (see chapters 3 and 5 for more on the tensions experienced by the students and women). This self-questioning is clearly an indicator of micro-transformations of Islamic ways of life, along with broader sociopolitical transformations in Turkey.

Rethinking the Linkages between the State and Islam

The spontaneous reconfigurations of inside/outside, core/periphery, private/public have put pressure on the insiders and created tension in their everyday lives. However, at the same time, they have helped the movement to adapt to the secular institutional milieu by facilitating integration into the Republic. Not only have the Islamic actors adjusted to the secular institutional milieu but the state has also learned to accommodate Islamic ways of life. The Islamic actors' rearrangement of their everyday lives has eased the state's accommodation of the sizable public presence and increasing powers of the Gülen movement. The smooth tuning between Islamic ways of life and the secular Republic should not be surprising. After all, "cultures and institutions belong together since institutions are both carriers and reinforcing mechanisms of culture."[104]

The movement has reconciled secular diversity in the public realm with uniform morality in the private sphere. It is important to note that these alternative rearrangements were caused neither by the state's patronage of Islam nor by Islamization of the state. Some studies have interpreted the increasingly non-confrontational overtones of Islam in Turkey as the products of statism.[105] There are a few analytical confusions that require clarification here. The followers of the Gülen movement are neither opponents of the state nor statist forces. First, *etatism* refers to the idea or practice that advocates the control of economic and political powers by a centralized state. This state-centered view leaves social actors with little or no power and influence on the state. Although the shifting links between the state and Islam in Turkey may seem as another incident of passive obedience to the authoritarian states of the Middle East, a closer look at Islamic agency suggests the opposite.[106] The mutual recognition of boundaries between religion and the state has provided autonomy for Islamic actors. More importantly, the new forms of compartmentalization in Islamic ways of life have endowed them with more freedom of mobility to move between and excel in all spheres of life, such as education, business, media and politics.

Second, the primacy of faith-reviving activity would be expected to put the Gülen movement into a conflict-ridden antagonistic relationship with the secular state, a relationship that would estrange the followers. Contrary to this anticipation, faith-based activities have motivated the followers to participate in rethinking the most rigid principles of the state more constructively. This was definitely not one of the goals or agendas of collective action at the window sites, which mobilized resourcefully for a variety of faith-reviving activities. Diversifying the public sites, for example, was one of the calculated pro-democratic ends that may have helped Islam to pass the test of pluralism.[107] However, the uniformity of the private sites has contradicted the diversity in the public sites and put pluralism into question.[108] Islam has contributed to democratization in an unplanned way. The reorganization of Islam in the public and private realms has had an unintended effect on broader transformations in Turkey. By changing the nature of secularization from top-down forceful to a bottom-up voluntary process, Islamic actors have eased the compatibility between the secular order and liberal democracy in a Muslim context.

Zubaida correctly emphasized that secularization was an "irreversible" process in the Middle East. However, he argued that "the recently resurgent political Islam [was] directed precisely against . . . the secularizing reforms that have occurred extensively in the region for two centuries."[109] As discussed before, the firmness of the walls that the Turkish Republic set between religion and politics have stood out among the inconsistent and hesitant trajectories of secularization in the Middle East.[110] Yet, at the same time, these secure walls also undermined the development of civil society and a liberal democracy in Turkey. Indeed, contrary to the predominant view of Islam as secularization-resistant in the West,[111] most authoritarian states of the Middle East have been forceful in separating religion and politics. The main problem has been that they have failed in creating friendly boundaries and interaction between Islam and the state.

Where formal and informal channels of interaction between Islamic actors and the state have been largely missing, public Islam may merely intensify the conflict, and undermine rather than strengthen democratic institutions in the Middle Eastern context. Indeed, public Islam and Islamic political parties in the Middle East have largely failed to promote democracies or have declined under authoritatively secular regimes. When

Refah came to power in 1996 in Turkey, it displayed high skills of local grassroots mobilization and horizontal networking. Similarly, Khatami's government managed to instigate a reform movement by opening a public debate on popular sovereignty, civil society and democracy in Iran. Al-Azhar in Egypt also used to be one of the most effective centers of Islamic knowledge and education that propelled civic participation.[112] However, in all of these cases the anticipated success of public Islam was blocked by authoritarian states. Refah was closed by the Turkish state, which hampered the hopes of a flourishing democracy in Turkey. Khatami lost his appeal as he surrendered to the orthodox clergy. Al-Azhar was co-opted by the Egyptian state, which undermined the seeds of a fragile civil society. Hence, whether or not public Islam can propel democratization is conditional. In the Turkish case, discomforts felt by Islamic actors invited them to separate and rearrange their private and public lives. Consequently, these discomforts of public Islamic actors have set the stage for an alternative secularization of Islam in Turkey. The 1980s and the 1990s have seen increasing numbers of Islamic actors who have voluntarily adapted to the secular institutional milieu. In turn, this voluntary secularization of Islamic ways of life is contributing to the transformation of the authoritarian laicist Republic into a more tolerant secular democracy.

CHAPTER 3

Contestations over Education

THE EFFECTIVE negotiation of boundaries between the state and the faithful has not entirely saved Islamic actors from tension and conflict. As this new turn endowed the Gülen movement with more public visibility and power, it has further puzzled and irritated the hardcore secularists. Following the soft military intervention in February 1997, the secularists started to openly attack the Gülen movement for betraying Atatürk's tradition, abusing "civil society" and undermining democracy. When I asked the adherents of the secularist organizations what they meant by "civil society," one explained to me eagerly: "Civil society in Turkey is the waged war against Islamists, who threaten our Republic." Another one replied: "Civil society is the civilization that Atatürk left to us and what Islamists are trying to ruin." The secularists' claims for ownership of "civil society" were provocative enough to activate competition from Islamic social forces.

This chapter analyzes selectively, not exhaustively, several instances and sites of contestation, sites that range from bitter dispute to negotiation. On the one hand, I analyze multiple layers of tension and conflict *within* and *between* the Islamic and the secularist social forces. On the other, I explore how the movement has negotiated over the schools without confronting the secular state. More importantly, I will look at how the secular state responded to these conflicts between the secularists and the followers of the Gülen movement. An in-depth understanding of contestations can shed light on the ways in which the political institutional framework accommodates dissent and consensus.[1]

Due to the growing number and popularity of the movement's schools, the major area of contestation between the state and the Gülen movement has been education. National education has been the main avenue of the nation-states to mold and unite the society.[2] Standardized national education is a powerful tool of nation-states for shaping fresh minds into a loyal citizenry and for instilling a widely shared feeling of belonging. Similarly in Turkey, secular national education has typically been one of the strongest arms of the Turkish state, by which it has not only penetrated the society but also demanded obedience to its staunchly laicist character.[3]

Clearly, it is not a coincidence that education has gradually become the main area of activity of the Gülen movement, both inside and outside Turkey.[4] Contrary to the secularists' common opinion, the Gülen schools integrate faith *not* into the curriculum but rather into the students' lives. The movement aims at revitalizing faith without challenging the secular character of national education. Contrary to public opinion, the most contentious issue about these schools has been not their threat to the secular order. What has disturbed the secularists most has been the growing influence of moral conservatism in Turkey in the last decades. The movement's remarkable accumulation of various sources of power has triggered anger among secularist organizations.

Upward Social Mobility and Transfer of Social Sources of Power

The traditional distance between the state and society in Turkey was not the only barrier to the development of a vital civil society in Turkey. Civil society was also largely undermined by the absence of middle-class ethics and "the timidity and the non-enterprising spirit" of the Turkish entrepreneurs.[5] The Gülen movement breaks both of these historical patterns that had caused a great deal of dependency of social actors on the state. Although the movement attracted people from various economic and social backgrounds, all followers shared the same ideal. They aspired to upward socioeconomic mobility and valued middle-class life styles and ethics. More importantly, they all agreed that this mobility could be attained through high-quality education. Their faith in social mobility gave rise to a strong incentive for cross-class cooperation. The movement attracted a large number of brave entrepreneurs, whose businesses ranged from small to large in size. Their strong sense of initiative had been nourished by Fethullah Gülen's encouragement for international networks of trade and business.

"One facet of Mr. Gülen's success is wealth creation. Many of his followers have become rich."[6] Since the mid-1980s, the movement has flourished immensely by taking full advantage of a growing free-market economy. Most followers are genuine proponents of economic liberalism.

Associational life in the movement seems to provide an affirmation of Adam Smith's worldview that commerce is innocent and distracts attention from political conflict while bringing prosperity.[7]

Fethullah Gülen states that the *müminler* (Muslim believers) will become increasingly influential in world trade and the global market. By invoking the image of the Golden Age of Islam, a time of vigorous trade when the Prophet Muhammad lived, he reinforces the expansion of networks at both the national and international levels.[8] The movement is in tune and actively involved with the global economy and international politics. While schools educate "morally superior" and internationally competitive generations, businesspeople create and strengthen international ties of commerce. This is how a moderate Islamic movement has found its way into the "international corporate bourgeoisie."[9] The new Islamic bourgeois bridges the faithful individual with the secular state and international world order. The Islamic businesspeople play an important role in making the state and bureaucracy responsive to the movement in particular, and the faithful in general.

The multiple spheres of activity and investments in the movement are neither separate nor distinct from each other. On the contrary, one of the greatest strengths of the movement is the smooth transferability of these resources from one sphere to another. The movement transfers economic power into human capital by connecting the capital accumulation of businesspeople and entrepreneurs with the knowledge accumulation of educators. Concretely, the adherents in the business community invest money in the schools and scholarships, which contribute to the accumulation of intellectual power, and that, in turn, produces more capital due to the academic success of the private schools. The increasing efficiency of the Gülen movement both in Turkey and internationally can largely be explained by the efficient connectedness of these separate outlets. The movement's networks facilitate cooperation between business, trade, education and the media in particular. The followers and friends of Fethullah Gülen own firms, hospitals, stock-holding companies, media outlets, newspapers, TV and radio stations and supermarket chains.[10] More importantly, these organizations voluntarily place their resources in the service of the movement. Hence, the movement has considerable and growing holdings of capital, both in the hands of individual followers and in the associations and foundations of the movement. Contrary to public opinion, the leader of the movement has nothing to do with this capital or any ownership associated with the movement. He insists that the schools are not *his* schools, saying, "I do not own them. Neither do I own anything that is associated with the movement."

Fuzzy boundaries help to accumulate and transfer different sources of power. The movement's economic power has been fortified, for example, through strong connections with national and local politicians in Turkey. The followers of the movement have also established new ties with local and national politicians in host countries, where it has opened schools. In Almati, Kazakhstan, for example, the Kazak-Turk Education Foundation maintains strong connections and close interactions with both the president and local politicians. As I witnessed phone calls from Kazakhstan's president, Nursultan Nazarbayev, in the movement's foundation, I also observed phone conversations with other political leaders in the movement foundations in Istanbul. Hüseyin Bey, a highly respected educator in Almati stated: "The president of Kazakhstan would never disappoint us and never turn us down." The movement is "connected" in the fullest sense of the term, as the *Economist* reported: "They are in the police, they have judges, and nobody is stopping them." The scope and influence of movement activities is striking. This has contributed to the growing fear of secularists that the movement has a conspiracy to take over the state (*devleti ele gecirmek*).

More than five hundred schools, both high schools and universities, were founded in the name of the Gülen movement around the world. More than one hundred of these high schools are located in Turkey, and the rest are in different countries and continents. The movement owns seven universities, two of which—Süleyman Demirel University in Almati and Fatih University in Istanbul—I visited during my fieldwork. The schools' quality, competitive standards, technology and curricula are affirmed by the distinct successes of the graduating students.[11] The movement offers scholarships to outstanding students and prepares them for competitive exams at the national and international levels. The aspirations for education in the movement are high. The best students are encouraged to pursue graduate studies in high-ranking universities in North America—such as Harvard, MIT, Princeton, McGill, Boston University, and the University of Massachusetts—and are supported in doing so.

The movement's schools do not offer a religious curriculum or an Islamic education. Science is taught almost exclusively, with the exception of a history course that covers world religions. Instruction in movement schools, both in and out of Turkey, is mainly in English and partly in Turkish. The schools are equipped with modern technology. Books and other course materials are imported from the West. Through education, the movement aims to adapt to the information age and to be competitive at the international level.

It is important to note, however, that scientific teaching in the classroom is accompanied by moral education in extracurricular activities. As boarding is obligatory in all movement schools, students spend much of their time in the dormitories, where a good deal of socialization and acculturation occur. As a result, the extracurricular activities in the dormitories effectively shape students' worldviews, and their identities. Outside the classroom and scientific teaching, students are given structure in their lives to save them from degeneration, immorality and decadence through moral education and discipline. Providing the structure is the responsibility of the devout teachers, who are unconditionally in the service of the movement. Their loyalties are so deep that when they are appointed by the movement, they voluntarily teach in high schools anywhere in the world. Often, these followers take their family with them. They are sometimes appointed to places with harsh physical conditions, such as Siberia, or to countries with limited infrastructure, such as in Africa and the new post-Soviet countries in Central Asia.

The leader, Fethullah Gülen has often made assurances that the schools are completely devoid of any traits of Islamism and fundamentalism and operate in line with the national education of the states.[12] Moreover, he has made a promise to close them down if any features of the schools are found to be against the secular Turkish Republic. By inviting high-ranking military officials to the schools, the movement has avoided the expected tension between the movement and the military. Several prominent politicians and high-ranking retired military officials have been welcomed and hosted by the movement schools.

Although the movement's schools have largely been accommodated by other host states, they have come under attack by the secularists in Turkey. They soon became the focus of public attention as well as an object of revulsion among hardcore secularists in Turkey. This dislike was intensified not only by the Gülen movement's increasing influence on education and the growing number of its schools but also by its claims to be part of civil society.

Contesting the Civilizing Project: Monopolizing the Civil Society

The late 1990s witnessed a growing interest in civil society in Turkey. On one side, secularists joined forces under the umbrella of "United Civil Society Organizations" (STKB, for Sivil Toplum Kuruluşları Birliği).[13] The STKB became the embodiment of a renewed enthusiasm for "rescuing" the secular Republic from the presumed "Islamic threat." On the other side, Islamic organizations and associations grew rapidly. They claimed to act as promoters of civil society, by revitalizing faith and legitimizing faith-based ways of life in the secular Republic. Whether through secularizing or Islamizing projects, both camps *claimed* to play a role in promoting civil society and democracy. The unspoken goal of each side was to shape the nation according to its worldview. Without admitting it, they contested the nature of the broader frame, the Republican project.

Although my requests for interviews were often rejected by leading figures of STKB, I had numerous daily conversations and informal chats with members in everyday sites. Art galleries, theaters and music halls— such as Atatürk Kültür Merkezi and Cemal Resit Rey—Istanbul art festivals, jazz clubs and membership clubs provided perfect opportunities to run into the actively involved secularists. There was a striking continuity between these conversations. The secularists expressed confidence in their sense of belonging to the Republic, while at the same time consistently excluding Islamic actors from belonging. Whether the framework was the nation, the Republic or civil society, the boundaries and meaning were defined and secured by exclusion of "Islamists."

Secularists' preoccupation with civil society echoed Atatürk's vision of progress and development as a civilizing project. Atatürk said: "Our thinking and our mentality will have to become civilized. . . . Take a look at the entire Turkish and Islamic world. Because they failed to adapt to the conditions [they] found themselves in such a catastrophe and suffering. . . . We have to move forward."[14]

The civilizing project meant a move toward Western civilization and away from the Islamic ones.[15] Like other secularists, the active members of STKB felt confident in holding the tenure of the state tradition. Taking over the role as guardians of the state, STKB felt very strongly that the Republic had been left to their trust. My interviews with the secular adherents of STKB suggested that they collectively shared a perception of the state as a fixed and monolithic entity. Most were in agreement that Islam was inherently an enemy of the secular state, and was therefore incompatible with civil society and democracy. They were reluctant to discuss the issue any further.

Secularist Republicans regarded civil society as their own national monopoly, which disqualified Islamic actors for civilizing projects. However the fast-growing Gülen movement provided a challenge to the self-assured quality of this monopoly. The Islamic movement started to contest the secularists' presumed territory of not only civil society but also national belonging. As Atilla Ilhan, a secular left-wing writer and public intellectual, correctly stated, "Fethullah Hoca is the child of the Republic (*cumhuriyet çocugu*)."[16] Feelings of belonging were non-negotiable, even with the self-assigned guardians of the state.

The secularists were not threatened by the unbridgeable gap between themselves and the movement. On the contrary, they were intimidated by the proximity of this moderate movement—closer than any other Islamist group in Turkey—to the Republican framework. This odd familiarity disrupted the secularists' comfort zone, the safe monopoly of the civilizing projects. However, the historically rooted divide prevented each camp from recognizing the proximity between them.

A closer look at the worldviews of Islamic actors and secularists unveils similar sensibilities and mentalities with respect to progress and civilization that can easily be traced to Atatürk's view of civilization. Although the Gülen movement and the STKB assume that they disagree on everything, in fact they agree on a long list of issues of central importance for the Republican project. They agree on the importance of science and Western scientific education in English, on the view of progress that is engaged with and inspired by the West, on civil society projects being at the heart of social engineering, and on combining nationalist loyalties with internationalist ambitions (which I analyze in the chapter 4) and on the central importance of having a "strong state."

The greatest difference between the secularist STKB and the Islamic movement is that the latter regard Turkish Muslim identity and morality as a central part of a civil society and the nation. Although the followers reconciled their pious communalism with secular faces of individualism in the public sphere, their alternative adaptations did not help to prevent deep conflict with the STKB. With increasing state repression in the late 1990s, the legacy of distrust peaked between these groups. They continued to fail to look beyond deep disagreements and long-lived hostilities. The struggles were often mistaken as clashes between Islamist and secularist ideologies, each having mutually exclusive agendas. In reality, however, both Islamic and secularist civil society organizations were competing over the authority and power in the same project—the transformation of the Republic that has been under construction.

DOES "CIVIL SOCIETY" LACK CIVILITY?

Fethullah Gülen states, "Turkey is a candidate to be a world's superpower, based on its past and present situation."[17] He specifies his educational agenda as the "protection of national pride and credentials." When I asked why the movement founded schools in European countries such as Switzerland, Germany and Denmark as well as in Africa, Australia and so forth, the followers gave similar answers: "Why would there be only American schools in Western countries? Why would the West be led just by American power and leadership? We do not want just to catch up with the West, but we aim to be respected, recognized and appreciated by the West. Were not our Ottoman ancestors the leaders of the world civilization once upon a time?"

Not surprisingly, the secularists took issue with the movement's representation of the Turkish nation at the international level. They asked, "Why would it have to be a "fundamentalist Islamist man" and "his brainwashed servants" who represented the modern secular Turkey at the international level?"[18] In their defense of Atatürk and Kemalism, the secularists directed their discontents primarily against the Gülen movement. Despite the conflict-avoiding attitudes of the movement, the STKB began to undermine the movement publicly and through media channels. The members called for the closure of movement schools "for the good of the Turkish nation." They presented it as a moral responsibility of every citizen of the Turkish Republic in order to rescue the future generations.

The secularists' main conviction was that the followers of the Gülen movement were committing *takiye* (dissimulation).[19] The former argued that "Fethullahists'"[20] secret agendas were so obvious that they would not be worthy of social research. The fact that the movement could be studied as a research subject of a Ph.D. dissertation was very upsetting for the secularists. It was simply not considered a worthwhile subject for scientific inquiry. Most secularists tried to convince me not to waste my time on the movement. When they failed to convince me, they excused themselves by saying that they "cannot be helpful" for my research. I was told by leading figures of STKB: "If you still could not discover the Community's hidden goals to overthrow the state, it is not your fault. They are professional liars and traitors. Of course, they do everything to mask their true intentions."

The secularists were in agreement that the movement, beyond the facade of civil society organization, is the biggest enemy of the Turkish nation. During my fieldwork, I found it hard, and often impossible, to discuss the issues about the movement freely and openly with the adherents of STKB. My several attempts to schedule interviews with them failed when they learned that I was studying "the Fethullahists." STKB's negative attitudes and discouragement of the study Islam, especially the Gülen movement, stood in sharp contrast to the Gülen movement's openness and encouragement for being a subject of social research. They collected and archived all of the news and research on the movement published in both academic journals and newspapers. They also prepared archives of Ph.D.

dissertations on Islam in Turkey. In addition, they shared these rich resources with social scientists who wished to study the movement.

I had a short phone conversation with a leading figure of the secularist civil society organization Çağdaş Yaşamı Destekleme Derneği (Association for Support of Modern Life) on 29 April 1998. When I mentioned my study on the Gülen movement, her first question was "Have you seen their real faces? Did they allow you in?" Her one and only motivation was to clarify on which side of the battle line I was standing. Just as anybody engaged in a war, she was distrustful and suspicious of anyone who did not announce her allegiance.

I asked if we could talk face to face rather than on the phone. However, she refused to share her "knowledge" with me: She told me to read the book that STKB published on this issue. She also added that, of course, I could communicate through fax if I happened to discover "the truth" about the movement, the nature of which had already become evident to STKB. After this failed attempt, I tried numerous times to get in touch with several STKB organizations in order to hear their adherents' views and reflections on the issue. Like most of my calls, these efforts to communicate were often left without a response. The adherents were often too busy fighting the movement, which did not leave much time, energy and recognition for "understanding" it.

After receiving similar rejections, I devised a pragmatic solution to this major barrier to my fieldwork. I decided to reach the adherents of STKB through my informal personal contacts, friends, family and acquaintances, rather than directly and formally through the associations of STKB. Because I was born into a secular family myself and had close ties to secularist circles through my Atatürkist parents and other family members, this solution worked efficiently.

A common response from the secularists was to informally attempt to convince me to reveal the harm and the evil of the movement. Most of them wished to validate and legitimize their own conspiracy theories through my work. If my thesis were to fail in satisfying these demands, they would be extremely frustrated and distance themselves from me. This was the extent to which the issue was personalized. These attitudes provided plenty of firsthand source information on the secularists' fears regarding my research. In a private dinner party with a group of female friends, I was attacked for purchasing and reading the Gülen movement's newspaper, *Zaman*. I attempted to clarify that I had to read it for my own research and that it was data for me. My justifications were not listened to, nor was there any sign they registered. Being unable to endure my sociological interest in *understanding* rather than judging, the host, who was a friend of mine, left the table and never talked to me again. She, among several other hardcore secularists, has chosen to cut all her ties with me since my fieldwork. This is how I started to realize the extent to which these contestations between Islam and secularism were deeply embedded not only in politics but also in people's personal lives. The depth of contestations transcended intimate relations, personal ties of friendship and even family ties.

My study was simply one of the tangible objects of contestation among many. Any potential knowledge to be produced about the movement was fiercely contested in order to make sure which side it was taking, the Kemalists' or Islamists'. Due to the heated nature of the confrontation, it has become difficult for the polarized camps to imagine a sociological analysis that goes beyond ideological debates. To my surprise, the contestations over the study between ideologically motivated audiences have not remained limited to Turkey but have traveled with me everywhere. This work has been questioned and pushed into taking sides in several international contexts, including even wider academic circles in the West, in venues such as conferences, lectures, job talks, funding applications and other competitions. Often implicitly and politely, but sometimes also explicitly and bluntly, I was asked if I was "an *objective* outsider" as opposed to being an insider.

Similar to social research, students became other "objects" of contestation. The following section narrates the story of how two of them were caught by the clashes between these two camps and were pressured publicly to take—or rather change—sides. These two students are the perfect examples of scapegoats of the so-called public debates between self-organized civil society associations. In order to critically assess mutual accusations between STKB and the movement, it is necessary to understand the rules of access to and exit from the movement, its schools and the followers' service.

Access to and Exit from the Movement's Schools

I visited several student houses and dormitories in different neighborhoods of both Istanbul and Almati where boarding was mandatory. Despite the tight individual space in these back stages, exit from the movement's schools is free and depends on the choice of the individual. I met several students who chose to exit from the movement and left the dormitory or simply quit their service. Most of them left because of personal issues; some could not tolerate the extent of the Community's control over their lives. They explained to me that they needed more individual freedom to test different worldviews and experiment with different life styles. Emine, a university student in history, discussed her discomforts with the movement:

> I need more room to explore. . . . Student houses create too many rules and discipline for my taste. . . . When I lived in the Işık Evleri, I found it very hard to step out of this well-protected, guarded space. It is weird, though, because the rules of the household are only a part of the story. I think the rest is very informal and perfunctory because without any further force you find yourself as a full member of the communal life. Perhaps it is nothing to be surprised at. . . . It is a community anyway. . . . I think I was not meant for any kind of community. . . . I just left.

It is important to note that Emine was a whole-hearted, radical Islamist who criticized the movement for "standardized mediocrity and conformism" and for impeding passion and radicalism within "the" Islamist movement. She was more an activist than a submissive follower of a non-confrontational pacifist community. She did not like the "walls" of the dormitories and the Işık Evleri. After having spent several years in the Community's *dershane*s (private establishments preparing students for various exams), schools, dormitories and Işık Evleri in different Anatolian cities, Emine was highly critical of all the fences surrounding student life in the Gülen Community. When she started to feel the implicit pressure to marry within the Community, although there was no formal imposition, she decided to leave. Shortly after her exit, she decided to marry an Islamist man from outside the Community with whom she had fallen in love. Emine's case is similar to that of many other students who abandoned the Community by their free will and who had various reasons for this decision.

Another woman, Vahide, whom I met during my stay in Almati, told me why she had to quit her service. She was the adviser *abla* of one of the girls' dormitories. She was a young, passionate and reliable woman in her mid-twenties. She was responsible for the application of rules and the discipline and order of the social environment of dormitories. As Vahide's family was in Germany, she devoted all of her time to being an active participant in the vital Gülen community in Almati. She had developed strong friendships and bonded not only with the followers, the teachers and other staff in Gülen's associations but also with the students. During my stay, she received an acceptance letter for a Ph.D. program in mathematics from a German university. She told me that this had always been her dream and that she was very excited about this new route. I asked if her departure would create any problem in the Gülen Community and if they might mind it. She looked at me and talked sadly:"These people have become my family, as my family is in Germany. They will be sad when I leave. However, they will understand my choice of departure, since they know how important it is for me to do a Ph.D. in mathematics. They can replace me immediately with somebody else, who, I am sure, is going to do her job very well."

Because the followers were organized in Germany, too, I asked if she was only leaving the dormitory or her service for the movement altogether. Her answer was prompt:"I am starting not only a new career but also a new life. I cannot be in service anymore. That is a full-time commitment. You cannot do service as a part-time activity. Besides, a Ph.D. in mathematics is pretty serious stuff in Germany."

The choice of exit was not limited to the staff in residence and university students but was open to anybody in service. Beril was a committed follower of the movement who had been in service for a long time. Instead of teaching in one of the movement's schools, she was teaching in a public Imam-Hatip (a religious high school that trains imams) in Eyüp, a relatively religious neighborhood in Istanbul. Over tea in her place, she told me that she was known as a very open-minded and tolerant teacher among other teachers in this school. However, due to her liberal attitudes towards the students, she was criticized by Islamists. She said, "They cannot understand the worldview of the Gülen movement. No matter what we do, we are too liberal for other Islamists. Even my relatively shorter coat disturbs them. What can I do? Should I change my style to fit their Islamist vision?" Beril was divorced from an Islamist man, who was from another Nur group, Okuyucular. She said that their worldviews clashed all the time. Becoming a single mother after divorce, she had a lot of pressure and responsibility and could not continue her active participation in *hizmet* and the movement's undertakings. *Hizmet* was too demanding for a single mother. She explained, "When you are *in*, there are high expectations and certain ways of conduct. . . . It is a way of life, . . . a big commitment. . . . I organized and coordinated educational and other public events for the Community for such a long time. However, I can no longer afford the time for it. I have to admit mine was not a smooth exit. Some friends were upset, as they needed me. But my son definitely needs me more."

When I asked Beril about relations between the movement and secularist organizations, she said: "It has recently become even more rocky than with our relations with the other Islamists." On one side, Gülen's followers' moderation and tolerant insights have estranged some of the radical Islamists. On the other side, the Islamic *dava* of revitalization of faith has galvanized secularists, STKB in particular. Summarizing the discontent of both sides, Beril smiled and concluded: "Despite our efforts to compromise peacefully, I guess we are too difficult to fit in anywhere comfortably. The more we wish to avoid conflict, the more we find ourselves in the midst of it."

Contesting the Students

In 1998, STKB waged a war against the schools and associations of the movement. The united force of self-organizations felt morally responsible to fight against "Islamic indoctrination" in the movement schools. They attempted to rescue several students from the "cages" of these schools, by claiming that these young souls had been tortured by the movement. The clash over students is extremely important to note, as it challenges the idea that the public sphere accommodates increasing diversity and recognition of differences. In contrast to this cozy view of a pluralistic public sphere, the codes of conduct and manners in these contestations seem to discard civility in the definitions of civil society.

Ongoing attacks reached a climax in February 1998 when the secularists began contesting and claiming benefaction of several students in Gülen's schools. Fueled by a heavy historical baggage of distrust between the Nurcus and early Republicans, the opposition between STKB and the Gülen Community deepened rapidly. Seven Kemalist civil society organizations came together to publish a book called *Hoca Efendi'nin Okulları* (Hoca Efendi's Schools—or if you discard the *o* in *Okullari*, Hoca Efendi's Slaves).[21] This term, *kullar,* was used to refer to the blind believers, the presumably enslaved students. The book opened an intense public debate. It consisted of interviews with two students of the movement, Ismail Özdemir and Serhat Özkan, who "bravely" stepped forward and made their shocking confessions about their experiences in the Gülen Community. Although the students' identities had been concealed for some time, they were publicized in a press conference in which the students openly attacked the movement. Both Ismail and Serhat had been the followers of the Gülen Community for some time but left the Community when they found support, "shelter" and financial aid in a major STKB organization, Çağdaş Eğitim Vakfi (Foundation of Modern Education). Under the leadership of Gülseven Yaser, a Kemalist member of the faculty at Istanbul University, several other members of STKB pursued this book project and promoted it by press conferences and television shows. They saw this as a moral duty of saving not only the two students but also the youth in Turkey.

The discourse of the book was dramatic. It claimed to unveil the "hidden truth," the agonizing events that Gülen students were subjected to in these schools. It was written in the form of questions and answers. The students answered the questions, which were prepared by members of STKB. The book's primary agenda was to present the "outcry" of the students. Its aim was to alarm the whole society about the evils of the movement. The book starts with a dark introduction: "These students are only twenty years old, but feel very old because of the painful times they spent in the Community. However, they could not publish their stories in one of the best-selling newspapers because the whole media was busy praising the Community and its leader."[22]

The Gülen Community was represented and labeled as a *Şeriatçi* (promoters of Sharia) and anti-state on the basis of the students' answers, stories and experiences. The students were quoted as they confessed the "hidden" aim of the Community, *Ila-yi Kelimetullah* (to spread Islam all around the world). Ismail and Serhat described how the movement called for rule of Sharia by presenting the Kuran as the main principle of both the sciences and social life.[23] Later in the press conference, they also confirmed the claims that they made in the book. They reaffirmed the argument that the non-confrontational and conformist outlook of the movement was a facade. They claimed that the Gülen movement served a hidden mission of Islamizing Turkish society as well as the whole world by overthrowing the state.[24]

In the book, Ismail is quoted as denying differences between different Islamic groups and various agendas.[25] This denial is interpreted by the STKB as dissimulation by the Gülen movement. As this issue lies at the heart of the mutual distrust between Islamists and secularists, it requires special attention. Ismail was quoted in his comparison of his years in Imam-Hatip (religious high school) and in the Gülen's educational institutions:

The aim of education in both Imam-Hatip schools and the Gülen schools was the same, that is, to create an Islamic society and Islamic state. . . . However, the methods and paths to reach this goal were different. While the Refah party and political Islamists presented themselves through their radical discourses and activities, the Gülen Community tries to present itself as a mild, moderate movement. We were taught a method, in order to avoid societal reaction, that is referred to as "*nabza göre şerbet verme.*"[26] For example, while other Islamists do not shake hands with women, we were asked to shake hands, in order to receive recognition from society. Another example would be Coca-Cola consumption. The students in Işık Evleri are not supposed to drink Coca-Cola, since it is *haram* (forbidden by Islam). . . . But when we were in presence of other people who were newcomers or potential newcomers, our *ağabeys* would accept the Coke, before we did.[27]

As I discussed in chapter 2, the followers have strong sensibilities for being accepted and recognized as members of society. Contrary to the accusation of dissimulation, however, the movement neither hides nor denies this collective need. On the contrary, the importance of self-presentation was often highlighted rather than denied in my interviews with the followers.

Shortly after the book came out, two representatives, Gülseven Hanım and Haşmet Atahan, the latter a Kemalist lawyer from STKB, brought the issue to a very popular late-night television show on 27 February 1998.[28] The goal of the show was to illustrate Ismail's and Serhat's confessions, this time in front of millions of opinionated and agitated people. Before and during the show, my phone did not stop ringing. The majority of secular people, by anticipating the end of the Gülen movement within the next couple of hours, were expressing mixed feelings of curiosity and revenge.

The discussion went smoothly for the first few hours. Surprisingly, however, after so many outspoken and bold confessions in the book and in the press conference, the boys did not come to the show. Initially, the idea was that they were late. In the absence of the students, the two representatives of STKB discussed their success in the "rescue plan" with pride. By also accusing the Community for Ismail's depression, Gülseven Hanım directly attacked not only the movement but also the leader. She spoke along the lines of the book: "The truth and the real faces (of Fethullahists) had to be revealed. . . . These children are *ours* and expect help from us. . . . This is going to be an awakening both for the parents and children, . . . especially the revealing of the true agendas of a person who presents himself as a representative of toleration and moderate Islam."

Because they still hoped that the boys would come, they kept trying to encourage the students on the air to come to the show. In their calls for the students, they were assuring the students' security, saying that the students would be "under their protection." Gülseven Hanım's and the lawyer's gradually increasing disappointment turned into anger and rough language that was used against the movement. After Ismail called the show from a cellular phone, the anger was also directed against the show itself. The audience heard Ismail talking on the phone, denying his confessions and accusations of the Gülen movement. He denied not only the illustrations in the book but also his own statements in the press conference. Surprisingly, he made claims that totally contradicted the ones he had presumably made before. He stated that everything Gülseven Hanım and the lawyer were saying were lies, that he had been forced to make false confessions about the Community, and that they had imposed emotional pressure on him to make him lie. He added that this was the reason why the questions were asked in written form during the press conference. Ismail also accused Gülseven Hanım and her colleagues of fabricating the book by presenting their own ideas, convictions and arguments as if they were Ismail's state-ments. He claimed to be emotionally abused and pressured to pretend to the public. Ismail bluntly confessed on the phone: "There is a disgusting game on the stage." He said: "Some people took our friendly discussions, created a scheme and filled in things that we never said. The writer of the book is neither I nor my friend." Speaking also on behalf of Serhat, he con-tinued: "They promised both material benefits and opportunities, such as to study abroad, but they also coerced us by using pressure. . . . They cre-ated such a scene and game that we could not find a way out."[29]

In addition to STKB's promises, Ismail's initial motive in approaching STKB has to be noted:

I entered Boğaziçi University in 1995–1996 through the national exam. The first term, I stayed in an apartment of the Gülen Community. Then I left the place because of personal problems. I underline "personal problems." Because the financial situation of my family was really bad, a friend of mine gave me the STKB Foundation's number and said, "If you want to have a scholarship from that foundation, tell them that you wish to exit from the Gülen movement and that you are in a difficult situation, and need their help". . . . Indeed, when I explained my situation, the STKB people showed great interest in my case. . . . Although I was not registered in school that term, they gave me a scholarship.[30]

When Ismail called the show, he was asked whose cellular phone he was using. He explained that one of the secularist businessmen gave him the phone as a gift. As Ismail freely admitted, both camps used material rewards and funding for education as a source of temptation for the stu-dents. Put differently, both camps used similar tools and strategies to attract the students. They tried to convince them about the good of their ideol-ogy and the evil of the other's, in order to shape these students according to their vision and agenda. As a result, they politicized both schools and students by locating them in the center of their own struggle. Although both camps were initially accusing the other side of using material means to tempt the students (such as money, accommodations, cellular phones), they ended up blaming the students for accepting them. However, rather than betraying each side, Ismail and Serdar were simply caught by the war between these camps and became rather disoriented by the impositions and demands of each group.

The surprising part of this incident is not so much the intensity and nature of confrontations. The real irony is that the contestations evolved around the discourse and the "virtues" of civil society. Both STKB and the Gülen movement tested the limits of the public sphere, by referring to it as *civil society* and pulling it in two different directions at once. Obviously, there was nothing civil about the deep distrust, suspicion, insults and

mutual accusation. The inner core of the Islamic movement is not different from that of the secular STKB with regard to its tendency to stifle and
mold human souls and fresh minds. Both failed to provide the students
with individual space in which they could freely experiment and make
their own choices. Both the Gülen movement and the STKB proved that
they regarded education as a tool to fashion the future generations after
their own image. Instead of being treated as autonomous subjects who
have free will, both Serhat and Ismail were patronized and co-opted by
both of these groups. This has nothing to do with the essence of secularism or Islamism but is more closely related to the illiberal faces and
authoritarian tendencies of the Republican project.

The next day, I was having a long walk with Nurten, who was a close
friend of active members of STKB. When we began to discuss the nerve-
racking incident, Nurten shook her head and said: "We really believed that
STKB was doing the right thing you know. Perhaps what all this *infighting*
does is simply to confuse, hurt and disorient the youth. I felt embarrassed
yesterday, not because I question my *faith in secularism* but because I realized that there is a problem with the way we handle it." Although the incident instigated some degree of self-critique, most people remained simply
angry towards the so-called other side. Following the politicization of the
students, the schools came to the forefront of contestation.

Contesting the Schools: Symbolic Negotiations between the State and the Movement

A retired military officer who joined the movement after his retirement
told me:

> The military has a serious concern about the fact that a religious community rep-
> resents Turkey abroad. A good friend of mine from the military says that the
> Community is "flirting" with everybody. According to him, this has to stop, as the
> Turkish nation strongly refuses to be identified with this new "*Ulama.*" On the
> contrary, I think they represent the Turkish nation better than any other Turkish
> organization or school did before. Anybody who is not content with them should
> have the power and ability to replace the schools. Otherwise, they should appre-
> ciate and leave the schools alone, because they are doing a real good job.

Some branches of the state, the military in particular, have traditionally
agreed with the STKB's position that Islam is essentially an enemy of the
Republic. As the secularists' discontent increased, the public started to
question the schools and why the Gülen movement was allowed to represent the secular Turkey abroad. Eventually, the Turkish courts initiated a
close scrutiny of the schools, making the movement accountable for their

finances and sociocultural agendas. The courses, curricula, and educational goals of these schools became the subjects of long-term inspection and evaluation.

Fethullah Gülen's immediate response to the state's inquiry was shocking. He announced without a hesitation that the movement was ready to decline its rights and transfer the ownership of the schools to the state. This caused conflicting reactions and disagreement from within the movement. The case was transferred to the highest advisory court, the National Security Council (MGK, for Milli Güvenlik Konseyi), which was dominated at that time by military officials. Fethullah Gülen announced through the media that "MGK is a constitutional institution. . . . My only contribution to the schools is encouragement and suggestions. They are under the state's control."[31]

Conservative public intellectuals who have been sympathetic to the movement, ranging from nationalists to Islamists, reacted against the leader's response. According to Nazlı Ilıcak, a right-wing conservative journalist, the response was an explicit injustice to the movement.[32] She argued that the movement should keep its schools. She also explained that Fethullah Gülen's non-confrontational attitude originated from his Islamic faith, tolerance, and patience. Many followers agreed that the transfer of the schools to the Minister of National Education would be a mistake. In my interviews, most argued that the staff in the schools were serving (teaching, educating and so forth) in the name of God. Their voluntary service was selfless and for no material return. It originated also from their love and faith in Fethullah Gülen. Most of the beneficiaries and benefactors stated that they were "voluntary servants" of only Hocaefendi and would not serve anyone else. Not only Islamic actors but others, even several prominent Jewish businesspeople, have supported the movement and its schools. The followers doubted that this hybrid constituent could be mobilized by anybody other than Fethullah Gülen. "How would the state replace the movement and its mobilization and management of the international networks?" Others said: "We will follow what Hocaefendi says. He is smarter than all of us."

Contrary to the STKB's expectations, the government and the military agreed on 27 March 1998 that "the Fethullahists" were "sincere" Muslims, and that they were entitled to maintain the schools.[33] By "sincere Muslims," the state actors referred to the people "who regularly practiced their religion in their personal and communal lives and acted according to the moral principles of Islam but otherwise had a secular discourse and praxis."[34] Having abolished Refah so recently and imposed a semi-military intervention with cautious attitudes toward Islamist activities, the state's final decision on the Gülen schools was interesting. Contrary to public opinion, the movement was neither betraying the state nor was it co-opted by it. Similarly, the state was neither attacked by the movement nor crushing it. What was at stake then?[35]

Indeed, the encounters between the state and the movement designated mutual recognition and readiness for negotiation. The issue of the schools' potential transfer was only an illustration of shifting dynamics between the state and the movement. Rather than a mere act of obedience to the state's control, the leader's surrender was an intermixed outcome of both his national loyalties and Islamic submissiveness. Similarly, the state's inter-vention was a symbolic act of reconfirmation of its authority and its reach in society. It is also important to note the symbolic quality of the com-munication between the state and the Gülen movement that is implicit in the use of terms such as *sincerity* and *loyalty*.[36] Symbolic negotiations served both the state and the Gülen Community to reassure their unde-clared, yet safe, spheres of influence and effectiveness. By experimenting with each other's limits of tolerance, they ended up mutually recognizing each other.

Not surprisingly, the state's responsiveness to and subsequent recogni-tion of Gülen's projects are conveniently omitted by public opinion as well as the literature. Parallel to the media, most of my secular and Islamic informants were quick to pick on the confrontations between STKB and the movement, while they often disregarded the non-confrontational quality of negotiations between the state and the movement. This pre-dominant neglect has had a selective rationality. On the one hand, the his-torically rooted distrust and fear between Islam and the state have obscured emergent linkages between the Republic and the Gülen move-ment. On the other hand, ideological motivation to maintain their image as enemies has also shrouded the shifting linkages between them. Clearly, the practices of both the state and the Islamic movement have deviated from the images that they have had of each other. Could these shifting practices potentially transform the mutually destructive perception of Islam and the state as part of a broader transition?

Ongoing Contestations: Making Sense of the State's Contradictory Behavior

Some social actors may find comfort in perceiving the state as a har-monious entity, as is the case with the STKB's symbiotic association with the monolithic image of the state.[37] However, neither the persistence of an official ideology nor the widely shared tenets of secularism and national-

ism of the state are indicators of the coherence of the state. Each of the
state's branches—such as the military, parliament, gendarmerie, police and
courts—represents only one dimension of the state, dimensions that often
disagree and fall into conflict in their attitudes towards social forces.[38]

The military has been the most resistant branch of the state against
Islamic movements. Despite its high suspicion towards the movement,
however, high-ranking military officials such as General Karadayı have visited Gülen's schools and have reported positive feelings and appreciation
for the successes of the schools.[39] The Gülen movement has also attracted
a large group of retired military officials who have openly expressed their
appreciation of the movement. However, these friendly overtones have
been interrupted by the gendarmerie's sporadic attacks on the movement's
dormitories. While the movement has occasionally had friendly relation-
ships with several state actors, including the police, these attacks have continued well into the new millennium. Although it is far from clear what
the gendarmerie was searching for, they have not been confronted by
another branch of the state so far.

The courts have also demonstrated contradictory attitudes towards the
movement. On one occasion, for example, the courts defended the movement against the police, which wiretapped the followers using illegitimate
methods. The chief police officer (Emniyet Müdürü) was expelled from
his position in 1999 as a result of this incident. He protested against the
courts' decision and complained that the state was favoring and protecting these Islamists at the expense of its own branches. "Any individual part
of the state may respond as much (or more) to the distinctive pressures it
faces in particular arenas as it does to the rest of the state organization."[40]

In other instances, the courts charged the leader, Fethullah Gülen, with
illegal activity. A videotape of Fethullah Gülen was aired on television,
which gave rise to another broad discontent in society. The videotape displayed an earlier speech by him, in which he spoke to his followers about
his religious views on being patient before taking action. This advice
caused fear and reaction from secularists, who had anticipated dissimulation and betrayal for a long time. Moreover, the religious clothing, a long
robe, that Fethullah Gülen was wearing upset the secularists as much as
the leader's religious preaching.

Ankara State Court (Ankara Devlet Mahkemesi) filed a lawsuit against
Fethullah Gülen in 2000, accusing him of mobilizing to change the state's
structure from a secular to an Islamic one. The court decided that he was
guilty and sentenced him to imprisonment for up to ten years. However,
at the time of the court decision, he was already in the United States, as
he had moved here in the wake of sporadic attacks in 1999. On 10 March

2003, the courts made a new decision, referred to as *şartlı salıverme* (conditional release). The decision removed legal barriers for Fethullah Gülen's return to Turkey with the condition that he was not to be charged with the same or a similar crime within the next five years. Put differently, the final decision was postponed (*erteleme*).

In 2005, the columnists of several newspapers started a new attack by questioning why Fethullah Gülen was still staying in the United States despite his permission to return. The leader told me, "I do not want to muddy the water (*suyu bulandırmak*) and cause another trauma by my return." It was clear that his potential return was going to provoke another public outcry and more societal conflict, which both the leader and his followers have always wished to avoid.

Since the time of his controversial preaching aired from a videotape, the ideas and other aspects of the leader's identity have changed dramatically toward compromise.[41] His traditional robe that he wore on the videotape has also long ago been replaced with Western clothing. When I visited him in Pennsylvania, he was wearing an ironed white shirt and a fashionable jacket, tokens that met rather important criteria for the secular elite of Turkey.

During the recent changes in Islamic actors' self-presentation and identity, the Turkish state has also gone through an intense reform period, which I will discuss in chapter 6. As a result of the legal reforms relating to the law of "counter-terrorism" (*terörle mücadele yasası*), the Ankara Criminal Court acquitted Fethullah Gülen on 5 May 2006.[42] He was found no longer guilty of committing a terrorist act and forming an illegal organization that aims to overthrow the secular state. At the time this book goes to press, the public curiosity and debate continues whether the leader is going back to Turkey or not.

Although contestations over the movement continue, their subject constantly changes. Recently, a prominent sociologist, Şerif Mardin, has also become the object of contestation. He has not only been very influential in shaping Turkish sociology and Turkish studies but has also greatly contributed to our understanding of Nakşibendi sect and the Nur movement in Turkey, among many other subjects.[43] In 2004, a columnist argued that Mardin's membership in the Scientific Academy of Turkey (Türkiye Bilimler Akademisi, TÜBA) was rejected because of his sociological study on the Nur movement.[44] Criticizing the conduct of science and knowledge production in Turkey, the columnist bluntly asked: "Böyle bir 'bilim'i ve böyle bir 'akademi'yi kim takar?" (Who cares about science and academia like that?) Another columnist who participated in the recent disputes on Said Nursi and Fethullah Gülen stated, "[The] good news for our country is that the military commanders finally acknowledge the fact that they can love their country *only* as much as the other citizens do, and that some of them can also make mistakes."[45]

As attention is exclusively paid to the tension between Islamic social forces and the state, the state's accommodating attitudes have often been left unnoticed by social actors. This neglect is reinforced further during transition periods because, like other institutions, the state's parts are transformed often unevenly at different paces. Although the subjects of contestations over the Gülen movement change, the sporadic nature of these disputes does not. The disputes explode, especially at crucial moments of uncertainty, as a broad transformation is taking shape through public debates. In addition to the state's multi-layered transformation, its contradictory responses to Islamic actors are caused by the changes within the movement itself.

What Turkish society is really debating through these sporadic contestations is the future direction of the Turkish Republic. The Turkish state, like many other centralized states, is indeed institutionally unified. However, it is a "unified disunity" to use Migdal's term. Its strength largely depends on the degree and capacities of cohabitation of different social forces as well as different parts of the state. Not only the social actors but also the state actors pull in different directions. "*Resistance* offered by other social forces to the designs of the state, as well as *incorporation* of groups into the organization of the state, changes its social and ideological underpinnings." [46] These dynamics are as influential in the formulation of state policy as political leaders' decisions and legislative processes.

These changes triggered by the politics of engagement reshape the overarching framework of belonging. Contestations occur when the Republican framework is shaken up in order to accommodate new Islamic identities and their sensibilities. While hardcore secularists misperceive these contestations as a threat to the Republic, these disputes are often organic extensions of a transition from authoritarian rule. Perhaps the Republican project has never been so eager for reform since the nation-building period. The balance between cohesion and disunity that the state is able to accommodate will largely determine the limits of cultural diversity and political pluralism in Turkey. I will return to this issue in chapter 6.

CHAPTER 4

The Appeal of Cooperation:
National Affinities and International Undertakings

THE MOST ILLUMINATING piece of evidence on cooperation between Islamic actors and state officials presented itself during my fieldwork in Kazakhstan. After becoming familiar with all of the followers in the movement's central organization, the Kazak-Turkish Education Foundation (Kazak Türk Eğitim Vakfı, KATEV) in Almati, I started to notice something odd. A group of gentlemen were visiting the organization regularly. Their visits were turning the center from a foundation into a community center, or a social club, where they would drink tea, have friendly chats, and laugh together. Despite the frequency of their visits, I was not introduced to this group of regular visitors. Initially, I thought that my gender could be a barrier and waited passively to be presented by a KATEV staff member. Finally, I had to make a conscious effort to approach them, and learned that these men were not from the Gülen movement. They were the teachers of the Turkish state. They were appointed to Kazakhstan to teach the Turkish language and history in Kazak schools and universities. In Almati, they worked under the Council of the Turkish Ministry of National Education (CTNE), which consisted of twenty Turkish teachers. Due to the heavy historical baggage of tension between Islam and the Republic, I initially expected some form of conflict, distrust or cleavage between KATEV and CTNE. I anticipated that the state officials of CTNE would monitor and control the movement's KATEV. However, it soon became clear to me that there was no such tension. A shared "unique form of social consciousness"[1] was overcoming any potential tension between them.

Nationalism is the primary source of mobilization among the Turkish Islamic actors in Kazakhstan. Once translated into an international context, the strength and primacy of Turkish nationalism surpasses other loyalties, such as the commitment to the Islamic *dava,* the Gülen movement or even the family. When the need appears for service in Central Asia, the followers, whether they take their whole family with them or leave them behind, go to the "Turkic lands."

The contestations within the national borders of Turkey translate into the international domain in the form of smooth cooperation between Islam and the state. This chapter demonstrates the major role that different forms and degrees of nationalism play in shifting state-Islam interaction outside the Turkish borders. The Gülen movement appeals to different faces of nationalism in Central Asia. These nationalisms facilitate the movement's cooperation with the Turkish state in mobilizing effective ethnic politics. The engagements in the international context reveal two important issues. First, nationalism is the key to explaining the elective affinities between the secular and Islamic Turks that overshadow the historical cleavage between them. Second, ethnic politics in post-Soviet Central Asia is the product of shared interests and agendas between the state and Islam.[2] Before illustrating how nationalism and ethnicity manifest themselves in the daily lives of the Turkish Community in Almati, a short background of Turkey's official interest in Central Asia needs to be introduced.

Central Asia and Kazakhstan

The official interest in Central Asia can be traced back to the Ottoman Empire. Abdülhamit II used Islam both as a strategy to expand into Central Asia and as a weapon against Western imperialism.[3] Later, the idea of a connection between the new and the old land of the Turks, that is, between Anatolia and Central Asia, was clearly articulated by the Young Turks.[4]

After the fall of the Empire, the founding fathers glorified the myths of descent from Central Asia in the formation of Turkish national identity.[5] The agendas for Central Asia took on a more state-framed form in the Türk Tarih Tezi (the Thesis of Turkish History). This thesis was created in the 1930s as part of the nation-building process and persisted as a cornerstone of official ideology. It claimed that the Turks contributed to civilization long before the Ottoman Empire, namely in Central Asia. Although the term *Turk* had a pejorative meaning until the late period of the Ottoman Empire, it became a source of pride to the Republic.[6]

In the early Republic, when Islam had become a national asset as opposed to being the basis of *Umma*, Atatürk glorified Turkic roots in Central Asia and anticipated Turkey's leading role in the future development of the Muslim majority in Central Asia. The early Republican elite recognized that in the modern world "religions [were] losing their political significance and power." The Turkist group believed that "religions [could] maintain their political and internal importance only by intermingling with and backing up the races."[7]

After the disintegration of the Soviet Union, the new states of Central Asia gained independence from long-term "Sovietization" without having the institutional, political and economic means to create democracies. In all of these five states (Kazakhstan, Kyrgyzstan, Turkmenistan, Uzbekistan and Tajikistan) authoritarian regimes emerged that helped to perpetuate the Soviet legacy of repression of religion to different degrees.[8] The new states are weak in infrastructure and authoritarian in their political rule. They have little or no interest in interacting with the society and severely restrict individual liberties and religious freedoms.[9] As the Kazak state continues to run elections through undemocratic means, the President, Nazarbayev, maintains his power to remove and reappoint the Prime Minister regardless of the outcomes of the elections.[10] Time will tell whether interaction with Islamic and other social forces may eventually transform the rigidly authoritarian states of Central Asia.

Although the newly independent countries of Central Asia have experienced a different type of secularization from Turkey because of their past under the totalitarian anti-religious Soviet regime, all of these countries have recently witnessed the rise of an entwined ethnic and Islamic consciousness.[11] The Kazak state has been particularly cautious about Islamic revival and has enforced rigid restrictions on the formation of religious self-organizations and movements.[12] Interestingly, however, while still regarding many other forms of Islamic action as threats, both the Turkish and Kazak states started to accommodate the schools and associations of the fast-growing Gülen movement in the 1990s.

In the post-Soviet period, the secular Turkish Republic has come to be seen as an obvious candidate to fill the power vacuum in the Turkic region. In this secular corner of the Muslim world, Turkey and the Central Asian countries were expected to opt for regionalization in order to establish an unshakeable buffer zone against the Islamic threat that Afghanistan and Iran posed. Paradoxically, however, instead of secular civic forces, the Islamic Gülen movement has attempted to build bridges between Turkey and Central Asia. The movement's projects have found fertile ground in Central Asia, where newly independent states are in the process of "nationalizing," and the civil societies are rudimentary. In this chapter I will discuss the ways in which national and ethnic sentiments have played a role in the Gülen movement's expansion in Central Asia. The movement's primary interest lies in revitalizing ethnic identities and Muslim ways of life among the Muslim-Turkic majority in Central Asia. Needless to say, those in the movement see faith as a primary component of Turkic identities.

It is extremely important to note that the post-Soviet period has witnessed the formation of new relations between home countries and host countries[13] that share large populations of co-ethnic (Turkic) and co-religious (Muslim) people. This new situation has proved very beneficial for the movement's exposure in the region. Since the mid-1990s, the Gülen movement has opened numerous schools and launched small- and mid-scale business and trade networks in these host countries in Central Asia.

The movement has 29 schools in Kazakhstan, 12 schools in Azerbaijan, 13 schools in Turkmenistan and 12 schools in Kyrgyzstan.[14] Uzbekistan is the only country that is hostile to the movement's schools; it has not only repressed Islamic action as a result of fear of Islamic threat but also banned the movement's schools since 1999. Among the Central Asian states, the Gülen schools in Kazakhstan are striking both quantitatively and qualitatively. Five out of 29 schools in Kazakhstan are located in Almati.[15] In addition to the striking number of schools, the quality and popularity of the Gülen schools has opened the way for a large-scale accommodation of Turks as well as for a vibrant business interaction between Turkey and Kazakhstan.

The high concentration of the Gülen schools in the Turkic Muslim world presents a sharp contrast to their weak presence, and often absence, in the Arab Muslim world. This is a strong indicator of the primacy of national loyalties and ethnic sentiments in the mobilization of the movement. When I asked the followers in Almati about the reasons for their presence in Kazakhstan, most answered that Fethullah Gülen had encouraged "the relations with the Turkic brothers" since the late 1980s. The leader himself told me that he always felt empathy for his *soydas* (people from the same ancestry), whose faith had suffered under Communist rule. "However," he said, "I have not much to do with these schools in Central Asia. Unlike you, I have not even visited them."

Ethnic Politics by Nationalist Islam

Outside the national boundaries, the Gülen schools have broader cultural and political agendas than the *dava* of revitalization of faith. While the schools in Europe attract Turkish immigrant families who aspire to raise their children in "the Turkish way," the appeal of the schools in the underdeveloped or developing countries of Africa and Asia originates from the quality of teaching, the technology, and the high standards of education. Finally, and perhaps most importantly, the high concentration of the movement's schools in Central Asia is part of the ethnic politics in the region.

The Gülen schools, which originally aimed to revitalize Turkish-Muslim ways of life, have also helped to create business networks between Turkey and Kazakhstan. The schools have become hospitable and accommodating to both Islamic and secular businesspeople who visit Central Asian countries from Turkey. The schools have provided different kinds of connections between the Turkish visitors and the locals. The Turkish community is linked with the parents who send their children to the Gülen schools and with others who develop personal or contractual ties with the followers. The Turkish businesspeople and entrepreneurs that I interviewed in Almati stated that they contribute to the finances of the schools in one way or another. They provide them with their products (most of the time equipment or food), offer scholarships to students and/or contribute to the salaries of the teachers.

A follower who owns a medium-size business, Yahya Bey, indicated that "Hocaefendi was the motivating force behind this Turkish exposure to Central Asia for a long time." He continued: "We have just followed his advice and tried to create a Turkish community here. The schools are the cornerstones of this community. Certainly, we do our best to support them." However, others, who were not the followers of Fethullah Gülen, also supported the schools. Vahid Bey was one of the presidents of a large Turkish firm in Almati. He was not a follower but was simply sympathetic to the activities of the Gülen movement in Central Asia. During my conversation with him, he explained his rationale for the charity:

The Kazak-Turk high schools mean human capital for me, for my business for the future of my enterprise. If I wish to transfer the same quality of human capital from Turkey to work in our firm in Almati, I have to pay much more. Besides, she or he will come here without knowing Kazak and Russian, probably not even English. These schools produce a well-educated, hard-working reserve army of labor. . . . I may be calculating my own interest. Obviously, my interest definitely does not contradict but fosters our national interest.

The national feelings of the Turkish community in Almati are closely tied to the idea of economic interest, which they see as part of national interest. As Greenfeld argues, "Individualism (as a moral and philosophical position) and nationalism (as a form of social consciousness) may be perceived as contradictory only if the individual is believed to be pre-social." Contrary to this view, she argues that individuality is the product of culture, not nature. "The individualistic ethic is the core and distinguishing characteristic of that communal identity." Greenfeld sees this type of nationalism as the "original inspiration for the economics of sustained growth."[16]

In the international realm, the Islamic movement smoothly transforms national affiliation into national*ist* identities.[17] The Islamic actors find motivation in the ideal of the Turkish nation as a means to expand economic and sociopolitical agendas outside of Turkey. Similar to Vahid Bey, most followers that I talked to in Almati did not see any conflict between the individual's welfare and the nation's. This is why they object to almost all collective identifications in the forms of "isms" (*sucu bucu olmak*), while they only embrace all kinds of national*isms*. During our long conversation about nationalism, Fethullah Gülen told me that nationalism is benign. Unlike other forms of ideologies, he said, nationalism "*connects* individuals rather than dividing them."

The Gülen Community in Almati aspires to be an ethno-religious community that welcomes and tries to incorporate the so-called Muslim "Kazak Turks." This should not be surprising if we note the irony of the "inclusive" nature of Turkish nationalism as opposed to "exclusive" ethnic nationalisms.[18] The nation is imagined as *inclusionary* of other ethnic groups and nations, such as the Kurds, in Turkey. However, this inclusion "happens" *only* if they comply with the tough condition that they assimilate and define themselves as Turks. Put differently, this "warm and neighborly welcome" to belong coincides with an implicit denial of the other's distinct ethnicity. This is a contrast to *exclusionary* ethnic nationalisms, which leave out and explicitly segregate other ethnicities that are perceived as a threat to a utopia based on ethnic election.[19]

Interestingly, Vahid Bey's business partner, Kaan Bey, said that he did not know much about the company's contribution to the Gülen schools. He suggested that I direct all of my questions about the "Fethullahcis" to Vahid Bey. When I probed further, he told me, "Look, I love my country, as do many other people who come to Central Asia. As much as I appreciate the Turkish community here, my partner and I share different views about 'the Islamists.' Quite honestly, they are free to do whatever they wish, and my business partner is free to support them as long as it benefits everybody. I just do not wish to hear about it."

However, when I brought up the movement's goal of reviving the Turkish-Muslim morals among the Kazak youth, Kaan Bey became immediately defensive of the movement. "*They* are not trying to consolidate the Kazak Islamic Republic. *We* are simply trying to fix a very degenerated society. It is hard to believe what the young are up to here."

While nationalist sentiments seem to bond Islamic and secular Turks, their wish to cooperate with Kazaks definitely does *not* cross religious lines. Specifically, the glorification of Turkic roots is addressed to Muslim Kazaks, not the Soviets or other non-Muslim groups in Kazakhstan. The Gülen movement tries to participate as effectively as possible in the nationalization of the post-Soviet Central Asian states by reconnecting the people with their "Turkic-Muslim origins." Within the bounds of this aspiration for unity, *religious* myths of ethnic election and *national* myths of shared destiny converge.[20]

Nevertheless, national loyalties and ethnic consciousness overshadow the Islamic undertone of the movement in the international realm. This is clearly reflected in the ways in which the followers of the movement emphasize their national loyalties more vocally than their Islamic agendas. In Kazakhstan, the fuzzy boundaries of the movement acquire a territorial consciousness of "we, the fellow Turks," which often dilute conflicts between Islamic and secular Turkish citizens.

Everyday life in the Turkish community in Almati revolves around the emphasis on ethnic pride in Turkicness. The Gülen movement glorifies—and to some extent invents—myths and symbols of commonality between Kazaks and Turks. One hears a generic and implicit reference to the myths, symbols and memories of common ancestry between Turks and Kazaks in the marketplace, on the street or in the corridors of the Gülen schools:

Tüpümüz bir (We have the same roots, in Kazak).

Aynı anadan süt emdik (We were nursed by the same mother, in Turkish).

Kankardeşiyiz (We are blood bothers, in Turkish).

The claims to a common pre-modern past are expressed through language and heroic stories as well as through customs, food and drinks, such as *kımız*. These elements, which constitute the "ethnie" in Smith's terms, are seen as the basis of a sense of solidarity between the Turks and Kazaks in Almati.[21] This solidarity based on imagined commonality appeals to and accommodates a remarkable diversity of ethnic and national sentiments under the roof of KATEV. The organization serves as a culture club, or rather a coffeehouse, for a vivid community in Almati. One of KATEV's primary duties is to coordinate and to organize cultural events.

Islamic and national loyalties often not only intertwine but also reinforce each other in the movement's educational projects. In the rather *areligious* context of post-Soviet Central Asia, the movement continues to attract sympathy for its Islamic goal of revitalizing faith. When I asked the followers in Almati what "the nation" meant for them, most followers emphasized that the nation is a sovereign collectivity of people who are "free to live their faith." As nationalism was incorporated into their faith-based projects, their *dava* was nationalized in the international realm.

Different Faces of Nationalism

The international sites of the Islamic activities not only prioritize but also *politicize* national affiliation.[22] In my interviews in Almati, all followers stated that their major aim was to "bring the Turkic cultures closer." However, how they wished to work on this differed dramatically. Many articulated this goal in terms of a multiculturalist identity politics, which supposedly calls for a peaceful recognition of differences.[23] But there is a paradox in the followers' communitarian claims for diversity. On the one hand, the followers believe in the unifying power of Muslim faith and Turkic culture. This belief aspires to bring homogenization rather than diversity to the region. On the other hand, their projects create the platform for various nationalist agendas and attract a broad range of nationalisms. At one end of this spectrum, everyday life in the Turkish community in Almati nourishes voluntary patriotism and individualistic forms of civic nationalism. This may propel not only capitalist growth and civil society but also democratization in the region.[24] On the other end of the spectrum, however, one finds clear expressions of collectivist ethnic nationalism and even ultra-nationalism that trace national belonging through the bloodline or biology of race rather than through one's will.

One of the teachers stated: "The aim is not to Turkishize Central Asia, as some of the locals have speculated, but to bridge a variety of the Turkic cultures and their resources." However, when further probed about this multiculturalist discourse, he added, "We do not simply teach the Turkish language but also the Turkish culture. . . . When the students are asked about their national affiliation, they say they are Kazak. They really lack 'ethnic consciousness.' In the future, they will define themselves as Turks, Kazak Turks. It only takes a decent education for them to realize their roots and how much we have in common. Is not education all about self-awareness and self-realization?"

At the extreme end of the continuum of ethnic nationalisms in Central Asia, one finds pan-Turkists who unconditionally support and finance the schools. One of my respondents, a Turkish restaurant owner in Almati, explained to me that he was moved and inspired by the encouragement of the leader, Fethullah Gülen, "to go back" to his Turkic roots in Central Asia. He was born into an ultra-nationalist family and thus was raised with this utopian view. Yet his vision has found expression only through his participation in the Gülen movement's undertakings in Central Asia. He stated:

My kin came from Central Asia, and I am so proud to be back to where I belong. . . . All these lands are sacred Turkish lands. . . . We are getting our land back with a huge Muslim population in it. . . . However, these things take time. It may take at least fifty years if we try to *türkleştirmek* (Turkishize) them through nationalist education. But if a smart political leader appeared who would cooperate and agree to consolidate Kazaks under the Turkish rule, we would save time.

Although this ultra-nationalism is not uncommon among the Turkish Diaspora in Central Asia, it must not be identified with the movement, its leader and organizations. Fethullah Gülen favors a mild form of patriotism, as he clearly expressed during our chat. While the extremists constitute a minority in Almati, moderate forms of nationalism are the main motivation of the loosely connected Turkish Diaspora in Central Asia.

"International Education Is Inherently Secular"

Linked to another organization, General Directorate, in the capital city, KATEV's major function is educational: it supervises the Gülen schools, teaching staff and curriculum.[25] It coordinates the teachers, experts on education, principals of the schools and the heads of the dormitories. The Turkish staff is fluent in the Kazak language as well as in English, the main language of instruction.

KATEV also forms extensive networks between the teachers, the parents of the students, the alumni and the businesspeople and entrepreneurs who financially support the schools and who provide scholarships to students. Consequently, the schools provide the students with relatively better standards of education, equipment and technology. All of the schools in Almati are considered to be highly prestigious. A nationwide exam is organized in order to select the best students in Kazakhstan. Moreover, during the orientation week (the first week before classes formally start), the staff identifies those students who have difficulty in adapting to the schools' norms and who display discipline problems. They refuse to enroll them in these schools.

The followers emphasize that "English is the universal medium of education and science." The openness to the West makes the schools more attractive for Kazaks. Along with the movement's recognition of universal principles of science, their goal is to make the Turkish language an international means of communication and science. As my chats with the students and the graduates of the Gülen schools illustrated, the students graduate with a proficiency in Turkish. The principal of the boys' high school in Almati stated that after graduation some alumni work for Turkish companies in Kazakhstan. Others become closer and friendly to the Turkish culture and consider moving to Turkey and searching for work there. The principal proudly stated that the graduates were "the bridges between Kazakhstan and Turkey."

Along with the secular curriculum and teaching, the movement's schools follow an overtly moralist and nationalist agenda in education. The educational project is divided into two parts that are implemented by two departments of KATEV, *eğitim* (education) and *öğretim* (teaching). The Teaching Department coordinates the courses, schedules and the curricula in collaboration with the Turkish and Kazak states, whereas the Education Department takes the initiative in resocialization and identity-formation of the students.

As in other Gülen schools, boarding is mandatory in the schools in Kazakhstan. Obligatory extracurricular activities aim at discipline and resocialization. The teachers do not compromise on disciplinary issues, either with students or parents. Students are taught Turkish–Muslim ways of life, customs, traditions, values and sanctions. Some of these activities intervene directly in students' privacy and personal habits, even including Muslim rituals of hygiene, bathing, clothing and so on. The students are made familiar with Turkish customs, traditional values, cultural codes and sanctions and the meaning and importance of Turkish national holidays. They are invited and encouraged to celebrate these customs. The aim of these activities is to spread a certain morality and culture of "Turkish Islam" to Kazak youth, who are viewed as the offspring of a society that morally degenerated under the so-called wicked Soviet rule. Moreover, the teachers take pride in sheltering the youth of the Turkish Diaspora, among a people who had been suppressed for many years under Soviet rule.

The schools have a distinct philosophy of education: they try to reconcile moral education with rationality.[26] Teachers see morality as rational. They all seem to agree with Durkheim's notion of moral education, that morality "sets in motion only the ideas and sentiments deriving from reason."[27] The goal is articulated as creating morally superior and internationally competitive youth. One of the teachers stated, "Turkish Muslim education helps the students to be internationally competitive. How would they study in self-discipline unless they are disciplined to respect the elderly and their customs?" Another one stated that "international education is inherently secular. . . . It simply has to be secular if we wish to join the global competition in science." In other instances, however, authoritarian tendencies surpassed the liberating agendas in my interviews. Over tea, another teacher told me, "These kids need discipline. What an unlucky destiny that they were born into a complete immoral disorder. . . . The anti-religious Soviet rule . . . cut people off from their spirituality, faith and morality. We know that it will take time, but they will gradually acquire the Islamic sensibility for moral order and discipline. . . . We have already started to see the change in their attitudes. Their parents report the rapid effects of our education and thank us."

Clearly, an ethnically conscious Islam is advocated, one that seeks "moral regeneration of the religious community,"[28] an Islamic cure for rootlessness and moral degeneration. These disciplining voices contradict the statements that emphasize international secular education. On the one hand, the success of secular teaching and its effects on revitalizing business life in Almati confirm Greenfeld's claim that nationalism is secular and propels capitalism. On the other hand, the collectivist Turkist teachings undermine individual liberties in education. The outcomes of nationalist projects depend on the "type of and specific character of nationalisms."[29] Like all other nationalisms, Turkish nationalism displays ambivalent tendencies when it is followed from the textbook definition of ethnic groups as "monoliths" to the messy realities of everyday life.

Parent-Teacher Collaboration in Discipline in the Private Sphere

As it does in the domestic and communal sites in Turkey, the movement has a clear interest in disciplining the private sphere of Kazak people's lives. Parents are encouraged to collaborate in this ambitious "educational" project. The parent-teacher collaboration is one of the most striking indicators of the "individualized" aspect of the Gülen schools.[30] The educators and teachers visit students' homes and monitor students in their family life and follow their progress by psychological tests and counseling. They not only make sure that the home environment does not contradict the discipline in schools. They also interfere with "order" in the private sphere if they do not find it conducive to the moral education that they are attempting to implement. It is an all-encompassing educational project that extends to all spheres of the students' life. Liberal concerns of freedom of experimentation and individual space to develop one's own path and identity are of no concern in this educational project.

Not surprisingly, the initial responses of the local people to the schools were negative. They were suspicious about the aims of the schools. Some thought that the Turks were "replacing the Soviet hegemony" and taking advantage of the power vacuum to dominate Kazaks through their missionary agenda. Their initial concerns made a rather minuscule difference in the movement's agendas. To relieve the locals' discomfort, the name of the schools was changed from Turk-Kazak to Kazak-Turk schools. I was told that the initial backlash and suspicion were soon replaced with "the trust, appreciation and cooperation of the parents as well as that of the Kazak state."

"The Schools Are of the Nation and for the Nation!"

The teachers have diligently worked on developing trust relations with host countries.[31] Their service abroad involves a high degree of self-sacrifice and self-denial.[32] The nature and degree of commitment are rather dramatic. Some of these teachers left everything behind and came to Central Asia to serve under harsh conditions. The legendary teachers who died for this goal in Asian countries are recalled often with pride and gratitude. Death appears as "the most radical manner possible" in which "the ideal pertaining to the *unity of state and nation* is realized."[33] In the idealization of this unity, service to the Gülen Community and the nation reinforce each other in the international domain. The majority of my informants stated, "If it were not for the nation, the difficulties we faced abroad would have been impossible to overcome." Here, it is important to note the homogenizing quality of modern nationalism, which not only fuses cultural communities with the political community of the nation but also integrates political and cultural identities.[34]

Modern nationalism intertwines incentives that are "from below" with "top-down" state-framed agendas. "By focusing only on certain aspects of nationalism, both culture- and state-framed views . . . underestimate the *interplay* between cultural aspects and political institutions."[35] The binary thinking "deflects attention away from engagements" between secular states and Islamic actors.[36] On the basis of empirical evidence from the Kazak context, I will illustrate below that Turkish nationalism is "not one object, but two; at best it can be described as a dual . . . structure," top-down and from below.[37] This dual structure of nationalism is an important factor that soothes state-Islam relations.

The Gülen movement tries to appeal to a culturally diverse "Turkic people" in Almati, people who also have diverse political orientations. As it does in its domestic patterns of public mobilization, the movement displays a high capacity to connect a heterogeneous constituency for common goals and projects—ethnic politics and moral education—in Almati.

This success has partly qualified the movement as a recognized international actor. However, it drives pro-democratic credentials largely from the unplanned outcomes of this ethnic politics. The movement's undertakings in ethnic politics help to mobilize a rather diverse collectivity for engagements with the nation-state.

A progressive daily newspaper, *Yeni Yüzyıl*, reported: "Four thousand teachers of Gülen schools operate like *diplomats* abroad."[38] *Zaman*, the movement's daily newspaper also applauded the teachers for their successful representation of the Turkish state.[39] "An international network in Central Asia would only strengthen *our* Turkic nation-states," said one of the KATEV's distinguished administrators, Hüsamettin Bey. He was a whole-hearted supporter of the ultra-nationalist party in Turkey. After serving as a teacher and later as a principal in the movement's schools, he was granted an award for being a "distinct education specialist" by the Kazak state. During my fieldwork in KATEV, I had several chances to observe his unconditional service to the Diaspora Turks, "the real Turks," as he referred to them. The families of these people had moved to Kazakhstan before the Soviet regime closed down its borders, and after the closing, they could not come back to their homeland. Mainly through his educational projects and community work among those who were part of the Turkish Diaspora, Hüsamettin Bey was connected to the leading politicians and bureaucrats in Kazakhstan, including the president of the country.

In my interviews, the teachers identified themselves not only as followers of the movement but also as "loyal servants of the nation," and good citizens of the Turkish Republic. More importantly, the schools in Almati are presented simply as "Turkish schools"—and not as the movement's schools—by KATEV and its followers. In the U.S., I met several alumni of the Gülen schools in Central Asia. They were often admitted to prestigious universities and had scholarships. They also referred to Gülen schools as "Turkish schools" and closely associated and socialized with Turks in America. Benefactors of the schools, both non-religious and religious, stated that they felt flattered and proud when they watched Kazak students, who were singing the Turkish national anthem and speaking proper Turkish fluently. They asked, "Who would not feel proud seeing the Turkish flag in the schools abroad?"

National culture is continually reshaped in reference to the "state of the nation."[40] As everyday life practices intertwine cultural and political forms, the preconceived idea of the nation by the founding fathers becomes a process that is constantly "happening."[41] The followers and the movement organizations participate in reformulating the nation by articulating a shared sense of belonging. This ordinary practice *repositions* the movement in relation to the nation–state. The ethnic affinities that the Turkish state and the movement share transform the interactions between them from contestation to cooperation in the international realm.

The followers of the movement are careful not to intimidate students and parents who already perceive Islam as a threat to Kazak society. The officers of KATEV and the teachers explained that they do not want the schools to lose their credibility because of the "Soviet-inflicted negative feelings against religion." In this rather sensitive post-Soviet context, the strong association with the nation and "its" secular state is not only comforting but also conducive to the movement's activities abroad. Some of the Kazak students and parents that I interviewed were not informed about the movement and its Islamic association. The new ethnic sensibilities nurtured by Islam were much easier to mobilize as they were legitimized by an adherence to the ideals of the secular state and rule of law.

The strong national feelings of the movement directly translate into commitments to the state institutions, including even the military. As a nationalist, Fethullah Gülen believes in the military for the security of the Turkish nation. During my interview with him at his current home in Pennsylvania, he told me that the state and the military were informed about the schools right from the start and that they approved them.[42] I also asked the leader about his personal feelings about military service. He smiled and explained to me that there was a special pleasure in serving as a soldier to one's country. Despite the burden and difficulties of the service itself, it was one of the most worthwhile endeavors of his life. Although his ideas on several issues have changed since the mid-1980s, his strong faith in the military can be traced back to pre-1980: "There are people who are born to be soldiers. They are soldiers by birth . . . and die as soldiers. They love their military duties, . . . the sacrificing . . . and the battles. In their everlasting struggles, . . . they reach from one continent to the other."[43]

Not surprisingly, the followers' usage of *millet* (nation) in the interviews was usually interchangeable—or almost identical—with the use of *devlet* (state) in Almati. As Beissinger argues, there are strong incentives for individuals "to accept dominant notions of nationhood and to work within the given parameters of the state. . . . States also shape imaginations about boundaries directly through their ability to inculcate ideas and shape expectations."[44] The quotations from Nutuk (Atatürk's speeches), which hang on the walls and doors in the schools in Central Asia, are indicators of the state's impact in shaping forms of belonging. At the same time, however, by embracing the state's image and the imagined community, previously marginalized Islamic social forces engage and reshape the state through everyday practices.

The political community is nationalized and the nation is politicized through the miniscule encounters where the movement engages the secular Republic. In this sense, Turkish nationalism has been the most successful, and the only complete, tenet of Kemalism.[45] The effectiveness of the Gülen movement's ethnic politics in Almati confirms not only the success of secular nationalism but also the alignment between Islamic and secular nationalisms.

Institutionalizing the Cooperation between Secular States and the Islamic Movement

In addition to the movement's loyalties to the nation and *its* state, it is also necessary to grasp the state's view of the movement and its schools. I focus on two organizations of the Turkish state that are responsible for the relations with the new states of Central Asia, the Council of the Turkish Ministry of National Education (CTNE) and the Turkish International Cooperation Agency (TICA). The state's teachers in CTNE explained in my interviews that they felt at home in KATEV and that they see it as a base for community. The interaction between Islamic teachers and state teachers is based neither on a civilized tolerance nor a calculated strategy. On the contrary, it is based on similar worldviews that originate from their shared belonging to a broader framework. One of the state's teachers in CTNE explained that "these schools do not undertake subversive activities. . . . Nobody can deny the advantage of having six or seven Turkic states in the United Nations that support and favor each other. We agree with KATEV that Turks deserve such an international privilege. . . . This cultural interaction . . . is accomplished not only by KATEV but also with the cooperation of the Turkish Embassy in Almati, and us, CTNE."

The yearnings for regionalization often came up in my interviews, both with Gülen's followers and with the state officials. The Turkish state's teachers expressed their appreciation for what KATEV does for the Turkish nation: "KATEV makes us recall our past and refreshes our historical memory." The director of CTNE chastised me for imposing "artificial cleavages between the state and the society. . . . These are the schools of the Turkish state. Nobody is teaching Islam in the Turkish schools . . . . Their mission has nothing to do with fundamentalism but everything to do with national loyalties."

The state officials are neither uninformed nor in denial of the Islamic basis of the schools. Similar to the followers, however, they highlight the primacy of national loyalties over other commitments, some of which they see as dividing forces in the society. The evidence speaks to the fact that the myths of descent have constituted the primary motivation for both Islamic teachers and the secular teachers of the Turkish state for their undertakings in Kazakhstan. They both inherited these myths from the founding fathers of the Turkish state. The affinities between Islamic and secular nationalists is manifest in their faith in the national myths, which reinforce the image of the state. This facilitates their yearnings and undertakings for political regionalization. Emphasizing the need for gradual reform and cultural changes, both Islamic teachers and teachers of the Turkish state underlined that schooling is the best and most direct way to shape fresh minds. It is the very nature of these overlapping agendas that have overshadowed the presumed hostility and/or tension between them.

More importantly, the movement has cooperated both with the Turkish state and the host states in Central Asia. The secular host states and the movement collaborate in establishing an international curriculum that fits each country's national education system. In Kazakhstan, KATEV collaborates directly with the officials of the Kazak state, who provide the buildings, the infrastructure and other facilities for the school. The followers indicated that they were on good terms with both low- and high-ranking officials of the Kazak state.

The accommodation of Turkish Islamic actors in the international order, especially in Central Asia and the West, suggests that modern forms of nationalism serve as successful forces to integrate Islamic social forces into the international world order. As Nairn suggests, "internationalism is an organic part of the conceptual universe of nationalism. . . . Internationalism has to be seen as a function of this principal's victories, rather than vice versa."[46] The Gülen movement became recognized as an international actor not only because of its capacity to engage the Turkish state domestically, but also because of its alliances with other secular states. Contrary to public opinion, these alliances have been facilitated by its nationalism, not by its abilities to overcome or supersede it. "The cosmopolitans . . . are *not* beyond the nation; and a cosmopolitan . . . will always depend, in the end, on the capacity of nation-states to provide security and civility for their citizens."[47]

Another institutional link between the state and the movement is the Turkish International Cooperation Agency (TICA). After the fall of the Soviet regime, TICA was founded in 1992 under the auspices of the Ministry of Foreign Affairs. It was eventually transferred from the Ministry to the direct control of the government, which endowed the ultra-nationalist party in the coalition (1999–2002) with a greater grip on TICA. Its projects aim at the socioeconomic and political development of the Turkic region. Similar to KATEV's performance in Kazakhstan, TICA has facilitated the activities of Turkish businesspeople in Central Asia. It has been particularly active in the sphere of banking, the training of officials and establishing computer networks.[48] In a recent academic publication by a TICA-funded research project, Gülen schools have been referred to as the "Turkish schools."[49]

The linkages between the secular state and the movement are facilitated largely by their overlapping ethnic discourses and nationalist agendas over Central Asia. The same issue came up in an interview with a hardcore secularist Turkish diplomat who was on duty in Central Asia. He admitted, with a subtle degree of discomfort, "As long as the state does not position itself against the Gülen movement, why would we?" In the international realm, several branches of the Turkish state perceive the so-called Turkish Islam as an international actor or an ally rather than as an enemy.

Needless to say, the cooperation of Turkish Islamic social forces with secular states challenges the prevalent dichotomy between religious and secular nationalisms. More importantly, it challenges the view that Islamic revival is an outcome of the failure of secular nationalism of the nation-states.[50] In contrast, the Gülen movement has excelled in the international realm to the extent that it has associated and collaborated with secular nationalists and the states. This suggests that the centrality of nation-states in the international world order persists in a world where several trends, such as globalization and the rising voices and demands of minority groups, provide challenges to the nation-states. "As far as political representation at the global level is concerned, nation-states are still the relevant units for the negotiation of transnational issues. . . . Political actors that engage in these treaties and organizations are still the formerly sovereign nation-states."[51]

It is important to note that collaboration with the nation-state does not undermine the movement's autonomy or weaken its Islamic character. To the contrary, the cooperative practices in the international sphere legitimize the movement's Islamic identity within the Turkish borders. While elective affinities between state and movement prevent confrontation and facilitate cooperation, Gülen's faith-based undertakings flourish independent of, but not in opposition to, the state.[52] The followers who are teachers enjoy a considerable degree of autonomy to implement the curriculum and full autonomy to conduct extracurricular activities in the host countries. First, the non-confrontational nature endows the movement with enormous bargaining latitude with secular states. This is clearly reflected in the movement's fast-growing international networks. Second, international recognition in turn increases the movement's bargaining power with the Turkish state. Third, by translating the capital from entrepreneurs and businesspeople into the schools and students, the movement creates its own resources, funding and financial independence. The outstanding accumulation of social, political and economic power inside and outside of Turkey also provides a conducive situation for the movement's autonomy from the state.

The Nation-State between Religious and Secular Nationalisms

Rather than simply pursuing a cohesive group identity (ethnic, civic or ultra-nationalist), the Turkish actors display *a wide range of individualist forms of nationalism* in Central Asia. These nationalisms are independent of, and cut across, group identification.[53] Although each and every person from CTNE and KATEV came to Almati upon appointment by either the Turkish state or the Islamic movement, a closer look reveals that their own *personal* ties to their nation and the state provided a strong motivation for their exposure and undertakings in Central Asia. Even the strong communal ties of the Islamic actors to the Gülen movement are diluted by their individualized attachments to the nation. I argue that the very diverse nature of nationalisms cuts across the Islamism-secularism divide and facilitates cooperation between the state actors and the Islamic actors.

In the Central Asian context, the spread of "Muslim-Turkish" ways of life provides a *shared* goal of education between the teachers of the Gülen schools and the teachers of the Turkish state. This should not be surprising, since Muslim ways and Islamic faith have appealed to many state leaders, including even such leading members of the military elite as Kenan Evren.[54] The *myth* of an ethnically unified Turkish state triggers feelings of belonging and familiarity between Islamic actors and state actors. Accordingly, the image of the state is reinforced by the shared consciousness between them. The evidence supports Gellner's claim that national education and the universalization of high culture shape the conceptions of nationhood. Moreover, states also introduce their preferred conceptions of nationhood "through their ability to dominate the public discourse and to enforce international norms."[55] In this way, they mold symbols of belonging and identification with them.[56]

The implications of the state's scope and influence over society have been perceived as the dark side of modernity.[57] Without denying the dark sides of the story, this study illustrates the *unintended* consequence of sharing some of the state's myths and committing to its image. Social actors' practices, which collude in the myth of the state, may also transform the state's image and its practices. The Islamic actors' loyalties to the nation-state have facilitated their collaborative practices with the Republic. Fortunately, this collaboration has extended the realm of the ethnic politics in Almati into unforeseen avenues. These loyalties have enabled the Islamic actors to cooperate with secular state officials as individuals in reimagining the nation and negotiating the framework of the Republic.

State-Islam cooperation unintentionally fosters *individualistic* ties between the state and social actors, Islamic and secular. The power of individualistic forms of nationalism renders intermediary forms of associations and non-governmental organizations almost redundant, even for Islamic actors, who have excelled in this realm. Whether Islamic or secular, the project-based undertakings—the underlying agendas and ideologies of non-governmental organizations—cannot fully account for the engagements between state and Islam. Clearly, this cooperation is not generated by inherent characteristics of either Islamism or secularism. To the contrary, as discussed above, both have had various illiberal authoritarian tendencies of their own. Here it is extremely important to differentiate the affective ties between Islamic actors and the state from the organizational strategies and preplanned projects of both. While educational projects of the movement that wish to "moralize" the society may have homogenizing and authoritarian tendencies, the spontaneous and unplanned state-Islam cooperation is likely to propel transition from authoritarian rule.

Why, then, have Islamic and national identities come to the forefront of transitions from authoritarian rule if they still maintain illiberal tendencies themselves? The relationship between religion, nationalism and democratization is contingent upon conditions, historical and contemporary. In times of political openings, Islamists and secular nationalists may come closer and even ally with pro-democratic forces as democracy becomes a common goal for these otherwise divided groups. Rather than providing a shared ideal, the anticipated promises of democracy appeal to and benefit these social forces in different ways. Still, an important question remains to be addressed. Did not fascism also expand by cooperating with the state? Indeed, cooperation with the states is not a guarantee of democracy. If we consider alliances such as the ones between the Mafia and the state, the cooperation between state and society may even seem to be an obstacle to democratization.

As Brubaker argues, there is nothing inherently wrong with state-framed nationalism, which simply designates the "congruence" of the nation with the state.[58] There is no intrinsic harm in Islamic actors' alignment of their national loyalties with secular nationalism. However, the intended and/or unintended consequences of these nationalist alliances will depend on two conditions. The first condition is that the "engaged" Islamic actors continue reconciling several types of nationalisms and internationalisms with moderate and tolerant forms of Islam. Second, the broader outcomes of the cooperation depend on its potential effect on the state's capacities to accommodate *other* marginalized groups, such as Islamic women and ethnic minorities in Turkey. The politics of engagement suggest elective affinities between Islamic actors and the secular Republic. However, it is still to be seen whether the shifting linkages between Islam and the state will facilitate the formation of other channels of interaction between the state and other underprivileged social actors. Until these conditions are fulfilled in the long term, there cannot be talk of a direct causal link between engagements and liberal democracy. I will discuss the improved treatment of minorities in recent years in Turkey in chapter 6.

CHAPTER 5

Compromising Women's Agency:
Bonds between Islamic and Secular Actors

THE SECULARIST founders of the Republic initiated gender reforms more than seventy-five years ago by handpicking and "inserting" Turkish women into the public sphere and politics. Considering the widely shared belief about Islam's "low score" on gender reform,[1] Atatürk and his followers seemed to distinguish themselves from the majority of male Muslim leaders by their "pro-women" attitudes.[2] Time has not really left them behind, either, as women's situation has worsened in recent years in Islamic states such as Afghanistan and Iran.[3] Nevertheless, the dispute has not been resolved as to whether Turkish women have ended up benefiting, either from the original intentions of the secularist founders of the Republic or the outcomes of their own actions that were mostly unforeseen by these gentlemen. Although the debate on the nature and outcomes of state-framed gender reform has continued in Turkey, this exclusive focus has left a recent trend largely unnoticed.

This chapter illustrates the ways in which the "engaged" Islamic male actors have recently inherited certain characteristics of male-initiated gender reform from the early Republic. First, despite many differences and disagreements, the "civilizing projects" of the secular and Islamic actors overlap in the way they locate women's public visibility at the heart of their agendas. Whereas the founding fathers were "nationalizing" secular ways of life, contemporary Islamic actors are nationalizing their faith-based ways of life. Second, women's place and role in society have played a major part in legitimizing both of these national projects that were engineered exclusively by men. Similar to the founding fathers, the Islamic male actors have not only inserted women into the public sites, these men have also proved to be successful in this endeavor. The continuity between the making of the state and civil society is most remarkable in the shared emphasis and prioritization of women's education. Interestingly, in line with their goal of enhancing Islamic female actors' public visibility and education, the male elites of the Gülen movement and the AKP have displayed a rather lethargic attitude toward challenging the state's headscarf ban.

Third, there is a national history behind male actors' attitudes. Male actors seem to determine women's interest by compromising women's agency for the sake of broader projects. The shared attitudes of Islamic and secular men have facilitated the formation of bonds between them in the short run. The flourishing ties between these Islamic and secular male actors emerge as another level of interaction between Islam and the state, a fundamentally cooperative one. However, these ties have left Islamic women out of the politics of engagement, and thereby outside of power structures. Women's remarkable presence in Islamic public sites conflicts with severe gender segregation and subordination in the private lives of Islamic actors. The evidence sheds light on the complexity of the link between transition politics and women's participation in the public sphere.[4] It is yet to be seen how these seemingly progressive gender reforms may benefit Islamic women in the long run. Specifically, the unintended consequences of the new cooperation between Islamic and secular males for the empowerment of Islamic women needs to be explored further.

Like most other nationalists, most Islamic and secular male actors in Turkey have shared a rather positive and benign view of the state in regard to gender relations.[5] From this perspective, the state is regarded as a force for gender reform, whether it was modernizing at the time of nation building or democratizing later during transition politics. Clearly, this view assumes that "women," like "the nation," was a category with unified interests. Feminists have rightly criticized these male-dominated projects for drawing a direct relationship between gender reform and broader political transformation.[6] There is *no direct* correlation between women's participation in transition politics and what they gain out of this participation. Quite to the contrary, women have participated both in revolutions and under and against authoritarian regimes, participation that did not reward but often undermined them.[7]

How do contemporary Turkish Islamic female actors relate to these overarching projects, the Republican and Islamic? Does their remarkable participation in the public sphere benefit them separate from national agendas? Does their public participation translate into the politics of engagement, and thereby their own independence and empowerment? Clearly, gender orders are embedded in the national culture, reinforced by national loyalties. Like nationalisms, they are the product of neither Islamic nor secular practices but are the outcome of interpenetrations between the two.[8] In order to explore the early historical legacy of the relationship between the Turkish state and women, I first discuss briefly the interactions between the early Republic and secularist women of that period. These earlier interactions shed light on the current and prospective situation of female Islamic actors in Turkey.

The Nation-Building Elite and the State as "Gender Reformers"?

For the founding fathers, women's public visibility designated a clear break from the Islamic Empire and its Islamic association with subordination of women. Gender equality was used for making the nation-state and legitimizing its modernity.[9] Although women in the West have struggled for their own emancipation and empowerment, Turkish women were inserted into the public and political sphere in the 1930s and were granted their political rights by the modernizing male elite. As early as 1925, Mustafa Kemal said in a talk in Inebolu, "Let women see the world with their own eyes and let the whole world see their faces."[10] Although the defense of women's freedom against the Islamic tradition is clear in this statement, the method of "letting women out" has not proved to be sufficient for women's emancipation.

Atatürk stated in his speeches that "Turkish women shall be free, enjoy education and occupy a position equal to that of men, as they are entitled to."[11] According to this modernizing mentality, women's freedom and empowerment was a direct result of their participation in the public sphere.[12] Paradoxically, there was no room for women's agency and a women's movement in this male-initiated gender reform. Not surprisingly, contemporary Turkish feminists refused to acknowledge the women's movement as an effect of the Republican male elite's incentive. Instead, they highlighted the origins of women's self-organizing in the late Ottoman Empire.[13] Women's sovereignty and the sources of their political power were easily traceable to the Imperial Harem, the so-called Sultanate of women of the sixteenth and seventeenth centuries. "The women of the Imperial Harem, especially the mother of the reigning sultan and his leading concubines, were considerably more active . . . in the direct exercise of power . . . [and] in what we might call the public culture of sovereignty."[14]

Despite the roots of the women's movement in the Empire, however, it should be noted that the secular Republic promoted women's rights dramatically in the 1920s and early 1930s. Major progress was accomplished in the areas of educational opportunities, marriage, divorce, inheritance, and property ownership. This progress was mainly the result of a comprehensive secularization of law, especially the adoption of the Swiss Civil Code in 1926. With the introduction of the concept of citizenship, women acquired civic and political rights that were relatively equal to those of men. In 1934, suffrage was extended to women, and Atatürk encouraged women to participate in the elections of 1935. They received formal equality under the legal framework, although the Constitution itself continued to discriminate against women in both explicit and implicit ways.[15] Turkish women entered not only the public sphere but also the government and the parliament earlier than female citizens in many other countries, Western or Muslim. However, gender equality was engineered at the mercy of a reform-oriented male elite. Not surprisingly, women's celebrated place in politics remained marginal and symbolic.[16] Very few women played politically significant roles, and even fewer acquired the sources of political power.

The male-initiated project for women's public visibility was an integral part of Turkey's commitment to Westernization and secularization as well as to nation building.[17] "The image of emancipated women [had to be] in line with 'true' identity of the collectivity—the new Turkish nation."[18] The Republican nation-building elite equated the interest of the Turkish nation with Turkish women.[19] However, neither the actual reforms nor the image of emancipated women led to a genuine empowerment and liberation for women.[20] This is mainly because gender reform led by the state was not really concerned with women's private lives[21] or genuinely supportive of women's empowerment in politics.[22]

As Yeşim Arat argues, the condition for women's introduction into politics was their exclusion from competition within power structures.[23] The legal system has been reformed only to recognize the *basic* equality of men and women, while it has continued to discriminate against women. "In this male-dominated society, women representatives benefited from men's power until they competed for office. . . . Once in politics, women confronted many problems because of their gender."[24] Moreover, the women who were initiated into this male-dominated realm needed "supportive husbands and fathers" at home in order to survive in politics, where the unequal distribution of power and discrimination against women was very explicit and persistent. Gender reform in Turkey has largely benefited elite women, while leaving out the majority of the female population from this privileged status.

It is important to note the voices of the Kemalist women of the early Republican period. Calling themselves the "women of enlightenment" (aydınlanmanın kadınları), these women of the older generation still identify entirely and passionately with the Republican project. They truly have faith in its universally emancipating nature for both men and women.[25] There is still a strong consensus among this older generation that they were much more equal than the new female generations, as they see the current Islamization as an attack on the equality that was granted to Turkish women by Atatürk. These "women of enlightenment" disagree with contemporary feminist critiques of Atatürk's gender reforms. Necla Arat cites Abadan-Unat, one of the leading female figures of that era: "All the progress I accomplished in my life was realized thanks to the civilizing reforms of Atatürk. That is why I call myself Kemalist."[26] Unfortunately, in assessing women of enlightenment, it is often disregarded that these women were the privileged female elite of their time, mostly professors and writers.

These women express their disappointment with the new generation of feminists' lack of appreciation for those reforms.[27] One of the female adherents of Kemalist civil society organizations answered my question about the rights and freedoms of Islamic women: "How unlucky that your mothers were born into an era of gender equality, and you, the children of those emancipated women, are searching for feminism in the bigotry of the actions of Islamist women."[28] The generation gap reveals an ongoing dispute among feminists with regard to their view of both the secularist founders of the Republic and the recent Islamization. What is even more important to note is that the deep loyalties of the women of enlightenment with the Republican project have not declined so far. Despite the declining numbers of the Republican feminists, they still see no difference between the Republican interest and their own. However, in the long run, the children of these women of enlightenment stood up and negotiated for their own rights.[29] As Yeşim Arat argues,

The relationship between the state and women in Republican Turkey has changed substantively since the early decades of the Republic. . . . By the 1980s and thereafter the defiant daughters of the older generation demanded liberation; they sought autonomy from tradition and the right to speak up as individuals. . . . Women have developed a language with which they can now redefine their relationship to the state as individual women who want to articulate their needs and priorities, independent of the state.[30]

For a long time, secular female actors have experimented within—and expanded—the tight boundaries of public and political realms that were granted to them by the Republican male actors. Clearly, this was not an intended or pre-determined consequence of the nation-building project. On the contrary, the women's movement took advantage of male-initiated reforms and rights and used the early Republican gender reforms to their own ends. Unlike their mothers, they at first distanced themselves from the Republican project and saw it with critical eyes. However, contrary to what their mothers' thought, they did *not* betray or attack the project itself. After all, they were also the children of the Republic, hence still attached to it. They engaged the illiberal authoritarian state in an effort to turn it into a liberal and tolerant one.

Not surprisingly, the engagements of the secular women have excluded Islamic women and their interests.[31] Nor have many secular feminists been supportive of the Islamic women's demands, needs and rights, such as the right to wear a headscarf. Although engagements take shape in the form of collective action, people do not engage as unified categories of sex, ethnicity or class. They engage as individuals. Evidence speaks to the fact that the conventional Islamic-secular divide has often cut across the lines of gender, ethnicity and class. Moreover, groups of individuals come to engage the state according to their own demands and interests and on their own clock. Engagements do not take place before individuals come to terms with the broader project that envelops them. Individuals engage once they sufficiently reconcile their sense of *distance and connection* to this overarching framework.

Conditions of Islamic Women's Public Participation
WOMEN'S OMNIPRESENCE IN PUBLIC SITES

As did the early Republican male elite, the male followers of the Gülen movement value and promote women's public participation and visibility. They prevent segregation of the sexes in the public sphere, as they perceive segregation as contradictory to the "civilized image" of public life. However, this has little or nothing to do with their pro-women agendas. Similar to enabling Turkish women in the nation-building period, having women in Gülen's public sites complements a certain civilized image. For the Gülen movement, the public sites are an obvious way of distinguishing their own Islamic projects from other ones and displaying that distinction to the outside world, both the Turkish Republic and the West. Indeed, in tune with the diversity in these window sites, they welcome women from different occupations, ages and religious and political orientations. The women-friendly nature of these sites completes the image of diversity in these public sites.

A leading male figure in the movement told me, "the women *were enabled* to be involved in most of the movement's projects as equal participants." Another male follower who was in charge of organizing some of window sites said, "what is left of civil society, if it consists of only men?"

The diversity of active, educated and professional women in these window sites echoes Atatürk's desire to make women a part of public life. This is consistently manifest in the movement's events, debates, charity dinners and conferences. Indeed, the Gülen movement encourages the education of girls as much as it does the visibility of women. When the headscarf ban prevented most of the covered girls from going to school, the Gülen movement was the first to insist on girls' schooling at the cost of compromising their headscarf. This issue will be discussed further later in this chapter.

In the window sites I met career women, academics and intellectual women who were giving speeches. Women were being allocated awards at ceremonies. These sites were hosting female celebrities such as actresses and singers who were wearing striking and extravagant outfits. Some women in these sites were wearing headscarves (in different styles), and some were uncovered. I also chatted with numerous working Islamic women who were doctors, nurses, teachers, writers, journalists, engineers and so forth. These women were the public faces of the Gülen Community, which legitimized their claim to be a civil society entity.

During my participation at those sites, the movement attracted several secular women who were passionate female sympathizers and defenders and who promoted the movement and the leader in the public debates and the media. One of the most vocal promoters was Nevval Sevindi, a journalist. When a video clip was released that showed Fethullah Gülen giving a provocative speech in traditional religious clothing, Sevindi, in her rather daring red evening dress, defended the leader openly in media. On one occasion she attacked the opponents of the movement by yelling at them on a TV show. Her highly dramatic devotion and emotionally driven defense of the Community has drawn a lot of attention for some time.

At the window sites, there was no pressure on the women with regard to their clothing, life style and political orientation. A variety of female actors were welcomed at numerous public events without feeling obliged to adhere to religious conduct or faith-based ways of life. Each time I would ask if it was necessary to wear a headscarf in order to participate in the events, the answer was, "No, no, not at all. You should behave as you feel and as you are. Covering is just a visual detail that may or may not express true faith." I also hesitated before shaking hands with men. Many other Islamists in Turkey would refuse to shake hands with members of the opposite sex. After a while, I realized that male followers in these public sites would even give friendly hugs to female colleagues, friends, or guests. A few of the leading male figures explained to me that "all these instances of restrictive conduct do not represent true Islam but are misinterpretations of it." When, with a glass of wine in my hand, I ran into a male follower in a bar and felt uncomfortable, he explained that he was used to the "night scenes" of Istanbul. Because he worked in public relations in one of the movement's foundations, he was used to dealing with a variety of celebrities in Istanbul nightlife.

During my fieldwork, the followers seemed glad that I, a secular Turkish woman, was studying the movement. Furthermore, they appreciated the presence of other secular or non-religious women in the public sites. These women expressed their appreciation of the movement's tolerant and accepting attitudes toward themselves and stated that they were impressed by the civility and open-mindedness of the movement. By bringing people from opposite worldviews together, these public sites have effectively diluted hostilities and overcome biases of secular actors.

When I asked my mother, a secularist and a lawyer, to accompany me to one of the movement's charity dinners in the Polat Rönesans Hotel, she was reluctant at first. As a strong defender of the impact of Kemalist reforms on women's emancipated status, she was deeply suspicious of Islamic social forces. Like many secularist women of her generation, she regards the headscarf as a betrayal of Atatürk's legacy to Turkish women. When we entered the huge ballroom in the five-star hotel where women and men were mingling and having dinner, she was not only surprised but also comforted.

Window sites are imbued with variety of symbols that pay tribute to Atatürk and the nation. A picture of Atatürk was projected on a huge screen. A documentary displayed the schools of the movement, in which could be seen quotations from Atatürk that expressed loyalty to his tradition and the secular state. Soon my mother started to relax. It was only then that she started to show interest in the Islamic women sitting at the same table with us. She was very happily surprised to find out that two of the covered women at our table were practicing doctors who had graduated from the medical school. According to the Republican mentality, women with careers were one of the most convincing proofs that Atatürk's reforms were still effective. After the dinner she told me that she was impressed by the tolerant way her questions were answered by the bright women whom she had met. Although she said that "they seem like open-minded people," she still disapproved of the headscarf because it was "so unaesthetic and visually awkward." "Surely, their faith deserves respect," she said but "why would a modern career woman wear this 'symbol of bigotry?'" She also disliked the promotional nature of the event, which seemed to pressure participants to join and/or support the movement financially or otherwise.

Similar to numerous other women at these sites, I was treated with respect as their *bacı* (sister).[32] This assigned gendered role proved advantageous to me in various ways. Despite the wide range of my questions and my extensive participation in the movement, my inquisition has been perceived as non-threatening. Contrary to my male colleagues' experiences in conducting their research in the movement, I was made very welcome to these public sites and was treated politely, albeit too protectively in some situations.[33] This caring, protective and patronizing attitude became more visible in Kazakhstan, where I was far away from both my country and family—the two basic preconditions for a woman's security, according to the male followers.

Similar to the early Republican male's wish to break away from the Islamic Ottoman Empire, Islamic male followers wish to dissociate from the predominant Western, and also Republican, view of Islam as a source of women's repression and oppression. Not surprisingly, public sites become the cornerstone of this illustration.

GENDER SEGREGATION IN PRIVATE LIVES
AND DOMESTIC SITES

Despite the wide appeal of the women-friendly public sites, my fascination with them did not last long. I soon discovered that the welcoming attitudes in the public sites were limited to female outsiders. During one of my interviews with Ahmet Bey, I was inquiring about his wife. I asked if I could meet her at the charity dinner that night. The answer was prompt and expressed a subtle tone of sarcasm: "Who . . . Ayşe? . . . Oh no, Ayşe does not go out at night," he replied with a smile on his face. I was confused because I had been told a few minutes earlier that she was "equal" to him. Trying to hide my astonishment, I asked if she attended communal events during the day. Apparently she was busy with the children. Besides, she did not want to participate in those events, either. "What would she have to do with that 'business' anyway?" At that time, I was not quite sure what business we were talking about. Digging further into this issue for a while, I soon discovered a long line of paradoxes about gender order in the movement.

The "business" meant the affairs of the Community, which took place in the non-private sphere where the wives and daughters of the followers did not necessarily belong. Indeed, most of the wives and daughters were regarded as irrelevant to the worldly pursuits of the movement. Similar to the male followers' statements, most of the wives also stated that they were "not interested in men's business" and justified their responsibility in the private sphere as a sacred duty of womanhood and motherhood. As the male followers claimed, women stated that they were not coerced to accept their "sacred duties." They simply preferred their kids to the crowded events of the movement. Very few female followers complained or showed a negative reaction to their absence in the window sites. Most of them seemed even to be content with and supportive of the segregated gender order. They appreciated having autonomy in the domestic sphere and enjoyed "a separate social life" with other female followers and their children. While they were voluntarily organizing the ways of life in the private sphere, they were also organizing communal activities among female followers that were separate from the projects led by men.

Gender segregation was a central part of social life on the "inside" of the movement. After many years of service for the movement, Osman, one of my interviewees, ended up working in one of the movement's organizations. I was very curious as to whether his wife ever participated at those activities. The moment I asked this question, he became defensive and mentioned the "good" qualities of his marriage and wife: "My wife is more beautiful and virtuous than all those celebrities that I work or socialize with. Her qualities, her virtue, her moral standards do not compare to any of my friends and colleagues." I asked him, "Does she accompany you anywhere? Can I meet her at one of the Community's events?" He said, "Serap does not like Community events. Besides, we have two little children. They take all her time."

In the middle of our conversation, his phone rang, and he started a conversation with a famous pop singer who, I understood, was going to sing at an upcoming public event. After his call, he continued talking to me. "You should understand. This is my work; I work for the Gülen movement. Serap should be, and actually is, proud of it." He said that all he was doing was "separating his work from home life." Many male followers made similar statements on separating the private and public spheres, statements that were actually setting severe gender segregation in motion.

Similar to the self-identification of the women of enlightenment with the Republican project, the female followers have completely identified with the so-called civil society projects of the movement. They have not only accepted ways of life that are based on gender segregation but have also voluntarily participated in compartmentalizing the public and private spheres accordingly. During my visits to their homes, I realized that women only socialized with other women. When their husbands came home after work, the women would close the doors so that there would be no contact between the sexes. Even if I had met the husband first and interviewed him several times before in the public sites, there would be little or no contact in the private sites. A close friend of mine told me that during her stay with a family from the movement in North America for two weeks, she did not see the male members of the family even once.[34] Men and women in the movement organize the degree and nature of gender segregation in the private sphere, often collectively. Similarly, the gender segregation can be observed in other organizations of the movement, such as the radio and television stations. The arrangement of space in the movement's organization differed from other Islamic organizations such as Refah. For instance, the television station of Refah incorporated women physically and socially into the organization. Although there has been a slow change in some of the organization of the Gülen movement within the last few years, the women who were integrated into these organizations were often "outsiders."

THE POWER OF THE ELITE WOMEN IN THE MOVEMENT

The very few exceptions to gender segregation were the female followers of the movement who were from higher social or economic standing. These women were either major benefactors of the movement's undertakings or the wives of relatively open-minded intellectual figures, such as famous professors, in the movement. Şahika Hanım, who was the wife of a prominent entrepreneur, supported the movement financially. She and her husband owned several companies and real estate. Despite her husband's affiliation with the Refah party rather than the Gülen movement, she was recognized as a powerful individual in the movement. In addition to her strong presence in the private lives of female followers and at *Risale* readings, she was also a highly respected public figure.

Other privileged women, the wives of the leading figures of the movement, were occasionally permitted to watch the meetings of their husbands while segregated in a different room. On one occasion, they observed—on a huge screen in the studios at Samanyolu, the Community's television station—a meeting in which Fethullah Gülen took part. The women told me: "It felt like the same as being there in the meeting, . . . even better, because we feel more comfortable among women."

Public sites have mostly accommodated women of privileged status who already have had the means and access to engage the state as individuals if they wished. How, then, can movement activities be conducive to reform and democracy if they exclude the majority of female insiders of the movement from the politics of engagement? In a few cases, I met and talked with men who acknowledged the contradiction between gender inequality and their civil society projects. An intellectual figure discussed the issue with me for hours. His positive attitude towards women's participation was a part of the "nice and neat" presentation of the movement's discourse on civility, progress and reform: "Women's situation is important to us. We know that we have a long road to walk. There are problems, but we have already achieved progress. We have high-standard schools for girls and encourage them to go to university. Change comes slowly and gradually. All we need is patience."

My insistent questions as to why there were no women in the production of ideas and projects was answered by men in similar ways: "It is not because women are excluded. . . . Did you ever think that women might simply not be interested in this business of ideas? Aren't we tired yet of the imposition of Western feminist discourse on our women? Can't they choose to be different?"

These arguments of relativism embrace a contradiction. On the one hand, the movement's civil society projects embrace Western practices in numerous realms, such as science, education in English, capitalism and the free market, Western goods and technology. On the other hand, the ways of life reflect a rather critical view of feminism, which is perceived to be Western.

DO FEMALE FOLLOWERS' SERVICE AND WORK LEAD TO EMPOWERMENT?

Are all the female followers constrained to the domestic sphere? Are the public sites open only to elite women or women with lesser or no ties to the Community? The answer to these questions is a clear and obvious "no." Although most female followers were primarily identified with the private sphere, not all of them were housewives. Some female followers, indeed, participate in the communal and public sites and organizations. As Walby argued in her brilliant work on the multi-faceted nature of patriarchy, it is particularly important to capture the interaction—similarities as well as tensions—between different manifestations of "patriarchy."[35]

Women are believed to possess inherent female qualities that enable them to educate the youth and to persuade benefactors for charity.[36] Hence, male followers particularly welcome female participation in specific areas such as teaching, educational advising and moral supervision in the dormitories. Female actors are particularly active in any form of unpaid service, voluntary work and cheap labor. While these jobs bring women into the public sphere, they hardly empower women either financially or socially. Traditional ways of conceiving femininity as innocent, pure and altruistic encourage people to see women as more appropriate to collect charity, as they are seen as the opposite of male followers, with their marketing strategies and business dealings. These conceptions render female participation in the public sphere as a valuable asset to the movement. The young female followers, most of whom were students in Gülen schools, work actively in the domestic, communal, and public spheres. This is often voluntary work such as undertaking small surveys in the households to find out who buys the movement's newspaper, journal, magazine, and so forth. It is labor-intensive in the sense that these girls are expected to enter people's private lives and visit homes. Their access to other people's private sphere is seen as easier for charity collection, as girls are regarded as more trustworthy and less threatening for most families.[37] Female followers' participation clearly blurs the boundaries between public and private, as they enter other people's personal spheres and are connected with others' domestic lives.[38] Moreover, they are expected to use their "female intuition and sensibilities" in order to reach out and connect with other people and expand networks. Usually, the female participants have no utilitarian expectation from these works, which are considered an altruistic service to the community.

Junior and single women participate in service in different fields. As already mentioned, some that I met were *ablas* (advising sisters), who supervised and helped the high school students, particularly the ones who were preparing for the university exam. Others worked in the associations and institutions of the movement "for the good of the Community." One of these duties is the promotion the movement. Female followers show videotapes or distribute textual documents that display the accomplishments and schools of the movement. These young women's skills are used to acquire and accumulate an enormous resource of economic and social power for the Community, although they get hardly any for themselves as individual female followers.

Although women are active in intellectual activities and in the ideational world, they share ideas and interpretations of the *Risales* mainly with each other. Due to gender segregation, their intellectual input often remains marginal. Women, their daughters, daughters-in-law, and friends gather periodically to read and discuss religious texts, especially the *Risales*. During my participation in the *Risale* readings, I observed a high-level awareness and sensitivity to the text among women's *Risale* groups. These women learn, discuss, explain, and teach each other and the younger students without making claims for power based on expertise. Women specializing in the texts say that they leave economic, organizational and political matters to their husbands. Put differently, while men concentrate on the formation of power networks, women develop expertise in the *Risales* as a daily activity.

My informal group interviews and participant observations among several male followers showed that they prefer to regard women's *Risale* readings as a sort of leisure activity along with tea, cookies and pastry as opposed to the men's organizational activities with substantial returns. In general, women's religious and spiritual activities were underrepresented in the movement. The Gülen school of thought was developed exclusively by the male intellectuals, particularly the circle around Fethullah Gülen and his best friends. As they do not collaborate with female followers in the private sphere, there are not many opportunities to exchange ideas between the sexes.

In addition to meeting women who were participating in women's local networks, voluntary work and service, I also met with a few working women in the Gülen Community who were pursuing a career. Most of them were single and therefore not yet bound by the sacred duty of motherhood. Their wages were strikingly low due to their unprivileged status in the workforce as "Islamist" women who wore their headscarves or prayed five times a day. In my interviews, these working women reported deep discomfort in the workplace, due to their exclusion from high-ranking offices and jobs of status, lack of trust, discrimination, and underappreciation for the work they undertook. Such treatment was justified because these women were regarded as temporary labor, who would soon leave their jobs for permanent maternal duties.

Other women who worked in the movement's organizations and schools also felt discriminated against. Nalan, an intellectual woman, was writing for one of the magazines of the movement thanks to her husband's tolerance and support. Despite her privileged situation at home, she expressed despair for her career and working conditions:

We are only a few women working in the production of this magazine. It is only me who struggles with the oppressive and unequal working conditions for women here. Other women comply. I have been confronting the managerial board for quite a long time for freedom of thought and expression. I want to write about women's situation in the Community. My years-long struggle has been futile, whereas men can write about anything they wish. There is strikingly less supervision and censorship on what they research and write. My husband is a very liberal, practicing Muslim who has nothing against my career. . . . But his positive support does not change the reality that my colleagues at work will not support or promote me.

Most of the time, women refused to acknowledge, let alone question, severe gender segregation in the movement. Only a few women expressed uneasiness about their situation. They stated that they had no female support or empathy from female followers, especially in cases where the women's interests explicitly conflicted with the movement's interests. In those rare cases in which women acknowledged that the situation was not fair, they eventually gave up. It was too hard to face the disapproval of both men and women.

Meral, a young graduate from medical school, told me about the job proposals she was receiving from several private hospitals. She had a hectic schedule because of her desire to be helpful to people. However, the Community was putting enormous pressure on her to continue with her service. In one of our meetings over coffee, she opened up and said that she really liked her profession and that her professors found her future options very promising. However, other female followers stated that her contributions to the movement were irreplaceable, and that "it would be a sin if she pushed the Community away for her own career ambitions."[39] She was one of the very few women who admitted that her devotion for the movement and her need for space and for individuality severely conflicted with the gender order of the movement.

In general, service seems to be a voluntary job for both men and women in a presumably equal way. But my interviews revealed that service is a gendered practice that disadvantages women. It is important to note that the male followers did not report any tension between the Community's demands and their own space and business. This is because their wives and families accommodate and support men's service unconditionally. In contrast, women's work outside the home is not recognized as essential. Regardless of their participation in the public sphere, women are excluded from networks of power. Exclusion is facilitated by the emphasis placed on motherhood and the arranged marriages for girls at relatively young ages.

PRESERVATION OF TRADITIONAL FEMALE ROLES

While the women-friendly public sites of the Gülen movement resonate with the Republican insistence on women's public participation, the movement has also inherited another view of the founding fathers. As both associate women primarily with the collective good, women's traditional roles in the private sphere are primary in each case.

Arat argues that the entrance of women into the public sphere in the early Republic took place simultaneously with the redefinition of traditional roles of women within the private sphere.[40] All women of the Republic, Islamic or secular, were expected to fulfill their sacred traditional roles and duties. The organization of the private realm and related domes-

tic issues seem to be immune to any exemption.⁴¹ Due to the strong association made between reproduction of the nation and nurturing in the
domestic sphere, it is not surprising that the Islamic and secular men agree
on associating women primarily with the traditional gender roles. This
shared attitude may endow Islamic women with more authority in shaping Islamic ways of life in the domestic and communal sphere. At the same
time, however, it leaves them out of the politics of engagement with the
state. The only exceptions to this, as I discussed above, have been the
Islamic elite women. Similar to a minority of secular elite women who
benefited from the nation building, a few Islamic elite women benefit
from the movement's activities. These cases of exception must not be generalized as "women's status" in Turkey.⁴²

In this respect, the Gülen Community is not that different from the
society at large in its view of motherhood. Fethullah Gülen states,
"Women's responsibility is to fulfill the domestic work, whereas men's
responsibility is to undertake the work in the non-private domain: The
woman raises new generations. She raises all the important figures of
human history. If the woman contributes with these capabilities and the
man with his abilities, this togetherness would create a family and virtuous society in a heavenly climate."⁴³

Islamic and Republican male elites share and promote the idea that new
generations should be raised by educated mothers. Clearly, rather than seeing women's education as an end for their individual development, liberation and empowerment, they see it as a means for them to become better mothers and educators.

According to the Islamic worldview in the movement, romance should
also not be the goal of marriage. The real goal is faith, and real love is love
for God. Marriage is seen as a responsibility to the collective good. It is
regarded as necessary for a secure home to have "companionship for a
lifetime" and reproduction of the next generations (*nesillerin devamı*).⁴⁴
Fethullah Gülen argues that there is a contemporary trend of romantic
marriage in society, which results in frustration and divorce. He claims that
marriage has to be based on reason and rationality and not on emotions.
Moreover, the idea of *hizmet* has to be primary and must not be overshadowed by the worldly passions such as the physical demands of the
body.⁴⁵

While marriage is regarded as a natural destiny and duty for every
woman, the Community reserves tolerance and reverence for the men of
Islamic knowledge and of extraordinary Islamic qualities who choose not
to marry. Fethullah Gülen and Said Nursi avoided marriage purposely and
rationally and avoided any romantic relationship with the other sex. Their

rational choice is very highly respected as they both justified this decision by arguing that their love for Islam and for their nation would not leave any space for marriage. Thus, it would be a sin to make a woman suffer because her husband's whole life was devoted to a sacred mission. However, it would be beyond imagination that a woman might choose a similar path, namely refusing to marry, for the same cause.

There is no strict age for marriage for girls, but if they do not go to university, it is likely to take place at any time after high school graduation. Even if the girl continues to study after high school, it is very likely that a match would be arranged with someone from the Community. Exogamy is discouraged so that one of the partners would not wish or try to give secondary importance to service or the good of the Community. It is for the Community's advantage that there is unity and agreement in the family. The most striking example of this was a young woman, Fatma, whom I met at one of the *Risale* readings. I saw her only once because, at the age of eighteen, she was always busy with her two babies. She told me proudly that she was married to Imam Hasan of the movement, who supposedly was known and respected by everyone.

Hasan was the Imam of a very large geographical area and thus responsible for never-ending sacred duties. Fatma told me that her husband was so busy that she might see him only once a week, or even less frequently. He was traveling very often and thus could very rarely sleep at home. Knowing that she was much younger than her husband, I was curious why she would choose this kind of marriage. Other women at the *Risale* reading explained that "he is a holy man of great importance for the Community. It is a great honor to be chosen as a wife for him. . . . Everybody would like to be in her place."

Moreover, a woman's association with the private realm is justified mainly by her physiology. Fethullah Gülen states that

a man can spend the whole year actively. Sometimes he works difficult and heavy jobs. Physiologically and psychologically, he is always stronger. The man is used to having more demanding jobs. . . . But a woman must be excluded on certain days during the month. After giving birth, she sometimes cannot be active for two months. She cannot take part in different segments of the society all the time. She cannot travel without her husband, father or brother. . . . The superiority of men compared to women cannot be denied.[46]

According to this perspective, gender segregation is the result of the Truth of Creation: women reproduce, nurture and mother, while men deal with worldly matters and earn money. While Fethullah Gülen's earlier emphasis on the biology of the sexes reflected his vision of gender segregation, his more recent views highlight that there is no reason why women cannot work outside the home.[47] In my interviews with his close associates Emir and Selçuk, they told me that their wives completed their undergraduate degrees in the department of divinity and were currently teaching in high schools. Both emphasized the fact that their wives were independent and powerful figures at home and career oriented at work. However, it is important to note that these career women still remain the privileged minority of the female population in the movement. Most female followers have conformed to the segregated gender order.

New Ties of Compromise between the Secular State and the Islamic Male Leaders

Atatürk and his followers advocated gender reform and female public participation in their attempt to import Western civility. Among many Islamic symbols, the headscarf was seen as a major contradiction to this goal and was discouraged. The state's official attitude towards the headscarf was rarely challenged until the mid-1980s. As Arat correctly observes, "when women began attending universities with covered heads during the 1980s, it was duly interpreted as an act of protest that triggered a tug of war between the secular state and Islamist women."[48] It is important to note, however, that these women were supported in their ongoing fight, demonstrations and boycotts by Islamist men. The Islamist men who gave real support to this cause were radical Islamists, who confronted the state and the laicist policies under the leadership of Refah and Fazilet. In 1984, the Council of State claimed that the headscarf was "no longer an innocent habit, but a symbol of a world view that opposes women's liberty and the fundamental principles of our Republic."[49] These girls' expulsion from the university would not contradict the ideals of the Republic, since their act was seen as against the secular state tradition.[50]

The official view of the headscarf as the symbol of an ideological war also regards veiling as evidence of women's subordination, and therefore as a handicap for gender equality. This male-dominated view, which does not take into account the agency of female Islamic actors, has been criticized widely as patriarchal, especially contributing to the persistence of the institutionalized gender inequalities.[51] Feminists highlighted men's wish to open the veil as an extension of a colonialist or orientalist attitude.[52] Göle sees veiling as the expression of an active engagement of Islamist women within the context of the Islamist movement. Veiling becomes a representation of "public and collective affirmation of women who are searching for recognition of their Muslim identity."[53] Accordingly, she argues that it endows them with social status, space and "autonomy" of action and a way to assert their difference.[54] While Göle was mainly interested in veiling as an alternative manifestation of modernity, Arat explored the female followers of Refah by focusing on their participation in urban setting and universities. She argues that their activism in Refah has an emancipating and empowering effect on these women's lives.[55] Another study undertaken by White in Ümraniye, a neighborhood of lower socioeconomic standing in Istanbul, showed that veiling did not have any effect on the "actual social and economic position of its wearers."[56] She also found little or no support from Islamist men in Ümraniye for veiled women's causes, as "men envisioned an ideal in which women were wives, mothers, and homemakers." However, while highlighting the patriarchal implications of the veil, White does not deny its effect on facilitating Islamic women's access to public life and political activism. Veiling, she argues, "established a kind of mobile honor zone from within which young women could interact with male students and teachers without feeling loss of reputation."[57] However, other feminists have disagreed on the issue of women's freedom and equality and veiling for different reasons. Some have defended universalistic views against relativistic and multiculturalistic approaches. They have argued that the latter might seem to tolerate women's veiling, although in reality it reinforces women's oppression in Islamic contexts.[58]

When Özal was the Prime Minister, between 1983 and 1989, his approach to the headscarf was more tolerant. The Constitutional Court, the parliament, parties in government, presidents continued to discuss the headscarf issue until covered students were expelled from universities in 1998. In the late 1990s, the Turkish state, with the cooperation of the Turkish army, tried to cleanse the public offices of veiled women, as they were perceived as the most striking symbol of Islamism. In the Fall term of 1998, threats of a headscarf ban led to severe enforcement at all universities, albeit with varying degrees of intensity. These enforcements discriminated against Islamist women, whereas they conveniently continued to overlook Islamist men who had a similar political orientation. Unfortunately, the ban forced Islamic women to make a difficult choice between giving up an important part of their identity, their headscarf, and giving up their university degree.

Interestingly, almost three-quarters of a century after Atatürk's secularizing reforms, another path-breaking gender statement came, from Fethullah Gülen. Rather than seeing veiling as a cultural right or an avenue for women's action or mobility, he popularized the idea that the headscarf was not *the* primary requirement of religion, and thus not mandatory in Islam. He justified his interpretation of the Kuran by explaining that the most important issue is faith, and there are many ways of expressing faith besides veiling. The movement's compromise on the headscarf, which predominantly affected young female university students, must be understood in the context of a non-confrontational politics of engagement. The Gülen movement avoided conflict between the state and female followers. During our chat about women's position in society, I asked the intellectual followers of the movement why the movement refuses to criticize the Republic. Male followers of previous Islamist parties, especially Refah, have supported the female followers in their resistance and protest to the state. In a context where secular feminists learned to criticize the state and negotiate for their rights, I asked, why would the movement not support the female followers' cause? Celal, a teacher in Gülen schools, answered my question: "Neither secular feminists nor Refah's male followers open schools for girls, but we do, and we would like to keep them open."

The Gülen movement's compromise eliminated a major barrier to Islamic women's and girls' participation in educational institutions and public offices. Along the lines of Republican mentality, the public faces of Islam were revised and "reformed" to fit a Western liberal image. Women's perspectives, feelings, interests, rights, and identities appear to have remained conveniently irrelevant in this seemingly pro-women act, while it brought Islamic and secular men closer together. Subsequently, the overlapping attitudes of the secularist and Islamic male elites in maintaining the "civilized image" has reinforced patriarchal practices.[59] However, this result is not caused by an anti-women action or conspiracy by these men. Neither should the consequence of this be seen as the ultimate defeat of Islamic women. Patriarchy defined as fixed relations of power fails to incorporate the concept of social change, as it disregards women's potential power and agency to transform social reality.[60]

In most cases, female student followers of the movement were given the choice of whether or not they were ready to take off their headscarf. However, most female followers smoothly internalized the movement's compromising attitude. The women at one of the *Risale* readings told me: "True faith is inside, in the soul and mind, and not in the outfit." When the headscarf ban was issued, I was working as a research assistant in one of the private universities in Istanbul, where the ban was enforced very strictly. The staff was obliged not to permit students with a headscarf into the university. As one of my respondents, a father of two female students with headscarves, said, "One must adapt to the requirements of modern times. My daughters will not give up their future careers to fight a cause that has not much to do with true Islam. These are the daughters of the Turkish nation, not of Iran." When I talked to the daughters, Sema and Selda, however, they did not express much excitement to continue schooling or willingness to give up their headscarf. They simply reiterated their father's idea that Turkey was different from other Muslim countries in supporting women's education. While still wearing their headscarf outside the university, they told me that their faith was not going to change if they took it off in the classroom.

Others convinced themselves not to cover until after university graduation. Günseli, a fourth-year psychology student, told me that "it felt naked and silly" when she was forced to take her scarf off by the authorities in the university. I reminded Günseli of other students who had protested the state's enforcements and/or left school. She indeed had a choice between quitting and protesting or conforming to the system. She expressed her sadness for many of her friends who did not have the flexible and "liberal" perspective on the issue that the Gülen movement advocated. She continued: "I was lucky. My family is enlightened by Hocaefendi's open-mindedness. But some students had to give up their education just because they did not have this vision of the Gülen movement."

In sharp contrast to the Gülen movement, the male elite of Refah supported confrontation between Islamist women and the state. Islamist feminists from the party criticized and attacked the "secular republican concept of women's citizenship" and asked for special rights.[61] As White noted, female followers of Refah were interested in the means by which the Islamist movement could allow them "to challenge the status quo."[62] Not surprisingly, Refah gave rise to a remarkable Islamic feminist consciousness and action through women's self-organizing, while the Gülen movement and the moderate and engaged AKP did not. I met, at the campus of Istanbul University, with female followers of Refah who refused to take their scarves off. They were critical of the compromising attitudes of the Gülen movement: "We have been treated like terrorists. The state does not care about our education . . . and about women's equality. . . . It is very hard for me to understand the students who easily gave up their headscarves. They did not even protest. This is what we have been taught by this society. When it is about women's rights, we are told we should be patient and quiet."

When the AKP came to power in 2002, it displayed similar attitudes to the Gülen movement with regard to the gender order in the Republic. Diverging from gender politics of previous Islamic parties, Refah and Fazilet, the AKP has remained silent, rather than being forceful on the issue of the headscarf ban. Similar to the Gülen movement, the party incorporated secular and uncovered women from conservative-right circles into its body. Female elites from privileged circles have been handpicked and invited to become active in the party. A few female Ministers of the party were "inserted" again into the political sphere, as long as they did not bring in feminist agendas. The AKP avoided any potential confrontation in the realm of gender politics. In contrast, Refah was harmed by the confrontational attitudes of its female representatives such as Merve Kavakçı, who insisted on wearing a headscarf in the parliament and as a result was expelled from the party and stripped of her citizenship.[63]

A female Minister of the AKP told me that she was surprised when she was invited to join the party, as she was neither an Islamic woman nor involved in Islamic politics. However, she explained to me that because the AKP brings together different interests, her secular background was not a problem for her participation. In my interview with her, rather than challenging women's traditional roles or the headscarf ban, she presented a conservative view of gender roles. Gender politics advocating traditional gender roles becomes increasingly the meeting point between the conservative right wing and Islamic social actors, whether they justify it by religion or not.

Islamic Women: The Politics of Engagement and Transition

Female participation in Islamic networks, like any other form of local participation, is a complicated concept. While it may appear as a progressive step towards female emancipation, in reality it often disguises the exclusion of women from the sources of power in the movement. Hence, local and civic participation should not be mistaken as engagement with the power structures, and eventual empowerment. Islamic women's active participation in the movement often does not liberate or empower them as individuals, since they are strictly identified with the collective good. They are excluded not only from networks of economic power but also from decision making. Consequently, Islamic women's public participation often remains at the local and horizontal level. It has not yet translated to vertical interactions with the state in order to negotiate gender issues.

Nor do male-dominated "civilizing" projects have feminist agendas or primary aims of women's empowerment. The success of these separate but interpenetrating gender regimes—early Republican secularist and contemporary Islamic—resides in their similar ability to present themselves as the basis for pro-women reform. In the Turkish context, their major accomplishment, female public visibility, has primarily fulfilled a role in completing the "civilized" image of these projects. Women's participation in these broader "national" projects, secular and Islamic, has delayed their organizing separately for their own interests. Although these projects (state-making and Islamic civil society projects) have benefited some elite women, they have temporarily disadvantaged the majority of the female population.

While submitting to the male-dominated agendas, the early Republican women and contemporary Islamic women were absorbed totally into these overarching projects. More importantly, men's exclusion of women from the politics of engagement coincided with women's reluctance and disinterest in all forms of political activity. In my interviews, they explicitly stated that they were not motivated to take part in any form of politics, communal or national. Similar to the women of the early Republic, the female followers of the Gülen movement and the AKP do not seem to engage in a dialogue for any gender-specific cause but leave the gender regimes in the hands of the male engineers of Islamizing projects. None of these women have expressed resentment over these projects that they are part of. On the contrary, they mostly agree on and commit to these projects without questioning them in terms of their own benefits and rights.[64] They are often convinced that they are better off than their contemporaries, as they belong to overarching "civilizing projects" of some sort, whether secularizing or Islamizing. I argue that while some historical continuity in terms of gender orders facilitates engagement between the Islamic and secular male actors, it keeps Islamic women momentarily disinterested in negotiating for their own terms, either with the state or the Islamic male elite.[65]

In contrast to moderate collective action, radical movements, as in the case of Refah, incorporated women into their struggle. However, this inclusive attitude was not a real sign of their feminist inclination, either. Anti-system movements, which envision transforming the social and/or political system, need women's collaboration. However, once the battle is won, and women's cooperation is no longer necessary, the male elite usually abandoned their women-friendly agendas. This has applied not only to the Muslim context but also to the West, as witnessed in the case of Eastern Europe. All revolutions were patriarchal in their betrayal of women's expectation and failed to replace the old order with a fresh democracy that benefits women.

Unlike radical movements, moderate movements, which engage rather than confront the system, do not need a great deal of women's cooperation. Hence, their primary need becomes to maintain women in their traditional role of serving the broader collective agendas. Accordingly, in the short run, moderation of Islamic action has benefited male Islamic social actors. Their shared views of gender issues have aligned secular and Islamic men, who historically have been enemies. The apparently pro-women discourses have diminished conflict between them, strengthened trust networks and reinforced their shared project of pro-democratic "reform." Regardless of the immediate returns of women, the overlapping parts of their gender politics have facilitated engagements between these historically divided male elites.

Despite their support for women's education and visibility, these seemingly pro-women projects have discriminated against women by keeping them outside of the politics of engagement and power structures. This side of the story is dark. There is no inherent link between *procedural* democracy and "democratization of the relations between men and women."[66] Just as illiberal democracies can survive simply by authoritarian rulers, women's participation and enfranchisement can be initiated and maintained by patriarchs. In contrast, a genuine gender equality requires institutionalized power sharing between women and men. Stated more specifically, gender reform necessitates women's engagement with power structures and their negotiation of their own terms.

However, there is also a bright side of the story. The cooperation of Islamic and secular men in undertaking reform is more likely to be favorable for Islamic women in the long run. Considering that these engagements are currently a major force of transitional politics in Turkey, if and when liberal democracy is consolidated, it is likely to benefit Islamic women. This bright side of the story remains to be realized, but if it happens it will result not from the male elites' presumably pro-women actions and projects but from the unintended consequences of their engagement with the state.

Hence, the male-initiated gender reform may potentially become useful for women. Similar to the secular Turkish women, Islamic female actors may find a way to turn this gender order to their own advantage in the future. As the density of communal life and networking among women blurs the boundaries between public and private, the strength of female bonding and trust are strong sources of power among female followers. Eventually, women have the potential to transform these horizontal strengths into the vertical politics of engagement. As striking progress has been achieved through the campaigns of secularist women's groups and movements in Turkey,[67] there is no reason to believe that genuine empowerment and equality for Islamic women cannot be achieved.

Certainly, whether female participation may or may not actually translate into women's empowerment also depends on their willingness to take advantage of the democratic processes and institutions.[68] Put differently,

Islamic women's empowerment depends ultimately on their own engagements and not on men's initiative. Hence, rather than focusing on the project-based undertakings and male-initiated gender reform, we must look closely at the historical and current nature of Islamic women's everyday life and activities. This may give us a better idea about prospective avenues for women's engagement and empowerment in the future. As discussed before, engagements are the outcome of a rather long-term experimental process, through which the individuals reconcile their sense of belonging and distance from the broader project, be it Republican or Islamic. Given the historical, cultural and political settings and conditions, there is no reason why women from the Gülen movement or the AKP would not in the long run translate their private and (limited) public participation into engagements with the state. The secular Turkish women's progress in empowerment provides support to the liberals' view on gender questions. "Women's movements are best advised to take on the state since it is there rather than in social relations as whole that progress can be made."[69]

The AKP Institutionalizes the Engagement: "Marriage of Convenience" between the State and Islam?

ALTHOUGH ENGAGEMENTS originated and ripened in historically specific contexts of the Republic, their success in several spheres of everyday life, unforeseen by the founders of the Republic, has had a transformative effect on the political processes and the state: "The new political rules are not so much invented de novo as translated, so to speak, from meta-rules of social, economic and cultural life. . . . Civil society, thus, plays a central role prior to and throughout the process of transition and consolidation. It is from this civil realm that the meta-rules of the political game emerge."[1]

The politics of engagement have become a pivotal force in the Turkish transformation into a liberal democracy. As formal political channels have continued to fail, which was evidenced by the ban of Refah in 1998, alternative codes of conduct have been formulated between the state and Islamic actors. Although the engagements originated in the midst of everyday life, where Islamic actors have created alternative ways to speak to and cooperate with the state, they have gradually expanded beyond the extra-institutional realm of daily life. Tocqueville provides the most illuminating analysis of the links between associations and political rule. However, although his theory of civic participation and associations as a cornerstone of civil society has echoed in the halls of academic institutions, the clear-cut link he drew between political rule and civic associations has not received the attention that it deserves.[2] Following Tocquevillean sociology, this chapter will examine the way in which the central role of religion in associational life and national culture links with institutional political processes.

As the diffuse patterns of engagements have penetrated the lives of both non-state and state actors in Turkey, they have smoothly transformed worldviews and ways of life at large.[3] The new codes and norms of non-confrontation have gradually transformed the political culture until they have finally been institutionalized by the AKP government. The pro-Islamic AKP government and the state have replaced the previously adversarial tones between the state and Islam with a new partnership and dialogue. In the face of EU pressure on Turkey to democratize, even the attitudes of the military, which was the most resistant branch of the state, towards Islamic actors have been changing.

As the engagements have shifted the power dynamics at the institutional level spontaneously and sporadically, their manifestation at the macro level has been not systematic but most uneven. Subsequently, institutional transformations have been noted and acknowledged by different social forces in varying degrees. No matter how erratically, both the staunchly secular political institutions and previously radical Islamists have gradually rethought and adapted their attitudes towards each other.

While the motivating forces of the broader transition are multi-faceted, Islamic actors have definitely come to the forefront of pro-democratic reform due to their engagements. Noticing the increasingly overlapping discourses of Fethullah Gülen and Erdoğan, I have followed the engagements from everyday life to the AKP government.[4] The continuity of the politics of engagement becomes clear when we compare the attitudes of the AKP and the Gülen movement. Here, it is particularly important to note the recent transformations of Erdoğan's identity and his rhetoric from one that was confrontational to another that is cooperative.

Linking Everyday Life in the Gülen Movement with the AKP's Party Politics

Fethullah Gülen strongly agreed with Said Nursi that Islam should not be a part of politics. Both leaders refused to form parties or to become part of a political party. However, their followers still "participated politically" by voting as citizens of the secular Republic. Dissociating from Erbakan and his Islamist vision, the followers of both movements have generally voted for moderate center-right political parties.[5] The main attraction of these parties for the Gülen movement has been their defense of a softer understanding of secularism against the rigidity of laicism.[6] While the followers disagreed with Erbakan's anti-system and anti-secular attitudes, they also dissociated from radical Islamic parties and social forces across the Muslim world that had a claim for state power. Not surprisingly, the movement's non-cooperative attitudes towards Erbakan and Refah have attracted a lot of reaction from Islamists who disapprove of Gülen's moderate position.[7]

When I interviewed Fethullah Gülen in his house in Pennsylvania in May 2005, we had a three-course dinner prepared and served by his companions. During our dinner, Gülen referred to Atatürk's ideas more than he did to any Islamic scholar from the Middle East. When I brought up Said Qutb and asked Gülen for his views, he said, "I find him too radical in his ideas that bring Islam into the center of politics."[8] He also explicitly referred to Erbakan in negative terms while expressing admiration for Turgut Özal (former Prime Minister from the conservative center-right ANAP) and appreciation for Bülent Ecevit (former Prime Minister from the center-left) and Süleyman Demirel (former Prime Minister and President from the center-right).

Up until the "soft" military coup d'etat in 1997 banned Erbakan, the dissociation and dislike of the Gülen movement for Islamist parties continued consistently. This recently changed. A large majority of the Gülen movement's followers voted for the first time for a pro-Islamic party, the AKP, in the 2002 elections.[9] Yet Fethullah Gülen explained to me that he had not had any contact with Erdoğan since he came to power.

Until he became the Prime Minister, Erdoğan (1954–) had already made a reputation as an Islamist. After being educated at a religious Imam Hatip high school, he studied economics and business at Marmara University in Istanbul. He started his political career in 1969 by joining the radical Milli Görüş, which was a think-tank of Erbakan's Islamist Milli Selamet (National Order). Later, he became a very popular politician under the roof of Refah and served as the mayor of Istanbul (1994–1998). With Refah's closure, he was banned from politics and sentenced to prison. When he became Prime Minister in 2003, he dissociated from Islamist organizations that he had participated in previously.

Throughout his political career, Erdoğan's discourse has changed and become not only more politically expedient but also more moderate. The most striking turning point in Erdoğan's position can be observed in his break from the Islamist faction Milli Görüş. While these changes are often associated with his personal experiences, such as his prison term and his current proximity and accountability to the West and the EU, we must also note that Islamic identities in general have changed along with structural transformations in Turkey.

The Minimal Consensus

After two decades of experimenting with the politics of engagement, at the turn of the millennium Islamic social forces and the Turkish state came to a *partial* agreement. Through their engagements and negotiations with the state, the moderate Islamic social forces have recently come to *selectively* agree on a few basic principles of the Republic. While still contesting matters relating to moral order, such as alcohol restriction, the AKP has started to engage various branches of the state. Rather than inventing the politics of engagement, the AKP has merely attempted to institutionalize the fine balance that already existed in society between negotiation and cooperation.

Prime Minister Erdoğan declared to the West, in his speeches in New York and at Harvard University, that his party relies on the "power of the secular regime."[10] The political leaders of the party, including Erdoğan, clearly stated that the AKP agrees on and respects fundamental characteristics of the Turkish Republic. Mainly, they agree on three major issues. Following Atatürk's tradition of national sovereignty, they agree on the secular source of political authority. This alone ensures the party's consensus with the state on the nature of the political community, which is the nation as opposed to the religious community, *Umma*. Similar to the Gülen movement, the AKP agrees on the need to reform (not to attack and abolish) the Republic. Finally, the party shares cooperative attitudes of the Turkish state toward the West, particularly the European Union and the United States. It promotes Western liberal democracy, science and technology.

Erdoğan is known to have objected to some, if not all, of these issues a few years ago. What caused this change at this particular time in history? Was it predictable, or random and accidental? When explanation of events become difficult, social science either tends to describe them as unpredictable or portray a big unforeseen break, which selectively ignores history.

Similarly, the new convergence between the AKP and the secular forces is often represented as being the result of a new behavior of the political leaders. Accordingly, the political elite bridges the gaps through a process of electoral competition.[11] Notwithstanding the importance of leaders and the political elite in bringing about short-term change and enforcing policies,[12] I argue that diffuse patterns of engagement between Islamic actors and the state preceded and facilitated the so-called elite convergence. The engagement with the state strengthened visibility, accountability and thereby legitimacy of Islamic actors, by also facilitating their dialogue and cooperation with a wide range of circles of secular actors.

Non-confrontational attitudes of Islamic actors have first soothed the conflict and bridged the divide between the secular state and Islam.[13] While this has minimized the distrust and content of disagreement between them, it has also expanded a limited consensus to the level of the nation at large. The formation of vertical links between civil society and the state has set the stage for a broader national spirit of societal compromise. Before changing the policies and strategies by the prominent political elite, the politics of engagement has diffusely transformed both non-state actors and state officials in the realm of everyday life.

The Inner Transformation of Islam: From Everyday Life to Political Institutions

CONFLICT AVOIDANCE AND LIBERAL DEMOCRACY

Similar to Fethullah Gülen, Erdoğan is known for his commitment to the community. After his successful service as the mayor of Istanbul, it was largely acknowledged that he cared for and served not only the religious community but also the nation. Just as Fethullah Gülen is the ideational father of the Gülen schools, which came to be referred to as the "Turkish schools," Erdoğan often envisions and proposes grand projects such as the building of a large mosque in Taksim square. However, when attacked by either the secularists or a branch of the state such as the military, neither of these religious leaders has insisted upon these projects. Submission, a core idea of Islam, appears to be a strong motivation for their non-confrontational attitudes. Throughout his political career, Erdoğan has learned to submit to the common will.[14] This has enabled him, like Gülen, to avoid conflict and to be able to align his ideas and worldview with broader national and global changes. Heper, a prominent political scientist stated: "Erdoğan's conception of a properly functioning democracy is informed by the Islamic institution of *shurah*, or consultation, . . . an exchange of ideas."[15]

SECULARISM AND FREEDOM OF RELIGION

Both Gülen and Erdoğan are proponents of the secular state, "provided . . . that the state in question [does] not discriminate against believers."[16] Neither Erdoğan nor Gülen challenges or disagrees on secularism as long as it does not pose a threat to religious freedom. This is a clear indication of two parallel transformations at the turn of the millennium in Turkey. As the rigidity of laicism is in the process of being replaced with more tolerant forms of secularism, Islamic social forces are moving from a marginal and counter-culture position[17] to a relatively more cooperative and mainstream one in Turkey. Similar to Gülen's respect for secular democracy, Erdoğan openly announced that his reference to Islam was at the personal level. He distinguished his political commitment to the secular constitution and democratic principles from his personal faith in

Islam.[18] Clearly, both religious leaders strongly yearn for a moral, virtuous and faithful society, but not an Islamic state. As my interviews with the voters of the AKP also suggested, the adherents of the party from wide-ranging political backgrounds share this secular (as opposed to laicist) understanding of the state.

Just as the Gülen movement has compartmentalized religion and scientific teaching between the classroom and the dormitories, the AKP has expressed loyalty to the principle of separation between religion and the state in its party program. Put differently, in the same way the Islamic movement adjusted to the secular order in the area of education, the pro-Islamic AKP adjusted to the secular institutional political milieu. The party's program depicts secularism as "an assurance of the freedom of religion and conscience" and rejects "the interpretation and distortion of secularism as enmity against religion."[19] In his speeches, Erdoğan often suggests that Turkey could serve as a model for the rest of the Muslim world. Not surprisingly, he also defends a softer and more tolerant secularism fashioned after the model of the United States, which does not restrict but nourishes the religious freedom of individuals.

This turning point in Islamic party politics has been interpreted in several ways. Some argue that Erdoğan's AKP was signaling the end of Islamism in Turkey. White, for example, sees the AKP as the inventor of a new Muslimhood model, which replaces the Islamists' communalism with new forms of individualism of Muslim actors.[20] The depiction suggests that new forms of individualism and communalism are mutually exclusive in religious ways of life.[21] Similarly, the terms "Muslim democrat" and "conservative democrat" have come to suggest in the Turkish context that the AKP is not only a temporary force of democracy but that it also has democratic ideals and worldviews. As a major characteristic of a democrat, the new Islamic actors have also been labeled "liberal."[22] From this perspective, the AKP appears metamorphosed, an entity that has undergone a complete change to the extent there is no continuity or even background to its transmutation. These views discard not only the sociocultural and historical background of the Islamic actors but also fail to situate them in the broader context that has accommodated the shifting power dynamics between the state and Islam in the post-1980 period. The AKP has not metamorphosed but is the result of decades of encounters between Islam and the state.

Some of the denial of the Islamic and community-oriented character of the party originates from the fact that the party has attracted people from diverse religious and political orientations. However, the denial is also derived partly from the Republican discomforts discussed in detail in the introduction and chapter 2. Just as the secularists refused to accept compatibility between Islamic actors and civil society, the coupling of a pro-Islamic party with reform has been difficult to swallow for many Kemalists and Western observers. Accordingly, *unless* Islamic actors abandoned their Islamic identity for a "Muslim" one that was in line with the Republican character, they could not participate in the transition to a liberal democracy. Although the numbers of hardcore secularists who insist on seeing the AKP as a continuation of Erbakan have decreased dramatically, some secularists at the extreme end of the spectrum still do think that the AKP hides its true agendas.

THE EUROPEAN UNION AND THE WEST: ARE ISLAMIC ACTORS THE NEW DESIGNATED DEMOCRATS OF TURKEY?

Although reform towards liberal democracy is likely to benefit all citizens, the Islam-inspired social forces in Turkey have definitely more to gain from the transition from authoritarian laicism.[23] Not surprisingly, they have become major forces of institutional reform, collaborating with the Turkish state, the EU and the United States in a joint effort for reform. There is no doubt that the interest of the international community in Turkish democratization has proved timely for the AKP. In my interviews, the voters of the AKP stated that the West's pressure on Turkey has played a role in the expansion of "reform-minded" Islam both inside and outside of Turkey. Notwithstanding the importance of international players, it would be wrong to attribute the source of contemporary transformations in Turkey exclusively to the EU's demands on Turkey. This EU-centric explanation of democratization neglects the historical and internal dynamics of the transition. Although EU membership has provided another major common goal for Islamic actors and the state on which to cooperate, this study has shown that Islam and the state have spontaneously cooperated in other realms that the EU could not influence or would not approve of.[24] Moreover, the current friendly terms between Islamic and state actors have also played a pivotal role in the EU's consideration of Turkey as a prospective member. Although Western powers have always had an impact on the Turkish transition, the cooperation between the state and domestic social forces has a longer history that goes beyond aiming solely at Turkey's integration to Europe.[25]

Much like the DP in the 1950s, the AKP aligned with the West in a limited way in terms of pro-democratic reform. The AKP attracts people from wide-ranging political backgrounds and bridges the gap between state and society. However, although the party pays lip service to the amendment of human rights and liberties in Turkey, its major interest is in reform for religious freedom. In its rhetoric, the AKP makes reference to the United Nations Charter of Human Rights by advocating human rights and basic freedoms. In practice, however, similar to the ethnic politics mobilized by the Gülen movement, as discussed in chapter 4, the party's views on ethnic politics and the rights of ethnic minorities merge with the Turkish state's attitudes. For instance, the "nationalists" of the AKP government blocked the first attempt at a conference in Istanbul on the Armenian genocide.

Although the Islamic actors of engagement are defenders of religious freedom, they are not fond of all liberties, individual or communal. Similarly, in spite of their current cooperation on pro-democratic reform and democratization, their appeal for liberal democracy is selective and limited. The fact that the Islamic actors of engagement have come to play a major role in the transition does not render them either democrats or liberals at heart. Their current proximity to the liberal democrats is motivated by their contemporary needs, demands and expectations from the secular Republic. This temporal cause also renders them best friends to the Western forces that pressure Turkey for reform.

SKILLS OF NEGOTIATION AND LIMITS OF DISAGREEMENT

Despite the agreement and cooperation, the consensus between Islamic social forces and the state is *partial* as opposed to complete. While this partiality is largely regarded as a flaw by the Kemalists, it is in fact the key to the flourishing of a liberal democracy. Because this limited agreement leaves space for disagreement between Islamic actors and the state, it also facilitates the articulation of partial discontents. Similar to the Gülen movement and its contestations, discussed in chapter 3, the AKP government negotiates controversial issues. In the process of rethinking the Republic and Atatürkism, both Islamic and secular forces continue disagreeing and developing different worldviews on ways of life, morality, and the role of faith in everyday life. However, unlike in Iran, Indonesia and Algeria, the disagreement in Republican Turkey does not extend to the fundamental principles of the Republic, particularly the secular political source of sovereignty.

The AKP continues to disagree with secular actors about what is moral conduct of life. In September 2004, shortly before the bill for legal reform was to be passed for Turkey's membership in the EU, a major disagreement took place between morally conservative Islamic actors and the secular actors (who were in favor of moral liberalism) over the criminalization of adultery. The legal reform of the penal code, Türk Ceza Kanunu, has been postponed as a result of the actions of the AKP's moralist factions, who wanted adultery to be included as a criminal act. This faction in the AKP should not be underestimated, as their moralist views are shared by a large base from not only Islamic but also conservative non-religious social forces. Not surprisingly, most of the followers of the Gülen movement supported the criminalization of adultery.

In response, a large liberal secular majority has bonded together to bitterly oppose what they see as the moral impositions of Islamists. During these debates, Erdoğan bluntly warned the EU not to interfere with the domestic affairs of Turkey and told the liberals not to use the EU pressure for their own agendas. These moral disagreements create large public debates and discontent between Islamic and secular actors. Although these social actors have agreed on the basics of political processes, they certainly do not wish to compromise on matters such as the terms of adultery and alcohol consumption. Turkey provides a contrast to the contemporary situation in many other Muslim and Arab countries, where controversy about political processes and the source of political authority continues while consent and compromises are largely reached over moral matters.

Both the Turkish citizens and the EU have great hopes for the party, as they have associated it largely with institutional reform. However, like every great expectation, this puts great pressure on the AKP. On the one hand, secular actors often conflate and misperceive the party's negotiation over moral issues as its failure in pursuing reform. On the other hand, Islamic actors have often seen its compromising and cooperative attitudes towards the state as evidence of a lack of strong leadership or passivity. The party fails to please both Islamic and secular actors in the fullest sense. This is because it is seeking a balance between contestation and cooperation within and between the society and the Republic. Hence, it is not surprising that it fits comfortably with the expectations of neither the secular or Islamic actors. In this search for balance, it occasionally hits the limits of agreement within the party, and the boundaries of disagreement within the bounds of the Republic. The AKP encounters and experiments with the borders of an overarching framework, the nation-state, in its negotiations. These experiments are often left unnoticed by the Islamic and secular critiques of the party. It is *not* the liberal democratic character of the party that makes it a force of transition but these widely neglected exercises of negotiation and cooperation. What differentiates the party from previous Islamic parties, including the Refah, is its negotiation and engagement skills rather than its liberal or pro-democratic character.[26]

The issues of contestation are many. These issues include, but are not limited to, states' accommodation of Imam Hatip schools and the lifting of the headscarf ban. Because the Constitutional Court used the headscarf issue as one of the justifications for closing Refah and Fazilet, the AKP has not pushed this matter too far. Although a large part of the AKP's constituents wish to see the abolition of the headscarf ban, the AKP has not been as assertive as the victims of the headscarf ban expected. The headscarf issue has remained unresolved, as the European Court of Human Rights (ECHR) upheld the state's ban of headscarves in June 2004.[27]

Another issue that the AKP is expected to fix is a dispute over the Imam Hatip schools. By extending compulsory primary school education to eight years, the Turkish state strategically diminished the years of education in Imam Hatip high schools. Moreover, although these high schools offer a similar curriculum to other schools (with the exception of additional courses on the Kuran), the graduates of Imam Hatip schools are not allowed to compete with the graduates of other schools to enter universities. The majority of Islamic actors have placed a good deal of pressure on the AKP, expecting the party to change what they see as an unfair state act. However, the party has not endorsed a change of policy so far.[28] In pursuing such controversial issues, the AKP government has experienced a good deal of bureaucratic resistance to reform. The difficulties that the AKP have encountered in negotiating with staunchly secular branches and officials of the state continue to raise further questions over the future of the party.[29] Can the AKP possibly continue diffusing tension between Islam and the state while also keeping its diverse constituents happy?

Within the party, the cooperative attitudes with the state have been marginally challenged only by a rather small radical group, the Milli Görüş (National View), which persisted from the Saadet (Felicity) party, mentored by Erbakan, to Erdoğan's AKP. While reinforcing the disputes on issues about moral order, the Milli Görüş group in the AKP refrains from upsetting the consensus on either the source of political authority or the nature of political community.

I argue that a shared frame of belonging and shared goals between traditionally opposed social forces facilitate capacities of minimal agreement not only within the state, but also between the state and society. This basic *accord* between the state and religious actors is a prerequisite of political pluralism and competitive politics. The absence of this minimum agreement on the political authority undermines the accommodation of cultural diversity and dissent. Different from cultural diversity, political pluralism is even more directly affected by the achievement of this minimum consensus on the fundamentals. In its absence, the political field often takes the form of societal fragmentation under an authoritarian and/or autocratic rule that imposes strict homogeneity by force. This kind of homogeneity must not be confused with the minimal harmony achieved through the platforms of engagement between the state and society.

The Inner Transformation of Atatürkism: From Secularists to the State

At the turn of the millennium, the decline of the radical voices of both Islamism and laicism opened the way for a constructive reinterpretation and adjustment of Atatürkism. Kemalism that was largely associated with the official ideology of the state has come to be replaced by society-framed forms of Atatürkism. On the Islamists' side, Erbakan's withdrawal from the political realm coincided with some of his followers' revision of their agendas and worldviews. Erdoğan's leadership has guided them to adapt to the secular order. On the secularists' side, even the leading military officials have started to loosen up their rigid understanding of laicism and Atatürkism.[30] General Özkök, the chief of staff, for example, mentioned the need for "reinterpreting Atatürkism." He stated that he "takes Atatürkism, the guiding light of the Turkish military, as a world view open to change, and not as an ideology, i.e., a closed system of thought."[31]

Though uneven, these instances render the distinction between Atatürkist thought and the distortion of it by the post-Atatürk bureaucracy imperative. "By converting Atatürkist thought into a political manifesto, [the bureaucratic intelligentsia] proved themselves less 'democratic' than Atatürk."[32] The recent changes even in high-ranking state officials' attitudes towards Atatürkism suggest that there has been a fresh rethinking of Atatürkism within and between state and society. In contrast to the intolerant top-down imposition of Kemalist principles, the post-1980 period witnessed the participation of many formerly excluded social actors in this debate. Different facets of Kemalism and laicism, and their presumably "unquestionable" quality, have been the subject of heated criticism. Interestingly, this critical public debate revived a voluntary bottom-up advocacy of Atatürkism. This can be observed by the increasing display of its symbols in both the public and private spheres.[33]

The more the rigidity of old-school Kemalism has weakened, the more the tolerant faces of Atatürkism have crossed the lines of class, ethnicity, age, gender and the urban-rural divide. Gradually, Atatürkism has even reached out and cut across the lines between pro-Islamic and secular circles. Clearly, Atatürkism was not abandoned as a result of these debates. Nor did these public discussions open a new post-Kemalist era, as some have suggested. On the contrary, these public debates have translated Kemalism from a rigid grand design to a more flexible frame of belonging. To the extent its legitimacy in Turkish society expands beyond its presumed confines among the secularist "Westernized" elite, [34] it facilitates the transformation and adaptation of the Turkish state to a rapidly changing world. Rather than abandoning the Republican project, diverse social forces have come to an unspoken agreement to "fix" it. Islamic and secular actors have joined forces in the formation and re-formation of a shared frame of belonging, by using the idioms of a liberal democracy.

Whether criticizing or defending the Turkish state, both Islamic and secular groups have addressed this overarching sense of belonging. Along with nationwide moderation, some radical secularists and Islamists have also come to share the very basic sensibility of belonging. More importantly, the call for a better democracy has increasingly become a collective endeavor. This has happened partly because of (and not despite) the highly contested nature of Kemalism and partly because of the disputed nature of Islam in Turkey. This is how the politics of engagement with the Republic has propelled the inner transformation of Kemalism along with an inner transformation of Islamism. While the transformation of Kemalism and Islamism has been noted separately in the current literature, the interconnectedness between these processes has been mostly neglected. A majority of historically divided people in Turkey, Islamic and secular, have converged through their shared interests in diverse matters. They have started to care collectively, for example, about the initiation of a mortgage system for homebuyers, and have become increasingly distracted from waging war against each other. Consequently, secular and pro-Islamic actors have joined forces on the streets to celebrate the beginning of the EU membership process for Turkey.

The portrayal of Turkish society as deeply divided along the lines of Kemalism and Islamism is becoming a problematic overgeneralization, which misses their parallel historical transformations.[35] Although Kemalism might have remained a persistent source of cleavage in Turkish society, a closer look reveals that the adherence to Atatürk—separate from the official ideology of Kemalism—has remained dynamic enough to adapt itself to changing conditions.

It is becoming less and less surprising to the Turkish society and the West to see Atatürk corners in the Gülen movement's schools, and to hear Fethullah Gülen and Erdoğan referring to Atatürk over the course of a conversation. The process cannot be explained by a one-dimensional or unilinear transformation, such as secularization of Islam, Islamization of nationalism, or the end of Kemalism or Islamism. The process must be understood as an outcome of multi-dimensional engagements between increasingly autonomous forces of a society and an increasingly responsive state. However, the uneven and multi-layered nature of these engagements makes it difficult for social actors to acknowledge them on a day-to-day basis.

Differentiating Cultural Diversity from Political Pluralism

The outcome of the politics of engagement is twofold. First, I argued above that the engagements have resulted in a "thinner" agreement—a consensus on a limited number of fundamental issues. This thinness facilitated its appeal for increasingly diverse social forces and state actors and enabled the agreement to stretch across the divide between Islamic and secular actors.

Second, the engagements have also led to increasingly legitimate disagreements, which have *not* amounted to fragmentation and polarization in society. Diverse societies are not intrinsically pluralist, as differences do *not* automatically translate into civilized and democratic modes of cohabitation.[36] Pluralism is not an inherent quality of a society with religious and ethnic cultural or group differences.[37] It needs to be achieved. Although diverse societies may not be more prone to become divided than homogeneous ones,[38] their solidarity depends more directly on a sense of public spirit or the achievement of public goals.[39] Whether diverse or homogeneous, societies become pluralistic and develop into democratic polities when a *considerable level* of cooperation is accomplished across the lines of differences and conflicts. Ethnic diversity and the primacy of local loyalties have led to fragmentation in Afghanistan,[40] whereas ethnic and national diversity among the people of Canada have formed the basis of political pluralism. Clearly, the linkages between social actors with the state are dramatically different in these two cases. While local affiliations with the tribes or warlords have preceded national loyalties and ties to the Afghan state,[41] Canadian citizens have associated and interacted with the Canadian government without contradicting their wide-ranging nationalities and ethnicities.

Although Islamic political opposition in Turkey has been contained institutionally in the competitive party system since the 1970s, and although elections have been free and fair, cooperation between the Islamic and secular actors remained impossible until the 1980s. After many decades of failure of the political system to accommodate this diversity, an emerging accord between Islam and the state brought secular and Islamic actors closer.[42]

Nationalism and shared international agendas have reinforced the dialogue and trust relations between Islamic and secular actors. Although increasing national sentiments have played a large role in the formation of cross-ideological cooperation, it was by no means the only affinity between Islam and the state. As discussed above, other public agendas also bridged the old Islamic-secular divide, particularly the membership of Turkey in the EU, democratization and economic liberation. The politics of engagement with the state encouraged societal compromise and cooperation to fix these goals collectively.

The moral, economic and political ties of the secular and Islamic actors surfaced in the Özal-led ANAP throughout the 1980s. Eventually, the platforms of *Nezaket* (politeness) in Fethullah Gülen's terms appealed to both moderate Islamic and secular actors, who developed cross-ideological cooperation. This cooperation can be observed explicitly in the Gülen movement's annual Abant meetings. Politicians, scholars, writers, journalists and intellectuals from a wide range of political spectrums and religious orientations come together to discuss major issues of Turkish politics. Not surprisingly, the problematic relation between laicism (as opposed to secularism) and democracy continues to occupy the center stage in these Abant discussions.

At the turn of the millennium, the cross-ideological and cross-class scope of these platforms of dialogue expanded dramatically. The political leaders of the AKP and the leading intellectual figures from the Gülen movement were not the only participants in these *Nezaket* platforms. Many prominent secular social actors from diverse political orientations, including even Marxism, also joined these circles of societal compromise. When I asked one of the highly respected Turkish public intellectuals, known for his leftist politics, why he regularly participated in and even led discussions in Abant meetings, he answered: "This is what this country needs most. We can finally talk and listen respectfully without carving out each other's eyes (*göz oymadan*)." The growing appreciation of these *Nezaket* platforms is reinforced by their historical absence in Turkey. This cross-ideological cooperation often appeals to individuals who suffered from the deep cleavages and ideological extremism that peaked during the 1970s in Turkey.

In the Abant meeting in Washington, D.C., in 2004, the Minister of the State, Mehmet Aydın, of the AKP delivered one of the most provacative speeches. With his eloquent English and his sophisticated reading of, and reference to, Western philosophers, Aydın argued that the secular state of Turkey was in a rapid process of democratization. He also detailed the AKP's active participation in this transformation. While clearly disagreeing on a variety of issues, the majority of participants from both Islamic and secular backgrounds talked within the boundaries of civility and agreed on the conditions of liberal democracy in the Abant meeting.

The Transformation of the Turkish State

THE MILITARY

The politics of engagement endorse the agency of peaceful and non-confrontational social actors, who are able to enact and influence the society and polity. These politics are a major difference between the AKP and the DP of the 1950s. Although both parties wished to break the unbridgeable distance between the state and the masses and tried to link diverse social groups to the political party in government, only the AKP succeeded in this without being regarded as a threat to the system. The DP government aimed at endowing the civilian rule with the upper hand over the military. However, it attempted to "divest the military of all authority."[43] The DP did not have a chance to learn from the two military coups (1960 and 1980) that the AKP's members witnessed. The military coup that overthrew the DP government in 1960 changed the civilian-military relations in favor of the absolute advantage and domination of the latter. Military domination over politics continued until the 1980s, when an expanding civil society under Özal's government started to challenge and transform this dynamic.

In contrast to the DP, and similar to the Gülen movement, the AKP reached a concordance with the military officers. The AKP acknowledges the autonomous sphere and central role of the Turkish military in terms of national security, as long as the military does not undermine the political autonomy of the government. Similarly, the military acknowledges the primacy of the government in political decision making, as long as the Islamic actors pursue secular politics. It is important to note that this conditionality of the concordance resonates with the partial nature of the cooperation between Islamic and secular actors. Although the AKP did not turn the military against it, as the DP had done, the cooperation between the AKP and the military is still fragile. As always, maintaining the sensitive fine balance takes constant work, communication and mutual compromise.

At the same time the Islamic actors have come to both negotiate and cooperate with the military, the military has started to rethink and adjust its inner workings. General Özkök has questioned the long-lived tradition of military intervention in politics in Turkey and has praised more democratic solutions. He has concluded that "military interventions are not panacea. We should have greater trust in people's judgment."[44]

Clearly, after agreeing on the basics, the AKP has gained more leeway to negotiate institutional reform with the secular Turkish state. With the support of the European Union, the AKP has launched a plan that calls for a series of institutional reforms in the legal, political and economic spheres, referred to as *uyum paketi* (package of harmony). The military's dominant role in politics has been restrained. A major decision was made to change the general secretary of the National Security Council, MGK, from a military official to a civilian council. The state security courts formed by the military were abolished.

OTHER INSTITUTIONAL REFORMS

The AKP's program makes a serious commitment to the principles of democracy by improving and extending basic rights and freedoms.[45] This commitment requires an amendment of several articles of the 1982 constitution, which was a product of the 1980 military coup. The AKP government revised the penal code by taking a radical stance against torture and giving more protection to women against violence. The Criminal Code was improved further by banning capital punishment. After the changes in the counter-terrorism laws, the Ankara Criminal Court acquitted Fethullah Gülen. The activities led by Fethullah Gülen were declared to be legal. Although discrimination against ethnic minorities is not thoroughly resolved, the Kurds and other minorities were permitted to learn and speak their own languages.

The AKP has made remarkable advances not only in domestic politics but in foreign policy and economics. The perennial issues over Cyprus seem to have come to an end. The AKP has been keen on maintaining good relations with the United States. Following the program implemented by the International Monetary Fund, the AKP reduced inflation to below 10 percent for the first time in twenty-eight years. After the economic crisis in 2001, the economy grew by 7.8 percent in 2002, 5.2 percent in 2003, and 9 percent in 2004.[46] After these economic advances and institutional reforms, the EU has finally acknowledged that Turkey has made sufficient progress to qualify for further negotiations for membership.

To what degree, then, have the "game rules" of the Republic either been reformulated or nullified? Migdal uses the term "game rules" to refer to a broader term than constitutional principles and law.[47] Game rules embrace acceptable attitudes and legitimate rhetoric toward the state. All Westernist architects of modern states—such as Nasser of Egypt, the Shah of Iran and Atatürk of Turkey—came under attack from dissenting social forces, which deviated from the founders' original plan. The grand modernization projects of the founding fathers have been criticized and discredited as authoritarian schemes discriminating against repressed and marginalized social forces. Similarly, the Republican project is perceived to be under attack by dissenting masses.[48] Contrary to this predominant view,

I argue that the game rules are transformed more effectively by the non-resistant and non-confrontational social actors than the previous confrontational ones. Rather than attacking the Republic, the reform-oriented social actors have transformed the state's practices by agreeing selectively on its most fundamental principles. As long as there is room for cooperation, conflicts are not threatening to the system, whether they cause contestation in religious, ethnic or gender politics.

The engagement of the non-confrontational actors was also facilitated by the state's historically ambivalent attitudes towards Islam. Contrary to its monolithic laicist image, the Turkish state's practices have not always pulled in a unilinear direction of laicism. Different state leaders and various branches have pulled in multiple directions, swinging periodically between periods of repression and tolerance of Islam. Hence, a close look at Turkish Islamic actors suggests that they are far from delegitimizing the game rules. On the contrary, by activating a process of rethinking and readaptation of these codes of conduct, and by prompting institutional reform, they have contributed to the current push towards liberal democracy.

Reflections on Democratization in the Middle East: The Ambiguities of Promoting the "Turkish Model" for Democracy

AT A TIME WHEN "the acceptance of democratic principles is still growing across cultures,"[1] democracy has increasingly come to be seen as a universal value.[2] Challenging the clash of civilizations thesis, a 2003 survey showed that the attitudes of Islamic and Western peoples were converging, especially towards the appeal of representative democracy.[3] However, despite the increasing consensus on the appeal of democracy both the practice of democracy and the challenges encountered in the democratization process have globally diverged.[4] The promising news about the global expansion of democratic values does not change the fact that the majority of the states in the Middle East have been the tardiest in terms of transformation from authoritarian rule.[5] Despite an increasing yearning for civil society and democracy, the future of the Middle Eastern states remains uncertain. The percentage of autocracies in the region is still the highest in the world.[6] It is even more unnerving to witness the persistence of rulers in maintaining their crowns for so many decades while civil societies remain fragile and weak under their dictatorships. The few cases that are considered to be in transition also seem to go in vicious cycles. One of the most promising political openings, led by President Khatami in Iran in 2002, came to an end as the ultra-religious forces were elected in 2005 with the presidency of hardcore conservative Mahmoud Ahmadinejad. Due to the dark political scene in the Middle East, the so-called Turkish model has become increasingly popular as a potential solution to the "Middle East problem." The recent steps that Turkey took towards a liberal democracy brought the country back to the center of attention. The studies that juxtapose the Turkish trajectory against the political stagnation in the rest of the Muslim world have become fashionable as a search has started for ways to *export* the Turkish model to other Muslim majority states.

As political scientists have discredited cultural arguments for their essentialist tendencies—as was explicit in Huntington's *Clash of Civilizations*—they have replaced them with political arguments.[7] Contrary to Huntington's warning that the West must not interfere with the menace of the Middle East, Western intervention has become increasingly deliberate in its attempt to "implant" democracies there.

Not surprisingly in the wake of 9/11, the Western fascination with Turkey, Atatürk and Atatürkism revived in a new form. Whereas Turkey's rapid and top-down modernization of the 1950s had previously captivated universalist modernists,[8] the transition in the new millennium appealed to a broader audience interested in the so-called globalization of democracies. Put differently, even though the fascination with modernization was replaced with a fascination with democratization, the idea of modeling the Middle East after Turkey seems to have persisted. Since we have learned in the meantime that modernities were multiple and that the Islamic Middle East redefined its modernity in alternative ways, perhaps democracy could provide a universal cure to the Middle East. As the ghosts of modernization theory have revived in the wake of growing American fear of Islam, the secular state tradition in Turkey and its "soft" Islam are turning into tourist attractions.

Among the many paradoxes of this idea of making a model out of Turkey, the most ironic one is the association, if not conflation, of the earlier top-down modernization and the current democratization. If Atatürk succeeded in modernizing Turkey from above, why cannot the United States democratize the Middle East from above, as it has already attempted in Iraq?

First, the current transition in Turkey is *not* an inevitable result of Atatürk's brand of authoritarian modernization. Atatürk's vision of a strong sense of belonging and indivisibility of Turkish society was undermined by the authoritarian characteristics of the Republic,[9] characteristics that eventually divided and polarized the society into many camps, including the Islamist and secularist ones. Hence, it is not a coincidence that the decline of authoritarianism coincides with the demise of polarization and rise of cooperation between state and society. Democratization is the product of the *failure* and decline of the authoritarianism of the Republican project. The current transformation is an effect of shifting dynamics between the state and society. As discussed at length, most of the underlying motives of these shifts have been unintentional, accidental and spontaneous.

While Atatürk's dealings with religion must be understood in their historical context, the complex evolution of the relationship between Islamism and secularism must be seen as a deviation from—as opposed to an extension of—Atatürk's original design for the Republic. Put differently, the current shape of state-Islam relations was not planned or foreseen by the founders of the nation-state or former politicians. It was not the unfolding of a determinate or predetermined path. This makes the idea of modeling a remote dream. Like any nation-building, this nation-building took place at the junction of several historical and sociopolitical realities; liberal democracy cannot be *transplanted* from any time to another time in history or from any place to another place across the world. Top-down modeling is unlikely to work in building nations and democratizing their states, especially the ones in the Middle East, which have a long history and collective memory. Because "models" are static, they cannot incorporate historically shifting power dynamics at the national and global levels and the unforeseen trajectory of state-society interaction into their scheme. Modeling the Arab world after "Atatürk's Turkey," in order to democratize the former, suffers from analytical confusion, empirical flaw and theoretical ignorance. While repudiating cultural essentialism, social research must be careful not to overestimate and essentialize the role of political engineering designed by the political elite, both indigenous and foreign.

Second, the idea of the "Turkish model" has gained popularity not only among Western powers but also among some Turkish social actors and scholars whose nationalist feelings were touched by it. Religious or secular nationalisms discussed before have converged in this regard, too. A strong argument along these lines has come from proud secularists, who insist on not tolerating Islam or compromising laicism. According to these secularists, the secular state tradition must be the basis of the model, as democratization depends on the state's success in controlling and taming Islam. In contrast, this study shows democratization as an effect of the gradual *taming* of authoritarian laicism into more liberal forms of secularism.

While some built the "Turkish model for a Muslim democracy" on the power of the secular state, others explained the Turkish trajectory as a product of its culturally specific Islam, the so-called "Turkish Islam."[10] Following Yavuz's line of thinking, scholars argued that Turkish Islam, unlike any other, was liberal, tolerant and inherently pluralist and pro-democratic.[11] Aras, for example, attributes the success of the Gülen movement in re-creating "a legitimate link between state and religion" to its *Turkish-Muslim identity*, as distinct from other Muslim identities.[12] In line with the nationalist assertions of Islamic actors, it is believed, as illustrated in chapter 4, that Turks share this "better" form of Islam with Central Asians of Turkic origin. This ethnic inclination has been so explicitly essential that it has made some of the Islamist intellectuals uncomfortable.[13]

Another attempt to justify the uniqueness and usefulness of the "Turk-ish model" is embodied by the idea of a specific kind of "Muslimhood." Accordingly, as Islam is a universal religion based on a universally shared text, the deviations across the Muslim world must be explained by Islamic ways of life and cultural differences.[14] Along these lines, the "Muslimhood model" of Turkey is argued to delineate the end of Islamism and the emergence of secularized Muslim actors. Put differently, the presence of pious Muslims in both the public and political spheres in Turkey is distin-guished from other Muslim countries by their "individual *personal* prac-tice."[15] However, when we look at daily manifestation of "secularization" in other Middle Eastern states, including even the theocracy of Iran, we see uneven yet similar patterns of secularization. As recent empirical stud-ies show, the majority of Iranians prefer to separate religion from the state and to confine it to their personal lives in the private sphere, where they can experience it individually.[16]

In general, the idea of Turkey as a model for the Middle East suffers from far too many flaws to be covered fully here. The Turkish trajectory cannot be explained by either the unique characteristics of Islam and Islamists in Turkey or by Atatürk's heritage of authoritarian modernization and the laicist Republic. Similar to the prophecies discussed in the intro-duction to this book, these approaches fail to incorporate the shifting power dynamics between state and society, dynamics that have been very uneven in the Middle East. Instead, they advocate for either society-centered or state-centered explanations. On the contrary, I argue that the source of change was the shifting linkages between the state and Islam, shifts that have motivated both sides to revise and readapt their attitudes and responses towards each other.

Similar to the multiple manifestations of Christianity from the United States to France, manifestations of Islam in Turkey differ from those in the rest of the Muslim world. However, the distinction of Turkey does not lie in the specific merit of Turkish Islam or the monolithic image of a time-less and staunchly secular Turkish state. As Zubaida correctly argues, polit-ical Islam is "integrated into *national* histories and cultures."[17] The nature of Islamic social forces cannot be analyzed independent of the shifting attitudes of the nation-states and changing political cultures.

The Neglected Agency of the Non-defiant Social Actors and the Illiberal States in Democratization in the Middle East

The politics of engagement is the outcome of continual experimenta-tion between the state and social forces. The feasibility of this experimentation depends on the availability and characteristics of settings that bring these forces together. Hence, the dynamics and channels will vary across time and space in the Muslim context. So, is every case an exception? Can we not hope to develop a theory of Islam and democratization on the basis of in-depth understanding of case studies? Put differently, are we doomed to collect separate, disconnected evidence of multiple trajectories of transition, trajectories that cannot be compared and contrasted?

The Middle East has suffered from the absence or weakness of the communication and interaction between Islamic actors and the authoritarian states. Despite highly vibrant local participation and expressions of discontent, the vertical channels that link states and societies have historically been cut off in the region. The majority of states have not only obliterated institutional channels of interaction with Islamic and other social forces but have also persistently undermined alternative pathways of negotiation. In the shadow of authoritarian rule, the Islamic actors were either muted or left only with the option of insurgency in order to make themselves heard by unresponsive rulers. This unequal power dynamic has created a selective focus on confrontational social actors as potential forces of change. The negative consequence of this focus has been a prevalent neglect, if not denial, of the agency of non-defiant social actors.

Indeed, did only the insurgent actors deserve agency in the authoritarian Middle East, while the non-confrontational ones were rendered passive? Contrary to this view, the revolutionary spirit and confrontational attitudes of the Islamic actors have been largely demolished by the dictators and autocrats in the region. No wonder that stagnation has been prevalent. The social and political transformations have often been entrusted to the failing attempts of the radicals and revolutionaries to fight against harsh political rule. Here, it is useful to remember Montesquieu, the father of the concept of separation of powers, who was a foe of both harsh rule and fanaticism and a fan of moderation.[18]

Some Muslim majority states, such as Jordan and Tunisia, have attempted to tolerate and incorporate Islamic social forces into the system. Although some states have moderated Islamic social forces, none of these states in the Middle East have transformed from authoritarian rule yet. In trying to incorporate Islam, Egypt largely co-opted Islamic social forces by depriving them of their autonomy and power.[19] The clergy in Iran also routinized and terminated the revolutionary and democratic spirit of the Islamists by institutionalizing an Islamic state.[20] Clearly, integration has proved to be a complicated project, as it has often undermined the agency of social and Islamic forces and their skills to negotiate.

Unlike the cases of co-option and authoritarian integration of Islam, the "politics of engagement" in Turkey has originated from unintended interactions between two separate groups of actors, the state and Islam. This does not by any means suggest that such engagements have gone smoothly in Turkey. On the contrary, they have had a stormy past and still continue to go through periods of instability. However, by keeping the state and social forces separate yet in touch and in tune with each other, everyday sites have offered a temporary alternative mechanism of interaction between them. These spontaneous encounters have created elective affinities between Islam and the state, and have facilitated cooperation between them. In the long run, the accepting attitudes and non-defiant characteristics of these actors have enabled them to actively participate in the transformation of the state from authoritarianism.

Hence, I have argued that Islam's major contribution to democratization has not been Islamic horizontal networking. I have highlighted the illiberal and authoritarian tendencies of the projects in which Islamic actors actively participate. I have also argued that although Islamic parties' participation in procedural democracy has played a role in their moderation,[21] the major contribution of moderate Islamic actors has been prepared by their unintended engagements with the state in everyday sites. The moderate Islamic actors have formed alternative vertical channels between society and the state. Similar to Turkey, other Middle Eastern countries may temporarily substitute alternative pathways for the absence or weakness of formal political channels between the state and society. The centrality of these channels is temporary, as the engagements eventually lead to a "marriage of convenience" in a formal contractual institution.

The key to the flourishing of these alternative vertical patterns is clearly the non-confrontational social actors, who have the potential to make sporadic changes in authoritarianism without threatening the system.[22] Although largely neglected so far, non-confrontation is the major characteristic of engagement and potential transition from authoritarian rule in the Middle East. However, engagements cannot be "made" or "engineered" beyond the historical spontaneity of the settings that the social forces and state actors participate in.[23] Although the terms of engagement cannot be strategically designed like the projects of civil society and the models of democracy, they can certainly be facilitated and encouraged through a better understanding of the power and agency of non-defiant social actors. The cooperative attitudes of Islamic actors, reinforced by their faith in submission to the collective good, are a conducive force to reach out to illiberal states.

I have illustrated several ways in which these vertical pathways of interaction gradually transform both authoritarian states and social forces.

Some—but not an exhaustive list—of the venues of state-Islam interaction that this book has discussed are national loyalties, ethnic politics, education, gender politics and international politics. I have identified these realms of activity as the meeting points of state and Islamic actors, in which they have developed the skills to *talk to* each other, as opposed to *talking past* each other.

A related problem in studying state-Islam interaction appears to be methodological. How do we study state-Islam interaction when most of these states are far from available or open for social inquiry, let alone accountable to society? How do we gain access to these states in which both the access to high-ranking political leaders and the availability of archival materials are limited by the authorities? Political ethnographies are imperative in these contexts to gain deeper understanding of how illiberal states and social actors meet each other in everyday life, in venues ranging from the streets to the households.

In the introduction to this book, I questioned the scholarly neglect of illiberal authoritarian states in the studies of civil societies and public sphere in the Middle East. I argued that this neglect originates from the divide between the political scientists' emphasis on political institutions and the political elites[24] versus the sociologists' and anthropologists' main interest in local grassroots and cultural aspects of Islam. This explains why Huntington's old thesis still remains the major source cited when theorizing about the link between political participation and macro institutions. Huntington argues that increasing political participation does not translate into democratization but rather feeds authoritarianism, which results when political institutions cannot keep up with the pace of mass participation.[25] The argument may still seem to hold when we consider the gap between vibrant public spheres in the Middle East and the stagnant political institutions. However, as it has been almost forty years since Huntington made this argument, it is time to rethink this old thesis in the light of fresh empirical evidence from the Middle East.

There is a widespread tendency in the literature to hold onto the continuities of authoritarianism and the failures of democratization in the region. This insistence clearly leaves the debate at the stage of never-ending "transition" by overshadowing the pro-democratic changes outside the formal institutional channels. In other words, the exclusive focus on the persistence of authoritarianism prevents research and scholarship from moving on and capturing emerging manifestations of democracy in the Middle East.[26] Sociological imagination needs to shift from the old habit of reiterating the failure of democracy towards the new reality of the failures of authoritarianism.[27] The Turkish case is a rather tough example, as it is the first liberal democracy yet to be consolidated among the many persisting Muslim-majority autocracies of the Middle East. The discourse of repressed and oppressed Islamic social forces by the authoritarian state has to be rethought and revised in the light of new evidence, such as that provided by this study, even if it may be too early to judge the consolidation of liberal democracy as of yet.

This ethnography has illustrated both the bright and dark sides of cooperation between Islam and the state and has discussed both the prospects and challenges. The fact that the shifting dynamics of state-society interaction have been largely neglected in the context of authoritarian regimes creates the illusion that this dynamic occurs only in Western liberal democracies. Similarly, from this perspective, the engagement with an illiberal authoritarian state may puzzle observers if it is seen mainly as a menace rather than as an accomplishment. However, it is absurd to assume that people do not have affective ties—positive or negative feelings, national loyalties and discontents—for the states that are not fulfilling the requirements of Western liberal democracies. The praising of Muslim societies, civil or not, at the expense of the authoritarian states of the Middle East helps neither the actualization of reform nor the development of theoretical insights on democratization.

The Partial Nature of the Accord between the State and Islam

Among the most important missing linkages between states and societies in the Middle East have been the distance and tension between the Islamic actors and the authoritarian states. The Middle East displays various patterns of discord between Islamic actors and states. Interestingly, however, this dissonance has often been regarded as impetus for a transition from authoritarian rule.[28] Moreover, the positive image of discord has become completed by a negative image of accord between states and social forces. Whereas disunity is associated with diversity, the "unity" between the state and society has been associated with co-option and state repression of social forces.[29] Moreover, the *harmonious* nature of these states has been associated with the persistence of authoritarianism in the Middle East. Is the persistence of autocracies actually a correlate of the harmonious nature of the states of the Middle East? Are these states in harmony in their actions within and between social forces and state actors? Furthermore, does accord between the state and society indeed originate from, or indicate, authoritarianism? Here, the nature and implications of state-society accord must be qualified further before we jump to quick conclusions.

Tocqueville's *Democracy in America* provides a useful insight—and definitely an alternative to the aforementioned one—on the accord between religion and politics. His analysis of the United States in the early nineteenth century provides a compelling insight into the role that religion plays in linking and aligning the state and society. While his contemporaries, other scholars of the Enlightenment, anticipated and collectively celebrated the unilinear decline of religion, Tocqueville emphasized the importance of the synchrony between faith and political institutions in propelling democracy and protecting freedoms.[30] He strongly believed that under certain conditions, religions could support freedom rather than undermining it.[31] Specifically, religions promote democracy only when they remain institutionally *separate* from politics, and *support* political institutions and values of freedom. Under these conditions, "religion increases its power over some issues and loses the hope of reigning over all."[32] This mutual understanding between politics and religion is the key for the accord between state and society.

Because Tocqueville experienced the consequences of the absolutist ancien régime during his life, his reading of the United States was against the background of France. He contemplated the nature and the impact of discord between the state and French society. He argued that distant and adversarial relations between the state and social actors was the outcome of authoritarian rule, which "divided and ruled" the society.[33] As a result, the French lost their ability to cooperate not only with each other but also with the state. Tocqueville's story of the ancien régime is a reminder of the clear-cut difference between "deeply divided" and "diverse" societies. The former results from failures of political processes while the latter is a characteristic of an accommodating democracy. Tocqeuville's analysis clearly illustrates that democracy is undermined by the discord between the state and society. Contrary to the separation in the American case, the split between religion and politics in France was hostile and resulted in resentment between state, society and religion. While religion declined in French society, the American society has remained distinctly religious, mainly because religion was perceived as a friend—not an enemy—of democratic institutions.

Competing visions of society and polity may propel democratization, but only when there is a minimal consensus on the nature of political authority. The minimum agreement on the secular (rather than divine) source of political sovereignty is imperative for the partial accord between state and society. Similarly, in the Muslim context a limited consensus on the national (rather than religious) basis of the imagined community fosters harmony between the state and Islamic social forces. Muslim majority states can tolerate disagreements and accommodate differences much more successfully after attaining a consensus on these basic principles of political rule.

As discussed in chapter 6, the *degree* of accord between the Turkish state and Islamic social forces plays a major role in translating sociocultural diversity into political pluralism. Here, it is important to note that neither in the Middle East nor in the West have the states and societies been in total accord or discord. Discord and harmony are matters of degree rather than defining characteristics of state-society interaction. Accordingly, instead of celebrating consensus or disagreement, social research must explore the nature and the *limits* of dissent and consent between states and social forces. These limits largely shape the nature and scope of political pluralism.

Chapter 2 pointed to other political openings in Turkey, such as the one led by the DP in the 1950s and the Refah in the mid-1990s. These political openings seemed to temporarily overcome the conventional disconnectedness between the government and social groups. For a limited time, the dogfights between the political elite made some space for the bridges between the masses and the state.[34] Why, then, were both of these experiments interrupted by military intervention? Both the DP and the Refah largely failed in communicating and negotiating with the state and the military. The distinction of the Islamic social forces represented by the Gülen movement and the AKP is that both have mobilized people from diverse backgrounds to engage the Republic.

This analysis follows Tocqueville's anticipation of the increasing role of religion in balancing state-society interaction in democracies. However, his optimism about the accord between religion and state has to be taken with some reservation. The nature and scope of cooperation between religion and politics must be rethought critically in light of current world politics and with historical and cross-cultural sensitivity. In Tocqueville's view, the alliance between state and religion propels democracy, provided that they remain separate and autonomous. Unlike Tocqueville's nineteenth-century America, however, the increasingly strong alliance between religion and the state raises new questions and concerns about whether it creates dissonance, and even polarization, in American society in the twenty-first century.

Although a certain level of harmony between the state and religion plays a positive role in broad transformations such as nation building and democratization, the persistence of a strong alliance between them may undermine democracy in the long run. Similar to nationalists, who "can stand close to liberalism *when* they struggle against a despotic regime,"[35] religious actors can occasionally temporarily join forces with democrats and help compel a transition to democracy. However, it is rather unlikely that the long-term implications of a strong and *permanent* alliance between the state and Islamists may propel democratization in the Middle East.

"Familiar theses in American cultural history go *beyond cooperation*, and propose the democratization of religion in America and the *religiosity of American democracy*."[36] At one level, the democratization of religion indicates the voluntarism of religious membership. At another level, the religiosity of American democracy reflects the strikingly high numbers of faithful citizens who organize politically on the basis of religion. In American history, the religiosity of democracy has not been seen as a major threat to secular institutions and the separation of church and state. It has rather been considered a matter of widely shared moral values embedded in the political culture. As Tocqueville clearly pointed out, religion reigned less as a doctrine and more as a common opinion in the United States. The question is would the American case travel to the Middle East and, if so, how? Does the contemporary engagement between the Turkish secular state and Islamic social forces also go *beyond* cooperation and indicate *religiosity of Turkish democracy*?

Although compared increasingly to religion in the United States, Islam in Turkey does not simply enter the public sphere to "Muslimize" the Turkish democracy and the political field. Rather than Islamizing the polity, Islamic actors acquire leeway to negotiate their religious freedom and to legitimize faith-based lives. Hence, Islamic actors' experimentation with the secular milieu correlates with the state's experimentation with liberal, secular democracy. Accordingly, I have argued that the sporadic disagreements between Islamic actors and the state must be seen as potentially valuable assets to liberal democracy in Turkey. As these discontents prevent the state and Islam from attaining complete agreement, they limit the nature and scope of cooperation between them.

Does State-Islam Accord Facilitate Cooperation between Islamic and Secular Actors?

Because despotic and authoritarian rule has a strong tendency to fragment and polarize social forces, people under despotic regimes often display anti-democratic or totalitarian tendencies.[37] Hence, neither the states nor Islamic social forces can be seen as the inherent enemies or friends of civil society and democracy in the Middle East. Islam and/or states may come to support democracy for different reasons that have little to do with democratic values or their genuine desire and inclination for democratization.

By endowing the Islamic social forces in Turkey with legitimacy, transparency and accountability, the politics of engagement set the stage for cooperation between social actors across the Islamic–secular divide. Parallel to the partial nature of the cooperation between Islamic actors and the state, the alliances between non-state secular and Islamic actors are temporary and are limited to some shared goals. These shared goals have enabled the two sides to transcend their group-specific agendas, world-views and conflicting political and moral orientations. These goals include Turkey's membership in the EU, economic liberalism and the transition to a liberal democracy. Clearly, these shared agendas are specific to a certain moment in the history of the transition. Is, then, the achievement or abandonment of these goals likely to weaken, if not obliterate, these ad hoc alliances? While these shared interests have provided an impetus for cooperation during a transition period, they definitely do not suggest a permanent alliance between Islamic and secular social actors. When I asked one of the leading intellectuals from the Gülen movement if cooperation was an ultimate end in itself, he told me: "There is no such a thing as 'ultimate cooperation.' One cannot cooperate with 'a somebody' and expect constructive change and reform. We cooperate *only if* it benefits the nation and advances the national interest."

What, then, makes this type of cooperation different from other kinds of overarching alliances between diverse social forces such as the ones that typically take place during revolutions? First, compared to the collective upheaval of the society against the state, as experienced in Iran in 1979, the contemporary cooperation between Islamic actors and the secular actors remain a relatively weaker bond in Turkey. It is not a trust network, as it still entails distrust with regard to several contested issues, which were discussed in chapters 3 and 6.

Advocates of social capital theory have often explained democratization and its failures by the rise or decline of a trust culture.[38] They have emphasized trust as an important asset of a democratic society. If that is the case, does the ongoing distrust between Islamic and secular actors undermine democratization in Turkey? Challenging this view, other scholars have argued that the lack of trust and even distrust might render democratic institutions necessary and indispensable.[39] Similarly, this study has suggested that the *transient* nature of alliances and *temporary* cooperation across the Islamic–secular divide have contributed to the institutionalization of engagements by rendering it indispensable. Because these temporary bonds do not correlate to a "generalized" trust between diverse social actors at large, people need to invest in and trust the political institutions of a strong democratic state.[40]

Aside from persisting distrust between Islamic and secular actors, there is another factor that prevents the alliance between them from strengthening. Despite the engagement with the state and cooperation with secular forces, Islamic actors have remained enemies of hardcore secularists, who still defend state control of religion in Turkey. The shrinking group of secularists has not changed its hostile attitudes and hatred towards Islamic actors, the Gülen movement and the AKP in particular.

After attending a talk at Harvard University in February 2005, I was invited to a dinner with the speaker and a few other Turkish scholars. I was seated next to a retired high-ranking bureaucrat who was in charge during the soft military coup in 1997 and who played a leading role in initiating the headscarf ban in universities. After a long and rather blunt discussion about the current situation in Turkey, he expressed his hatred for Islamists, especially followers of the Gülen movement. Disappointed by my detached and rather analytical approach, he said, "Do you know why your generation fails to have the insight that your parents' generation had? It is because our own kids are too apologetic to see the truth, the threat of Islam and how it is undermining a sound tradition of democracy in Turkey."

Heper anticipated in the late 1990s that "a marriage between Islam and democracy in Turkey can be consummated if the radical secularists stop trying to impose their preferred life-style and set of values upon the Islamists, and if the latter do not undermine by word or deed the basic tenets of the secular democratic state in Turkey."[41] As illustrated in chapter 3, the hardcore secularists are holding onto their antagonistic position while most of the moderate secular actors have either softened their views, or sympathized and cooperated with Islamic actors. The politics of engagement have transformed the Turkish state but largely failed to affect the hardcore secularists, such as the members of United Civil Society Organizations, STKB.[42] Ironically, however, their non-compromising attitudes and radical laicism may not necessarily be a barrier to democratization after all. Under the conditions of partial accord between the secular state and Islamic social forces, distrust between hardcore secularists and Islamic actors may even be beneficial for democratization. The hardcore secularists not only maintain a bitter opposition, but their intolerant antagonism also renders the institutional reform imperative if Turkey is to consolidate liberal democracy.

The key to cross-ideological cooperation is that, regardless of the attitudes and feelings towards each other, the collaborating parties must have a certain degree of trust in the state. Currently, a "marriage of convenience" between the state and the Islamic actors is in process, although the hardcore secularists have not ceased their imposition of laicist ideology on Islam. Rather than remaining as the state ideology, however, laicism has become a group ideology of the "laicists" among many other ideologies. Aside from refusing any form of cross-ideological cooperation, some of the hardcore figures in this group, including a minority of state officials, even object to institutional reform and EU membership. Their objections are motivated by the fact that reforms are undertaken under the political leadership of a pro-Islamic party.

Because of (not despite) these challenges, the politics of engagement are empowering as a major force of democratization. On one hand, they align the state and society to a certain degree. On the other, they facilitate partial cooperation and limited agreement between previously divided social forces. Eventually, engagements enable them to express both affinities and discontents within the boundaries of a widely shared frame of belonging. As Hall argues, "Liberal regimes may achieve very great stability by diffusing various conflicts through society rather than concentrating them at the political center. Pure democratic participation will destabilize, unless it is channeled through social institutions that contain, manage and regulate conflict."[43]

When the linkages between the state and Islam are largely absent, the unarticulated or miscommunicated discontents of social forces are likely to accumulate as anti-state feelings. These discontents may amount to overthrowing the state, as was experienced in the case of the Iranian Revolution. The formation of an Islamic theocracy was an unintended consequence of this kind of cross-ideological cooperation between diverse social forces, cooperation that is clearly not conducive to democracy. The Turkish transition stands in sharp contrast to such cases where conflict concentrates at the center while cooperation is limited to the interaction between social forces that are all resentful of the state.

First, the discontents and disagreements can be communicated through alternative social channels and political institutions in Turkey. Second, although the hardcore secularists' non-cooperative attitudes temporarily undermine the principles of democracy, they also serve a temporary purpose. They render cross-ideological cooperation an incomplete project and prevent it from taking a totalizing form. More importantly, as long as cooperation across the worldviews of Islamism and secularism exists as a viable option and one can choose not to cooperate, it remains a positive force for the future of democracy. Under these conditions, alliances that cut across group affiliations, religious orientations and conflicting worldviews can shift periodically and remain fluid. Time will tell if the current cooperation between Islamic and secular actors will maintain its intensity once contemporary agendas, such as Turkey's EU membership, are resolved, for better or worse.

Notes

Introduction

1. See for example, Rubin, Michael. 6 August 2004. "Talking Turkey. She Is a Democracy," *National Review Online*, http://www.meforum.org/article/624/.

2. I chose to use the term *Islamic actor* as it effectively highlights Islamic agency.

3. The statement that caused Erdoğan's sentence was delivered in his speech on 6 December 1997. "Minarets are bayonets, Domes are helmets, Mosques are barracks, Believers are soldiers."

4. See Barsalou, Judy. 2005. "Islamists at the Ballot Box: Findings from Egypt, Jordan, Kuwait, and Turkey," United States Institute of Peace Special Report No. 144. United States Institute of Peace, www.usip.org/pubs/specialreports/sr144 .html. In the report, Tepe is cited for defining the AKP's identity as an elusive one. She correctly argues that the ideology of the party shifts between Islamic and un-Islamic. My interviews with sympathizers of the party, both from Islamic and un-Islamic backgrounds, suggest that this elusiveness seems to have helped the party to increase its acceptability and popularity, especially among the moderate secular groups in Turkey. However, Tepe also correctly reminds us that this may lead to the failure of the party in the long run.

5. Author's field notes, July 2004, Istanbul.

6. Mardin observes a similar trend in scholarship, a "dearth of studies investigating in depth the Islamic component in the life" of Erdoğan. Mardin, Şerif. 2006. "Turkish Islamic Exceptionalism Yesterday and Today: Continuity, Rupture and Reconstruction in Operational Codes" in Çarkoğlu, Ali, and Rubin, Barry (eds.) *Religion and Politics in Turkey*. London and New York: Routledge, p. 3.

7. Ibid., p. 4.

8. Author's interview, December 2005, Odakule-Istanbul.

9. In this study, I use the terms *Islamic* and *secular* as distinctly different from *Islamist* and *secularist*. The terminological distinction originated from the need to differentiate the agency of non-confrontational Islamic actors from Islamists who challenge the secular state ideologically. In contrast to the latter, Islamic and secular actors disagree on religious and secular worldviews, ways of life and morality. They passively or actively promote freedom for their own views and lives, and thereby engage in a negotiation of the boundaries between religion and politics.

Contrary to the Islamic and secular actors, the terms *Islamist* and *secularist* (used interchangeably with *laicist*) indicate active advocacy of ideologies *of Islamism* and *laicism* in order to transform and fashion the social order and the polity after their own religious or secular blueprints of the world. There is little or no concern for making space for opposite ideologies and views. Clearly, the major interest of this work is in the former groups, the Islamic and the secular.

10. See especially Bozdogan, Sibel and Kasaba, Reşat (eds.) 1997. *Rethinking Modernity and National Identity in Turkey*. Seattle: University of Washington Press.

11. For a discussion of the role of Islam in the state in Shi'ite and Sunni traditions, see Arjomand, Said. 1988. The *Turban of the Crown. The Islamic Revolution of Iran*. New York: Oxford University Press.

12. For a discussion on the gap between the state-making projects and their limits in practice, see Migdal, Joel. 1997. "Finding the Meeting Ground of Fact and Fiction: Some Reflections on Turkish Modernization" in Bozdogan, Sibel and Kasaba, Reşat (eds.) *Rethinking Turkish Modernity and National Identity*. Seattle: University of Washington Press.

13. One of the most illuminating discussions of these shifts can be found in Sakallıoğlu, Ümit-Cizre. 1996. "Parameters and Strategies of Islam-State Interaction in Republican Turkey," *International Journal of Middle East Studies*, 28: 231–251.

14. As an anti-system party led by Erbakan, Refah received the protest votes not only from Islamists but also from the urban poor in the shaky political milieu of the 1990s. The party won the elections with 21.1 percent of the votes, and came to power in a coalition government in 1996.

15. Geertz's distinction between science and ideology is important to remember here. He argues that the attitude of science towards the subject matter is disinterested, spare, analytical, whereas ideologically motivated attitudes are committed and deliberately suggestive. While social science seeks "intellectual clarity," ideology searches for motivating action. Geertz, Clifford. 1973. *Interpretation of Cultures*. New York: Basic Books, p. 230.

16. For exceptions, see Zubaida, Sami. 2000. "Trajectories of Political Islam: Egypt, Iran and Turkey." *Political Quarterly*, 60–78; Norton, R.A. 1995. "Introduction" to *Civil Society in the Middle East*. Leiden: E. J. Brill; Toprak, Binnaz. 1995. "Civil Society in Turkey" in Norton, ed. *Civil Society in the Middle East*. Leiden: E. J. Brill; Salame, Ghassan. 1994. "Introduction: Where Are the Democrats?" in Salame, Ghassan. (ed.) *Democracy without Democrats: The Renewal of the Politics in the Muslim World*. London, New York: I. B. Tauris, pp. 1–23.

17. Schwedler, Jillian. 2004. "The Islah Party in Yemen: Political Opportunities and Coalition Building in Transitional Polity" in Wiktorowicz, Quintan (ed.) *Islamic Activism: A Social Movement Theory Approach*. Bloomington: Indiana University Press; Ismail, Salwa. 2003. *Rethinking Islamist Politics: Culture, the State and Islamism*. London, New York: I. B. Taurus, p. 24. Ismail emphasizes that "Islamist discourses have been articulated within state structures."

18. Mardin, Şerif. 1973. "Center Periphery Relations: A Key to Turkish Politics," *Daedalus*, p. 102.

19. Heper, Metin. 1985. *The State Tradition in Turkey*. Beverly, UK: Eothen Press, p. 98.

20. White, Jenny 2002. *Islamist Mobilization in Turkey. A Study in Vernacular Politics.* Seattle: University of Washington Press; Tugal, Cihan. Forthcoming. "The Appeal of Islamic Politics: The Ritual and Dialogue in a Poor District of Turkey," *Sociological Quarterly.*

21. Mardin 2006: 6.

22. See especially Yavuz, Hakan. 2003a. *Islamic Political Identity in Turkey.* Oxford: Oxford University Press, p. 199; Yavuz, Hakan. 2000a. "Cleansing Islam from the Public Sphere," *Journal of International Affairs,* 54 (1). Yavuz juxtaposes state-centric and society-centric Islamic movements (pp. 28–31). In Yavuz's view, Islamic movements that do not challenge the state are falling under the category of state-centric, as they believe that "the ills of the society are best corrected by the control of the state through its enforcement of a uniform and homogenous religious ideology" (ibid. p. 28). This explains why he sees non-confrontational Islamic movements as "co-opted" by the state (2003a: 199). This view clearly misses the agency of the non-confrontational social actors.

23. Not only state-centered accounts but also bottom-up approaches that brought in the voice of Islamic actors leave emergent linkages between Islam and the secular state unstudied. See, for example, Saktanber, Ayşe. 2002. *Living Islam: Women, Religion and Politicization of Islam in Turkey.* London: I. B. Tauris, p. 18–21, 27.

24. For an exception see Kasaba, Reşat. forthcoming. "Modern Turkey" in Robinson, Francis. (ed.) *The Islamic World in the Age of Western Dominance.* Cambridge: Cambridge University Press. In his thought-provoking article, Kasaba explores the history of state-Islam interaction in Turkey. His analysis suggests that the 1950s witnessed the first opening where the state and society set the bridges for a dialogue. He sees a similar trend in contemporary Turkey, in which the gap between the state and society is again being recovered for a more constructive interaction.

25. Not only the focus of most anthropological work but also of political science remains on the oppositional forces as a source of political change in the Middle East. See, for example, Posusney, Marsha Pripstein. 2006. "The Middle East's Democracy Deficit in Contemporary Perspective" in Posusney and Angrist (eds.) *Authoritarianism in the Middle East.* Boulder, CO, London: Lynne Rienne Publishers, pp. 12–14; here, note the exclusive interest in human agency as a force of resistance to authoritarian regimes. See also Brownlee, Jason. 2006. "Political Crisis and Restabilization: Iraq, Libya, Syria, Tunisia" in Posusney and Angrist (eds.) *Authoritarianism in the Middle East,* pp. 43–63.

26. Mardin 2006: 19.

27. For a debate on the hostile and friendly separations of religion and politics, see Stepan, Alfred. 2000. "Religion, Democracy the 'Twin Tolerations,'" *Journal of Democracy,* 11 (4): 37–58.

28. Here, I am following Migdal's anthropology of the state, which explores the state as a multi-layered social organization. As Migdal clearly highlights, states' multiple parts often fall into conflict with each other in their interaction with diverse social forces. Migdal. 2001. *The State in Society. Studying How States and Societies Transform and Constitute One Another.* Cambridge: Cambridge University Press.

29. The Nur movement was formed in the early years of the Turkish Repub-

lic under the leadership of Bedüizzaman Said Nursi, who came to be regarded as a threat to the secular order and spent most of his life in exile. See especially Mardin, Şerif. 1989. *Religion and Social Change in Modern Turkey: The Case of Bedüizzaman Said Nursi.* Albany: State University of New York.

30. I interviewed a large number of secular actors in 2004 and 2005 who admitted to being in either one of these categories.

31. These observations are based on the author's interviews and fieldwork with the followers of the Gülen movement since the late 1990s.

32. Here, a few exceptions apply. Author's interviews with the leaders and followers of the Gülen movement and the members of Ministers of AKP since 2002 in Istanbul, Ankara and the United States.

33. Özdalga, Elisabeth. 2005. "Redeemer or Outsider? The Gülen Community in the Civilizing process," *Muslim World* 95 (3): 429–446; Gülalp, Haldun. 1999. "Political Islam in Turkey: The rise and fall of the Refah Party," *Muslim World* 89 (1): 22–41.

34. Islamist mobilization by loosely organized Islamic groups (sects and movements) and the Islamic parties Refah and the AKP have remained largely disconnected in the literature. This is mainly due to a predominantly analytical distinction between civil society and political society, which leads to a divide in perception between social forces in the political and apolitical fields. The ethnography of the state, which sees states as social actors, overcomes this analytical dichotomy.

35. See, for example, Longhor, Vickie. 2005. "Too Much Civil Society, Too Little Politics? Egypt and Other Liberalizing Arab Regimes" in Posusney and Angrist (eds.) *Authoritarianism in the Middle East.* Boulder, CO, London: Lynne Rienne Publishers, 193–218; White. 2002.

36. Starting in 1997, I conducted multi-sited ethnographic fieldwork and some two hundred interviews (formal and informal), oral histories and group discussions and life stories. The real names of the social actors are kept anonymous. Instead, I consistently use pseudo-names.

Chapter 1: The Politics of Engagement

1. After the coup in 1980, the Council of Higher Education was established, which put an end to the autonomous self-administration of the universities. In the early 1990s, the headscarf issue was largely left to the judgment of the university's president. Since 1997 when the regulations were tightened, the dress code, decreed by the Council of Higher Education, has banned headscarves at universities.

2. Yeni Asya group is one of the smaller offshoots of the Nur movement. The daily Yeni Asya provided a platform appealing to most of the Nur followers, and gave them an opportunity to express their discontent with the Gülen movement. Like all Nurcus, the Yeni Asya group follows the teachings of Said Nursi, founder of the Nur movement. Its activities are mainly supported by Yeni Asya Foundation. In my visit to their center in 1997, the group's followers tried to persuade me to focus on their group and activities rather than the Gülen movement and gave me a long list of reasons why I should disregard the Gülen movement.

3. Işık Evleri accommodate approximately four to six students, who live to-

gether in an apartment. These apartments are usually financed by benefactors of the Gülen movement, and are shared by same-sex students.

4. See especially Navaro-Yashin, Yael. 2002. *Faces of the State: Secularism and Public Life in Turkey.* Princeton, NJ: Princeton University Press. Foucaultian approaches tend to see social actors' performance (practices) as simply doomed to underpin the so-called "mythical" power and legitimacy of the state.

5. Migdal 2001: 19. Like Foucault, Migdal differentiates the practices and images of the state. However, unlike Foucault, his work focuses on precisely those practices that "*batter* the image of a coherent, controlling state." Hence, while Foucaultian works conflate the realms of the state and society, mostly by deconstructing both, Migdal leads a school of thought that maintains the analytical separation between them.

6. In my interviews in 1997–1998, the followers from each of these groups expressed explicit dislike and disregard for each other. Even the followers of each offshoot of the Nur movement—such as the Gülen, Yeni Asya, Okuyucular and Yazıcılar—disagreed strongly about worldly issues and politics.

7. The two small branches of the Nur movement, Okuyucular and Yazıcılar, were very difficult to reach. Each time my appointments with their adherents were cancelled, I was told that they were "intimidated" to talk with outsiders. In contrast to the openness of the Gülen movement, these groups felt threatened by the state's control, sudden invasion and inspection of their centers and forced inquiries about their Islamic agendas.

8. Ismail 2003: 22.

9. For other studies that place the Gülen movement into the debates on civil society and democracy, see Aras, Bülent. 1998. "Turkish Islam's Moderate Face," *Middle East Quarterly,* 5 (3): 23–29; Özdalga, Elisabeth. 2003. "Secularizing Trends in Fethullah Gülen's Movement: Impasse or Opportunity for Further Renewal?" *Critique: Critical Middle Eastern Studies,* 12 (1): 61–73; Başkan, Filiz. 2005. "The Fethullah Gülen community: Contribution or Barrier to the Consolidation of Democracy in Turkey?" *Middle East Studies,* 41 (6): 849–861.

10. Zubaida 1996. "Turkish Islam and National Identity," *Middle East Report,* April–June, p. 11.

11. For other studies on the Nur movement, see Mardin 1989; Abu-Rabi, Ibrahim. 2003. *Islam at the Cross-Roads: On the Life and Thoughts of Bediüzzaman Said Nursi.* Albany: State University of New York. Yavuz. 2000b. "Being Modern in the Nurist Way," *ISIM Newsletter,* October, p. 14-1; 2003b. "The Case of the Nur Movement" in Yavuz and Esposito (eds.) *Turkish Islam and the Secular State: The Gülen Movement.* Syracuse, NY: Syracuse University Press. See also Yavuz 2003a: 181–185. Although Yavuz sees the Gülen movement as a continuation of Nur, my findings reveal sociological differences between the two movements. The historical and political embeddedness of the Nur and the Gülen movements in two different periods of the Turkish transition will be discussed further in chapter 2.

12. Uzbekistan has been an exception. The dictator, Kerimov, banned the Gülen schools, as they were found threatening to the secular rule. See Balcı, Bayram. 2003. "Fethullah Gülen's Missionary Schools in Central Asia and Their Role in the Spreading of Turkism and Islam," *Religion, State and Society,* 31 (2): 151–177.

13. Author's interviews with followers in Massachusetts and Pennsylvania, 2004–2005.

14. Tepe 2005. "Turkey's AKP: A Model 'Muslim-Democratic Party'?" *Journal of Democracy*, 16 (3): 76.

15. See, for example, Mirsepassi, Ali. 2000. *Intellectual Discourse and the Politics of Modernization*. New York, Oxford: Oxford University Press.

16. *Risale-i Nur* (Epistle of Light) is the title of the volumes, which are collected letters written by Said-i Nur Bediüzzaman, the leader of the Nur movement. It is his interpretations of the Kuran, in which he mainly tries to reconcile religion with science, faith with reason and rationality. *Risales* are read widely by the followers of the diverse Nur groups. The followers of Gülen also get together to read, interpret and discuss the *Risales*, along with many other contemporary religious texts.

17. For example, there are Fem *dersaneleri* (private establishments preparing students for various exams) and a high school, Yesilvadi, in Ümraniye, a neighborhood with lower socioeconomic standards in Istanbul.

18. The generational change is analyzed more in detail in chapter 2. It is important to note that a rather large proportion of my informants were born into secular families that either did not accept their children's Islamic identities or had difficulty in understanding their Islamic motivations. I also had many informants who indicated that they came from religious families, which they defined as "traditional Muslim" or "socially unconscious" about their faith. This was the way the new Islamic actors differentiated themselves from the older generation of the devout. With regard to the reproduction of Islamic everyday patterns in every generation, see Zubaida, Sami. 1993. *Islam, the People and the State*. London: I. B. Tauris, p. 123.

19. Çarkoğlu, Ali, and Toprak, Binnaz. 2000. *Religion Society, and Politics in Turkey*. Istanbul: TESEV Publications. In the late 1990s, a national survey revealed that the majority of Turks continued to be faithful believers and practice religion. However, "religious belief and practice is considered to be limited to private life and the idea of religious involvement in public life is not supported."

20. Arat, Yeşim. 2005. *Rethinking Islam and Liberal Democracy*. Albany: State University of New York Press, p. 9.

21. For a view that sees Islamists as products of governments' attitudes and actions, see Anderson, Lisa. 1997. "Fulfilling Prophecies; State Policy and Islamic Radicalism" in Esposito John (ed.) *Political Islam: Revolution, Radicalism or Reform*. Boulder, CO: Lynne Rienne Publishers, pp. 18–31.

22. See for example Mozaffari, Mehdi. 1988. "Islam and Civil Society" in Ferdinand, Klaus, and Mozaffari, Mehdi (eds.) *Islam; State and Society*. London: Curzon Press, p. 106. In his discussion of sporadic patterns of secularization in the Muslim world, Mozaffari highlights the Turkish experience as "unique to its kind to the extent that it was a total secularization that affected, power, institutions and life-style all at once."

23. Hefner, Robert. 2005. *Remaking Muslim Politics: Pluralism, Contestation Democratization*. Princeton, NJ: Princeton University Press.

24. Bryant, Christopher. 1992. "Civil Society and Pluralism: A Conceptual

Analysis," *Sisyphus*, 1 (7), p. 110. Bryant argues that the exclusive focus on ideological struggle has proven largely unhelpful in explicating "the conditions of democratic reconstruction."

25. Gellner, Ernest. 1994a. *The Conditions of Liberty: Civil Society and Its Rivals.* London: Hamish Hamilton. 1992. *Postmodernism, Reason and Religion.* London, New York: Routledge, p. 5. There have been strong critiques of Gellner's view on the incompatibility of Islam and secularism, nationalism and the nation-state. See especially Eickelman. 1998. "From Here to Modernity: Ernest Gellner on Nationalism and Islamic Fundamentalism" in Hall, J. A. (ed.) *The State of the Nation.* Cambridge: Cambridge University Press; Zubaida, Sami. 1995. "Is There a Muslim Society? Ernest Gellner's Sociology of Islam," *Economy and Society*, 24 (2): 151–188; Asad, Talal. 1996. "The Idea of an Anthropology of Islam" in Hall, J. A., and Jarvie, I. (eds.) *The Philosophy of Ernest Gellner.* Amsterdam, Atlanta: Rodopi. Asad particularly criticizes Gellner for the absence of actual people's agency and voices in his "dramaturgical" anthropology.

26. Haldun, Gülap. 2005. "Enlightenment by Fiat: Secularization and Democracy in Turkey." *Middle Eastern Studies*, 41 (3): 351–372.

27. Sachedina, Abdulaziz. 2001. *The Islamic Roots of Democratic Pluralism.* Oxford: Oxford University Press; Yavuz and Esposito (eds.) *Turkish Islam and the Secular State: The Gülen Movement.* Syracuse, NY: Syracuse University Press; Esposito, John and Voll, John. 1996. *Islam and Democracy.* Oxford: Oxford University Press.

28. Gellner 1994a; Huntington. 1996. *The Clash of Civilizations: Remaking of the World Order.* New York: Simon and Schuster; Lewis, Bernard. 2002. *What Went Wrong? Western Impact and Middle Eastern Response.* Oxford, New York: Oxford University Press.

29. Beinin, Joel, and Stock, Joe. 1997. *Political Islam: Essays from Middle East Report.* Berkeley, Los Angeles: University of California Press; Hann, Chris, and Dunn, Elisabeth. 1996. *Civil Society: Challenging Western Models.* London and New York: Routledge; Özdalga, Elisabeth, and Persson, S. 1998. *Civil Society, Democracy and the Muslim World.* Istanbul: Turk Tarih Vakfi Yayinları. These studies challenge the heavy historical baggage that the Western models of civil society have carried and imposed on the non-Western variants.

30. For a particular understanding of civil society juxtaposed *against* the authoritarian states of Eastern Europe, see Keane, John. 1988. *Civil Society and the State: New European Perspectives.* London: Verso.

31. Chazan, Naomi. 1994. "Engaging the State: Associational Life in Suburban Sahara" in Migdal, Shuh, and Kohli (eds.) *State Power and Social Forces.* Cambridge: Cambridge University Press, pp. 256. For a similar defense of a rigorous definition of civil society that is not a blank where anything goes, see Hall, John. 1995. *Civil Society. Theory, History and Comparison.* London: Polity Press.

32. Gellner 1994a: 29.

33. For exceptions, see Zubaida, Sami. 1993. *Islam, the People and the State.* London: I. B. Tauris; Arjomand 1988; Toprak 1995.

34. Western scholarship has brought back the state into society-centered approaches. See, for example, Evans, Peter, Rueschemeyer, Dietrich, and Skocpol, Theda. 1985. *Bringing the State Back In.* Cambridge, New York: Cambridge Uni-

versity Press. For her critique of the society-centered neo-Marxist approaches, which fail to theorize and incorporate states as autonomous entities, see Skocpol, Theda. 1979. "Introduction" to her *States and Social Revolutions: A Comparative Analysis of France, Russia, and China*. Cambridge, New York: Cambridge University Press. In contrast, states and state transformation in the Middle East has remained as an understudied subject matter in contemporary discussions on Islam, civil society and even democracy. This is mainly because these states and political institutions have been regarded as either too authoritarian and illiberal or too weak and incompetent to be considered as a key to the development of civil society and democratization. For exceptions see, Arjomand, Said. 2000. "Civil Society and the Rule of Law in the Constitutional Politics of Iran under Khatami," *Social Research*, 67 (2): 283–301; Anderson, Lisa. 1986. *States and Social Transformations in Tunisia and Libya 1830 to 1980*. Princeton, NJ: Princeton University Press.

35. The voluntarism and activism around project-based activities is far from being unique to social actors in Turkey. According to Walzer, "civil society is the *project of projects*; it requires many *organizing strategies* and new forms of state action." Walzer, Michael. 1995. *Toward a Global Civil Society*. Oxford and New York: Berghahn Books, p. 27. He refers to civil society as the "setting of settings" as it brings all small-scale projects together.

36. Tepe 2005: 75.

37. Chaichian, Mohammed. 2003. "Structural impediments of the Civil Society Project in Iran: National and Global Dimensions," *International Journal of Comparative Sociology* 44 (1): 19–50; Boroumand, Ladan and Boroumand, Roya. 2000. "Illusion and Reality of Civil Society in Iran: An Ideological Debate," *Social Research* 67 (2): 303–344.

38. See Gellner, Ernest. 1981. *Muslim Society*. Cambridge: Cambridge University Press, p. 1. He regards Islam as a "blueprint of a social order" that has a claim to organize every sphere of life.

39. Saktanber 2002: 234.

40. Hefner, Robert. 2005. Remaking Muslim Politics: Pluralism, Contestation, Democratization. Princeton, NJ: Princeton University Press, p. 2. Hefner sees "Muslim interest in democracy and pluralism" as a strong indicator of "the creation of a civil society with genuine pluralism and freedoms." While "genuine interest" in pluralism is clearly a positive attitude, it is far from clear whether this yearning is a sufficient force to strengthen civil societies and democracies in most Middle Eastern countries. The conception of the term as a project runs the risk of conflating prescriptive hopes and descriptive accounts of civil society.

41. Saktanber 2002: 238.

42. For an opposite view, see Yavuz's reading of the Gülen movement. Yavuz 2003a: 204. Fethullah Gülen's "distinct conception of Islam vis-à-vis other Islamic groups promotes pluralism in Turkey."

43. Heffner 2005: 9. He argues that "forging pacts and alliances with influential actors and agencies in the state" is of a great importance for "pluralist participation" in Muslim politics. Still, the question remains whether Islamic networks become pluralistic as part of their deliberate commitment to the civil society project or through their "pacts and alliances" with other actors and the state.

44. Chazan, for example, argues that civil society shapes the state through its interactions with it. Chazan 1994: 255–289.

45. Bakhash, Shaul. 2003. "Iran's Remarkable Election," in Diamond, Larry (et al.) *Islam and Democracy in the Middle East.* Baltimore: Johns Hopkins University Press. Bakhash correctly argues that Khatami's efforts to create a vital public debate and civil society could not lead to institutional reform and transformation. In the absence of linkages between the state and social actors in Iran, Khatami's civil society project and reform agendas came to an end.

46. See, for example, Hattox, Ralph S. 2002 [1985]. *Coffee and Coffeehouses: The Origins of a Social Beverage in the Medieval Near East.* Seattle and London: University of Washington Press; Göle, Nilüfer. 2000a. *Islamin Kamusal Yüzleri.* Istanbul: Metis Yayınları.

47. See especially Casanova, Jose. 2001. "Civil Society and Religion: Retrospective Reflections on Catholicism and Prospective Reflections on Islam," *Social Research,* 68 (4): 1041–1081. Casanova uses civil society as interchangeable with the public sphere in his comparative work on de-privatization or "going public" of Islam and Christianity. For a more detailed analysis of public religions, see Casanova. 1994. *Public Religions in the Modern World.* Chicago and London: University of Chicago Press.

48. Recently, the literature on Islam and the public sphere has flourished. See, for example, Öncü, Ayşe. 1995. "Packaging Islam: Cultural Politics on the Landscape of Commercial Television," *Public Culture* 8 (1): 51–71; Göle, Nilüfer. 2000b. "Snapshots in Islamic Modernities," *Deadalus,* 129 (1), pp. 91–119; Navaro-Yashin 2002.

49. Mardin 1989: 229. Mardin observed that the Islamic Nur movement was expanding the private sphere under rigid privatization of religion in the Republic.

50. For discussion on public Islam elsewhere, see Eickelman, Dale. 2005. "New Media in the Arab Middle East and the Emergence of Open Societies" in Hefner (ed.) *Remaking Muslim Politics: Pluralism, Contestation, Democratization.* Princeton, NJ: Princeton University Press; Hoexter, Miriam, Eisenstadt, Shmuel, N., Nehemia, Levtzion (eds.) *The Public Sphere in Muslim Societies.* Albany: State University of New York Press.

51. Tepe 2005: 70. Tepe finds that the AKP's reform activities are undertaken at the cost of "undermining its own commitment to *intraparty* democracy" (italics added).

52. For an exception, see White 2002. The leading theorists of public religions acknowledges this problem: "What we need are better theories of intermeshing of public and private spheres" (Casanova 1994: 7).

53. Özyürek, Esra. 2004. "Miniaturizing Atatürk: Privatization of State Imagery and Ideology in Turkey," *American Ethnologist,* 31 (3); Altınay, Ayşe Gül. 2004. *The Myth of a Military Nation.* Basingstoke, UK: Palgrave Macmillan; Özdalga, Elisabeth. 1998. *The Veiling Issue, Official Secularism and Popular Islam in Modern Turkey.* Richmond, UK: Curzon Press.

54. Emirbayer, Mustafa and Sheller, Mimi. "Publics in History." *Theory and Society* 27 (6): 727–779.

55. See, for example, 1994. "A Time and Place for the Non-state: Social Change in the Ottoman Empire during the 'Long Nineteenth Century'" in

Migdal, Joel et al. (eds.) *State Power and Social Forces.* Cambridge: Cambridge University Press; Arjomand, Said. 1999. "The Law, Agency, and Policy in Medieval Islamic Society: Development of the Institutions of Learning from the Tenth to Fifteenth Century," *Comparative Studies in Society and History,* 41 (2): 263–293; Hefner, Robert. 1998. "A Muslim Civil Society? Reflections on the Conditions of Possibility" in Hefner (ed.) *Democratic Civility: History and Cross-Cultural Possibility of a Modern Political Idea.* New Brunswick, NJ: Trescoton Publishers, pp. 285–323.

56. Eisenstadt, Shmuel N. 2002. "Concluding Remarks. Public Sphere, Civil Society and Political Dynamics in Islamic Societies" in Hoexter, Miriam, Eisenstadt, Shmuel N., Nehemia, Levtzion (eds.) *The Public Sphere in Muslim Societies.* Albany: State University of New York Press. An important question in this regard is whether or not social actors have been sheltered by a stable legal-rational bureaucracy and a lasting tradition of rule of law, something akin to its early burgeoning in the late Ottoman Empire. See Toprak 1995: 89.

57. Wood, Richard L. 2002. *Faith in Action: Religion, Race and Democratic Organizing in America.* Chicago: University of Chicago Press. Wood discusses local networks and participation in religious associations in the United States. See also Singerman, Diane. 2005. "Rewriting Divorce in Egypt: Reclaiming Islam, Legal Activism, and Coalition Politics" in Hefner, Robert (ed.) *Remaking Muslim Politics.* Princeton, NJ: Princeton University Press.

58. See especially White, Jenny. 1996. "Civic Culture and Islam in Urban Turkey" in Hann, Chris and Dunn, Elisabeth (eds.) *Civil Society: Challenging Western Models.* London and New York: Routledge; White (2002) makes a strong argument that Islamist mobilization has acquired its major strength from local sources of participation and the vernacular dynamics of Islamic action.

59. Putnam, Robert. 1994. *Making Democracy Work: Civic Traditions in Modern Italy.* Princeton, NJ: Princeton University Press. He argues that social capital makes democracy work, while its decline undermines it.

60. Tocqueville. 2000 [1835–40]. *Democracy in America.* Chicago: University of Chicago Press, p. 489.

61. Ibid.

62. For an excellent critique, see Berman, Sherry. 2001. "Civil Society and Political Institutionalization" in Edwards, Bob, Foley, Michael W., and Diani, Mario. 2001. *Beyond Tocqueville. Civil Society and the Social Capital Debate in Comparative Perspective.* Hanover, NH: University Press of New England; Jamal, Amaney and Heydeman; Steven. 2004. "Social Capital: Rise and Decline in the Immediate Post 9/11 Environment." Paper for SSRC Project.

63. For a critical review of the debate, Edwards, Bob, Foley, Michael W., Mario, Diani. 2001. *Beyond Tocqueville. Civil Society and the Social Capital Debate in Comparative Perspective.* Hanover, NH: University Press of New England.

64. See, for example, Singerman, Diane. 1995. *Avenues of Participation: Family Politics and Networks in Urban Quarters of Cairo.* Princeton, NJ: Princeton University Press. Singerman successfully demonstrates the daily patterns in which the ordinary people in Egypt participate socially and politically. However, it is not clear how effectively the informal networks negotiate with the persistently authoritarian state.

65. Eickelman, Dale. 1995. "Foreword," in Norton, R. A. (ed.) *Civil Society in the Middle East.* Leiden: E. J. Brill, p. xi. Eickelman argues that "civil society can

exist without formal political organizations because pervasive informal organizational structures often serve as the framework for effective political, social and economic action." See also Eickelman, Dale, and Piscatori, James. 1996. *Muslim Politics*. Princeton, NJ: Princeton University Press.

66. The independence from the state has been a central issue for the development of civil society across the world. For similar discussions, see Holmquist, Frank. 1980. "Defending Peasant Political Space in Independent Africa," *Canadian Journal of African Studies*, 14 (1): 157–167.

67. Can, Eyüp. 1996. *Fethullah Gülen Hocaefendi ile Ufuk Turu* (A Tour with Fethullah Gülen Hocaefendi to the Horizon). Istanbul: A. D. Yayıncılık, p. 135.

68. Ibid., pp. 27–30.

69. Rubin, Barry. 2003. *Revolutionaries and Reformers. Contemporary Islamic Movements in the Middle East*. Albany: State University of New York Press, p. vii. See also Roy, Oliver. 1994. *The Failure of Political Islam*. Cambridge, MA: Harvard University Press; Sivan, Emanuel. 2003. "Why Radical Muslims Are Not Taking Over Governments" in Rubin, Barry (ed.) *Revolutionaries and Reformers. Contemporary Islamic Movements in the Middle East*. Albany: State University of New York Press.

70. Skocpol, Theda. 1999. "Between State and Society: Roots of American Civic Engagement. How America Became Civic," in Skocpol, and Fiorina, Morris P. (eds.) *Civic Engagement in American Democracy*. New York: Russell Sage Foundation, p. 33.

71. For exceptions, see Migdal, Joel. 1988. *Strong Societies, Weak States: State-Society Relations and State Capabilities in the Third World*. Princeton, NJ: Princeton University Press; Vitalis. 1994. "Business, Conflict, Collaboration and Privilege in Interwar Egypt," in Migdal, Joel, Kohli, Atul, and Shuh, Vivienne (eds.) *State Power and Social Forces*. Cambridge: Cambridge University Press; Abrahamian, Ervand. 1988. "Structural Causes of the Iranian Revolution," in Goldstone (ed.) *Revolutions: Theoretical, Comparative and Historical Studies*. New York: Harcourt; Arjomand 1988: 14–18.

72. For a well-substantiated critique of the same trend in the literature, see Ismail 2003: 13–15.

73. Migdal, Joel, Kohli, Atul, and Shuh, Vivienne (eds.) 1994. *State Power and Social Forces*. Cambridge: Cambridge University Press.

74. For examples of recent ethnographies, see Altınay 2004; Özyurek 2004.

75. Lindholm, Charles. 1996. *The History of the Islamic Middle East*. London: Blackwell, p. 267. Reflecting on the history of the Islamic Middle East, Lindholm correctly argues: "Without a legitimate state sphere . . . Middle Eastern traditions of democracy, equality and participation in the rivalries of the local polity trained men to value their freedom from domination, but did not lead to any wider sense of citizenship or community beyond the local necessities. . . . We should be careful not to romanticize democratic and egalitarian local structures in themselves; when individuals lack . . . a legitimized *governmental framework* . . . local independence may easily coincide with national repression, and democratic communities may produce aspiring dictators rather than participatory citizens."

76. Turam, Berna. 2004a. "The Politics of Engagement between Islam and the State: Ambivalences of Civil Society," *British Journal of Sociology*, vol. 55 (2).

77. Turam, Berna. 2006. "What Has the Secular State to Do with Islamic

Revival?" in Rabo, Annika, Utas, Bo (eds.) *The Role of the State in West Asia*. Swedish Research Institute.

78. Hall 1995.

79. See Hall, John A. 2002. "Disagreement about Difference" in Malesevic, Simisa, and Haugaard, Mark (eds.) *Making Sense of Collectivity, Ethnicity, Nationalism and Globalization*. London: Pluto Press; 1998b. "The Genealogies of Civility" in Hefner, R. W. (ed.) *Democratic Civility: The History and Cross-Cultural Possibility of a Modern Political Ideal*. New Brunswick, NJ and London: Transaction Publishers; Hall, J. A. 2000. "Reflections on the Making of Civility in Society" in Trentman, F. (ed.) *Paradoxes of Civil Society*. New York: Berghahn Books.

80. In the late eighteenth century and the nineteenth century, *civil society* was originally used to refer to "limited government" under "rule of law" with an emphasis on individual freedom; see, for example, Montesquieu. 1909 [1748]. *The Spirit of Laws*. London: George Bell and Sons; and Tocqueville 2000 [1835–40]).

81. See especially, Kazemi, Farhad. 1995. "Civil Society and Iranian Politics" in Norton A. R. (ed) *Civil Society in the Middle East*. Leiden: E. J Brill, pp. 119–153.

82. Mann, Michael. 1993. *Social Source of Power*, vol. 2. Cambridge: Cambridge University Press.

83. For a similar approach, see Perez Diaz, Victor. 1993. *The Return of Civil Society*. Cambridge, MA: Harvard University Press, p .56. In its original Eurocentric sense, civil society was "civil as much as its *autonomous* agents [were] 'citizens' (as opposed to mere subjects of a despotic ruler or a ruling caste)."

84. Roy 1994; Sivan 2003.

85. Brumberg, Daniel, and Diamond, Larry. 2003. "Introduction" to Diamond et al., *Islam and Democracy in the Middle East*. Baltimore: Johns Hopkins University Press.

86. Tamir, Moustafa. 2000. "Conflict and Cooperation between the State and Religious Institutions in Contemporary Egypt," *International Journal of Middle East Studies*, 32, pp. 3–22; Zubaida, Sami. 1997. "Religion, the State and Democracy: Contrasting Conceptions of Society in Egypt" in Beinin and Stork (eds.) *Political Islam*. Berkeley, Los Angeles: University of California Press; Brumberg, Daniel. 2001. *Reinventing Khomeini*. Chicago: University of Chicago Press.

87. Angris, Michele Penner. 1999. "The Expression of Political Dissent in the Middle East: Turkish Democratization and Authoritarian Continuity in Tunisia," *Comparative Studies in Society and History* 41 (4): 730–757.

88. See, for example, Toprak, Binnaz. 2006. "Islam and Democracy in Turkey" in Çarkoğlu, Ali, and Rubin, Barry (eds.) *Religion and Politics in Turkey*. London: Routledge, p. 29.

89. Ibid., pp. 25–26.

90. See, for example, Özbudun, Ergun. 1996. "Turkey: How Far from Consolidation?," *Journal of Democracy*, 7: 131–132; Heper, Metin. 1997. "Islam and Democracy in Turkey: Toward Reconciliation?," *Middle East Journal*, 51 (1).

91. See especially Koğacıoğlu, Dicle. 2004. "Progress, Unity, and Democracy: Dissolving Political Parties in Turkey," *Law & Society Review*, 38 (3), 433–462.

92. In an attempt to differentiate civil society from political society, scholars have argued that the actors of civil society are defined by their disinterest in com-

ing to power. See, for example, Schmitter, Philippe. 1997. "Civil Society East and West" in Diamond, Larry, et al. *Consolidating the Third World Democracies: Themes and Perspectives.* Baltimore: Johns Hopkins University Press, p. 240.

93. See also Ismail. 2003: 25 for a similar critique of the definition of the political field: "Complex processes involving state and non-state actors and different forms of interaction are also productive of the political."

94. Tepe (2005) argues that although the AKP's agenda was to limit the state's power, its actions may paradoxically have served the opposite purpose. See also Saktanber 2002: 238. For a long time, both Islamist and secularist groups have shared the conception of the state as an "unshakeable agent possessing repressive power." However, most of the reform bills that the AKP has passed have aimed to specifically curb the intolerant and authoritarian tendencies of the state, such as the domination of the military in politics. Whether they may succeed or not, the institutional reforms aim exactly at shaking this repressive power of the state. This would create a "stronger" rather than weaker state.

95. Here, Michael Mann's (1993) separation between infrastructural and despotic powers may be useful to remember.

96. Secular liberal feminists, for example, have also negotiated successfully with the Republic. Arat, Yeşim. 2000a. "Gender and Citizenship in Turkey" in Suad, Joseph (ed.) *Gender and Citizenship in the Middle East.* Syracuse, NY: Syracuse University Press, pp 275–287; Arat, Yeşim. 2000b. "From Emancipation to Liberation: The Changing Role of Woman in Turkey's Public Realm," *Journal of International Affairs,* 54 (1). However, unlike the Islamic actors, the secular feminists shared a worldview and secular way of life that was central to the Republic. This certainly facilitated their engagements with the state and their outcomes. Clearly, Islamic female actors have not enjoyed this advantage.

97. In attempts to make sense of the recent role of Islam in the democratization process in Turkey, scholars have invented terms of *liberal Islam, Muslim democrat, conservative democrat.* See, Yavuz, Hakan. 1999a. "Towards an Islamic Liberalism: The Nurist Movement and Fethullah Gülen," *Middle East Journal,* 53 (4); White, Jenny. 2005. "The End of Islamism? Turkey's Muslimhood Model" in Hefner (ed.) *Rethinking Muslim Politics.* Princeton, NJ: Princeton University Press. These ideal types highlighted—if not exaggerated—certain characteristics of Islamic action at a certain time in history. However, these categories are less reliable to make sense of both hybrid everyday practices and broader transformations over a longer time period. In Islamic activities and identities, liberal and tolerant tendencies have often existed with conservative and restricting ones at different sites and in different moments.

98. Zubaida 2000: 63.

99. Brumberg, Daniel. 2003. "Is Iran Democratizing? A Comparativist's Perspective" in Diamond et al. *Islam and Democracy in the Middle East.* Baltimore: Johns Hopkins University Press; Hefner, Robert. 2000. *Civil Islam: Muslims and Democratization in Indonesia.* Princeton, NJ: Princeton University Press.

100. Mann 1993: 23 and 42. Mann highlights a major problem in the debate, the severe decoupling of states and societies. In his study of the rise of the West, he correctly argues that "civil societies were always entwined with the states."

101. Mardin 2006: 19.

102. I borrow the term from Goethe's famous novel *Elective Affinities*. Rather than mere emotional ties, the term refers to a subtle harmony, a mutual compatibility between two parties that facilitates the appeal and interaction between them.

103. Piscatori, James. 1986. *Islam in a World of Nation-States*. Cambridge: Cambridge University Press; Heffner, Robert, and Horvatich, Patricia. 1997. *Islam in an Era of Nation-States*. Honolulu: University of Hawaii Press.

104. Affinities differentiate the sites of engagement from the sites of policy-making and grassroots mobilization, where actions are often goal oriented and outcomes are calculated. Here, I follow Migdal (2001: 11) as he differentiates between macro-level policy analysis and micro-level studies of state-society interaction. Migdal argues that "domination and change were not best understood in terms of the outcomes of purposeful, goal-oriented loci with overpowering resources and ideas at hand, such as the state, as we found in prevailing theories. Perhaps we should look at *multiple* sites to understand dominations and change—and at results that did not fit any of the parties' designated policies."

105. For an enlightening discussion on the topic, see Hall, John A. 1998a. *The State of the Nation*. Cambridge: Cambridge University Press.

106. For another manifestation of the link between national sentiments and the state, see Wedeen, Lisa. 2003 "Seeing Like a Citizen, Acting Like a State: Exemplary Events in Unified Yemen," *Comparative Studies in Society and History*, 45 (4): 682. Wedeen's brilliant work reveals how "experiences of national belonging may actually be shared in the breach of state authority—in the moments when large numbers of people . . . long for its protection."

107. Here, it is useful to make a distinction between ethnically motivated Islamic actors, which are the subject of this study, and the Islamists, for whom ethnicity and nationalism is of a lesser importance. See especially, Avcı, Gamze. 2006. "Religion, Transnationalism, and Turks in Europe?" in Çarkoğlu, Ali, and Rubin, Barry (eds.) *Religion and Politics in Turkey*. New York and London: Routledge, p. 67. Her analysis shows that while the Diyanet İşleri Müdürlüğü (Directory of Religious Affairs) has followed a more ethnically motivated Islam outside the borders of Turkey, Milli Görüş (National View) was organized and mobilized primarily by an Islam-based agenda in Europe.

108. Mandaville, Peter. 2005. "Sufis and Salavis: The Political Discourse of Transnational" in Hefner, Robert (ed.) *Remaking Muslim Politics*. Princeton, NJ: Princeton University Press; Voll, John O. 2003. "Fethullah Gülen: Transcending Modernity in the New Islamic Discourse" in Yavuz and Esposito (eds.) *Turkish Islam and the Secular State*. Syracuse, NY: Syracuse University Press, pp. 238–251; Balcı 2003: 11.

109. Here, I am using Brubaker's concept of "nationness," which redefines the "nation" as a contingent event constantly "happening." Brubaker, Rogers. 2004. *Ethnicity without Groups*. Cambridge, MA: Harvard University Press, p. 21. The term is helpful in analyzing nationness as an everyday life practice, both in cultural and political forms.

110. Turam, Berna. 2004b. "A Bargain between the Secular State and Turkish Islam: Politics of Ethnicity in Kazakhstan," *Nations and Nationalism*, 10 (3).

Chapter 2: The State and Islam

1. For an enlightening discussion on the issue, see Gülalp, Haldun. 2003. "Whatever Happened to Secularization? Multiple Islams in Turkey," *South Atlantic Quarterly*, 102 (2/3): 382.

2. Gellner 1994a: 29.

3. Migdal, Joel. 2004. *Boundaries and Belonging*. Cambridge: Cambridge University Press, pp. 5–6.

4. For a broader historical analysis of the conditions that facilitated the interpenetration of Islam and secularism starting from the late Ottoman period, see Mardin 2006: 7–17.

5. Casanova 1994: 7. "In particular we need to rethink the issue of the changing boundaries between differentiated spheres and the possible structural roles religion may have within those differentiated spheres as well as the role it may have in challenging the boundaries themselves. . . . At least since the emergence of the modern state, the public character of any religion is primarily determined by the particular structural location of that religion between state and society."

6. Migdal 2001: 11.

7. Berkes, Niyazi. 1999 [1964]. *Development in Secularism in Turkey*. London, New York: Routledge, p. 16.

8. Mardin 1989: 30; see also Berkes 1999: 133.

9. Mardin (1989: 18–19) states that "Islam first coalesced into a religious community. . . . [The] Kuran defined with some detail how the religious community was to operate, although it was not so precise concerning the structure of the state."

10. Toprak 1995: 89.

11. The *Tanzimat* Charter (Gülhane Hatt-ı Hümayun) put a limit on arbitrary executive powers of the *padisah* (the sultan). Although the charter did not introduce a concept of popular representation, it established the idea of the inviolability of life, property and honor as legal fundamentals.

12. Berkes 1999: 145–147, 155.

13. Berkes 1999: 169–188. Although religious and secular law coexisted in the Empire, this period witnessed the first attempts to establish public law distinct from *şeriat* (Islamic law) as well as secular education separate from religious education.

14. Berkes 1999: 218. Anti-Westernism of anti-reformist forces reached its climax after the fall of the Tanzimat in 1871 and failed attempts of the first Parliament and Constitution in 1876.

15. Mardin, Şerif. 1983. "Religion and Politics in Modern Turkey" in Piscatori, James (ed.) *Islam in the Political Process*. Cambridge: Cambridge University Press, p. 143. According to the Young Ottomans, Islam was "a principle of cohesion for the Ottoman, and the Tanzimat statesmen had undermined this element by their secularizing reforms in the judiciary"; see also Berkes 1999: 214.

16. Berkes 1999: 250

17. Berkes 1999: 326.

18. Atabaki, Touraj, and Zurcher, Eric. 2004. "Introduction," in Atabaki and Zurcher (eds.) *Men of Order: Authoritarian Modernization under Atatürk and Reza Shah*. London: I. B. Tauris, p. 10.

19. Kasaba. Forthcoming.

20. Kasaba, Reşat. 1997. "Kemalist Certainties and Modern Ambiguities" in Bozdogan, Sibel, and Kasaba, Reşat (eds.) *Rethinking Modernity and National Identity in Turkey.* Seattle: University of Washington Press.

21. For a detailed portrayal of the Shah and his distant image from the society, see, for example, Zonis, Marvin. 1971. *The Political Elite of Iran.* Princeton, NJ: Princeton University Press.

22. Parla, Taha. 1991. *Siyasi Kültürün Resmi Kaynakları.* Istanbul: Iletisim Yayınları, pp. 65–72.

23. See Parla 1991: 51–55, for Atatürk's other speeches in 1927.

24. Parla 1991: 172. Atatürk often stated in his speeches that he saw his people as a "monolithic conscience and one heart" (speech in 1925, cited in Parla 1991: 26, 30), and that *his* people were "*with him* with all their conscience and heart" (speech in 1922, cited in Parla 1991: 25, 30).

25. Migdal 2001: 16–21.

26. For a discussion of symbolic submissive identification with the "father state," see Delaney, Carol. 1991. *The Seed and Soil: Gender and Cosmology in Turkish Village Society.* Berkeley: University of California Press.

27. Karal, Ziya. 1981. "The Principles of Kemalism" in Kazancıgil, Ali, and Özbudun, Ergun (eds.) *Atatürk, Founder of a Modern State.* Hamden, CT: Archon Books, p. 11.

28. Parla 1991: 100, 173. He did almost all the planning without much consulting with his colleagues. When he decided to declare the Republic, for example, he gave them a short notice one night before the declaration and said: "I did not even find it necessary to inform the closest allies and colleagues. I was quite confident of their reaction" Atatürk, M. K. 1927 [1962]. *Nutuk* (Speech). Istanbul: Devlet Matbaası, 495.

29. Atabaki, Touraj. 2004. "The Caliphate, the Clerics and Republicanism in Turkey and Iran: Some Comparative Remarks" in Atabaki and Zurcher (eds.) *Men of Order: Authoritarian Modernization under Atatürk and Reza Shah.* I. B. Tauris, p. 45. See also Mardin 1991b. *Türkiye'de Din ve Laiklik Makaleler 2.* Istanbul: Iletisim Yayınları, p. 142.

30. Karal 1981: 13.

31. Mardin 1983: 143; Mardin, Şerif. 2000. *Türkiye'de Din ve Siyaset Makaleler 3.* Istanbul: Iletisim Yayınları, pp. 16–17; see also Lewis, Bernard. 1975. *The Emergence of Modern Turkey.* Oxford: Oxford University Press, p. 412.

32. For a collection of Atatürk's published speeches on religion, see Aytaç, Kemal. 1986. *Din Politikası Üzerine Konusmalar.* Ankara: Ankara Üniversitesi Basımevi.

33. See Atatürk's *Nutuk* 1927 [1962]: 685.

34. See, for example, Yavuz, Hakan. 2000a. "Cleansing Islam from the Public Sphere," *Journal of International Affairs,* 54 (1).

35. Parla 1991: 110.

36. See Avcı, Gamze. 2006: 65–66. *Diyanet İşleri Bakanlığı* (Directorate of Religious Affairs) has managed religious affairs, such as administration of mosques and preachers since 1924.

37. See Hattox (2002), for an example of the resistance against the introduc-

tion of coffeehouses in the sixteenth-century Ottoman Empire as areas of potential political disorder.

38. Mardin 1989: 229.

39. Şahiner, N. 1996. *Bilinmeyen Taraflariyle Said Nursi.* Istanbul: Yeni Asya Yayınları.

40. Taussig, Michael T. 1997. *The Magic of the State.* New York: Routledge. Taussig argues that the "mystical" powers attributed to the states create "state fetishism," which enforces the perception of states as "transcendental entities." The authoritarian tendencies of the Turkish state have also been the motivation for similar approaches.

41. Migdal 2004: 19. Some state leaders, including Atatürk, have managed to convince the people that "the state and society are undistinguishable in purpose, if not in form."

42. Migdal 1988; Mann 1993.

43. Diaz 1993: 57. "The distinction between the state and civil society appears to be a logical historical precondition for analyzing the relations between them, while blurring the distinction seems to lead to analytical and normative confusion."

44. Atabaki and Zurcher 2004: 10–11.

45. Berman 2001: 39. "The more complex and diverse a society, the greater the need for strong political institutions capable of bringing together people with a variety of interests and associational affiliations, and mobilizing them in the service of societal, rather than individual goals."

46. Diamond, Larry. 2002. "Elections without Democracy. Thinking about Hybrid Regimes," *Journal of Democracy* 13 (2): 21–35.

47. There is ongoing disagreement among scholars with regard to the role of Islamic actors during the early period of multi-party politics (1946–1960). Toprak (1981) and Mardin (1989) represent Islamic actors of that era less as reactionaries and more as cultural actors who gave passive support to the Democrat Party rather than actively mobilizing political Islam. Gencel Sezgin's recent research based on several Islamic publications issued in that period challenges these views by revealing Islamic actors' political agendas and activities. Gencel Sezgin, Ipek. 2005. "When Islamists Vie for Votes," paper presented at MESA conference, Washington, D.C. She argues that "Islamic actors in these accounts were taken into consideration as political actors only when they established a political party in 1969." This view, according to her analysis, reduces Islamic political movements to the actual existence of an Islamic political party.

48. Kasaba. Forthcoming.

49. Toprak 2006: 29.

50. Mardin 2006: 16.

51. Kasaba. Forthcoming.

52. The followers of the Gülen movement refer to the leader, Fethullah Gülen, as Hocaefendi (the knowledgeable master).

53. Rosenblum, Nancy. 1998. *Membership and Morals: The Personal Uses of Pluralism in America.* Princeton, NJ: Princeton University Press, p. 73.

54. See Arat 2005: 59. Arat also noted that some women who were active in Refah came from secular backgrounds, from middle-class secular families.

55. Berman 2001: 36.

56. For discussions on the limits of social capital and "unsocial" capital, see Levi, Margaret. 1996. "Social and Unsocial Capital: A Review Essay of Robert Putnam's *Making Democracy Work*," *Politics and Society*, 24; Stolle, Dietland. 2003 "The Source of Social Capital" in Hooghe, Marc, and Stolle, Dietlind (eds.) *Generating Social Capital*. New York: Palgrave Macmillan; Jamal Amaney and Steve Heydeman. 2004.

57. Toprak, Binnaz. 1984. "Politicization of Islam in a Secular State: The National Salvation Party in Turkey" in Arjamond, S. A. (ed.) *From Nationalism to Revolutionary Islam*. Albany: State University of New York Press; 1981. *Islam and Political Development in Turkey*. Leiden: Brill.

58. For an illuminating discussion of the historical and ideational background of Milli Görüş and its links to Islamic forces, see Atacan, Fulya. 2006 "Explaining Religious Politics at the Cross Road: AKP-SP" in Çarkoğlu, Ali, and Rubin, Barry (eds.) *Religion and Politics in Turkey*. New York, London: Routledge, pp. 45–57.

59. For the radical and anti-state positioning of Refah, see, for example, Toprak 2006: 31.

60. After the demise of the DP, Demirel came to power as the Prime Minister of the successor central-right Justice Party, *Adalet Partisi* (AD). Unlike the DP leaders, he soon associated with the Kemalist establishment and Anatolian industrialists, rather than the rural poor.

61. Author's interview with Süleyman Demirel, Ankara 2003.

62. Heper and Toktas 2003.

63. Karmon, Ely. 2003. "Radical Islamist Movements in Turkey" in Rubin, Barry (ed.) *Revolutionaries and Reformers*. New York: State University of New York Press.

64. Zubaida, Sami. 1996. "Turkish Islam and National Identity," *Middle East Report*, April–June, p. 10.

65. Göle, Nilüfer. 1997. "Secularism and Islamism in Turkey: The Making of Elites and Counter-Elites" *Middle East Journal*, 51 (Winter), p. 47.

66. Yavuz 2003a: 70–75.

67. Rosenblum 1998: 7. The strengthening of associational life is generally associated with liberal democracy under certain conditions. Membership in religious associations can actually become an act of freedom when the associations restrain the government "from prohibiting one or other religion or requiring adherence to any. . . . In a liberal democratic state, neither affiliation nor non-affiliation affects our standing as citizens."

68. Tilly, Charles. 2004. "Trust and Rule," *Theory and Society* 33 (1): 1–30.

69. *Artı Haber*, 1997, no.1. Although the Gülen Community's separation became the focus of media attention for quite a long time, these fragmentations have been neither explored sufficiently nor situated analytically into the broader transformations in Turkey.

70. As the followers of the Gülen movement do highly respect the *Risales*, it may seem that the religious text (*Risales*) was a common denominator between the Nurcus of the 1950s and the followers of Gülen of the 1980s. However, the role and meaning attached to *Risales* have changed along with broader transformations in Turkey. Many benefactors, especially the entrepreneurs and businessmen that I interviewed, stated that they have not read the *Risales*. One of the lead-

ing intellectual figures in the movement, who has been close to Fethullah Gülen, stated: "Although *Risales* are magnificent, they are no longer irreplaceable. However, nobody will prevent or discourage you from reading what you prefer and choose. There is more Islamic publication now. During the 1950s, they were banned. That scarcity made *Risales* unique. Today, *Risales* are still a valuable source, but no longer the only one."

71. Although several people may have moved from previous Nur networks to Gülen associations, their ways of life and identities have changed along with the changing social and political processes in Turkey. Another follower, who pays regular visits to Fethullah Gülen told me that "Hocaefendi himself admits that the movement adapted to the new world order, which is dramatically different from Said Nursi's times."

72. Erdoğan, Latif. 1995. *Fethullah Gülen Hocaefendi: Küçük Dünyam* (Fethullah Gülen's Biography). Istanbul: Dogan Kitapcılık, p. 33.

73. This information is from my oral histories with a few followers who had been to the household where Fethullah Gülen was raised.

74. It was a privilege for Fethullah Gülen to meet with Nursi's students when they came to Erzurum to join a *sohbet* (dialogue). See Erdoğan 1995: 45.

75. Erdoğan 1995: 44. He describes his initial feelings about these Nurcus: "There was a depth in their prayer. Their *namaz* and praying seemed so different to me."

76. See especially Mardin 1989: 8–9. While Said Nursi "combated materialism because it negated Islam, he also realized that the influences of Western ways (ideas, institutions, practices) were destroying the cultural frame that Muslims used to establish a rapport with the everyday world."

77. See Özdalga, Elisabeth. 2000. "Worldly Asceticism in Islamic Casting: Fethullah Gülen's Inspired Piety and Activism," *Critique: Critical Middle Eastern Studies* 17: Fall: 83–104.

78. Author's field notes and interview with the leader, May 2005, Pennsylvania.

79. Author's field notes, May 2005. One of these houses is used as a guesthouse, where I stayed. It hosts a large number of guests from a wide-ranging political and religious spectrum from all over the world.

80. *Hürriyet*, 19 January 2005. Ahmet Özhan, a famous Turkish singer who is known for his Sufi involvement, has turned Gülen's poems into a music album, *Hüzünlü Gurbet*. All lyrics of the album belong to Fethullah Gülen and reflect feelings of homesickness.

81. From author's interview with Fethullah Gülen, Pennsylvania, May 2005.

82. Gülen, Fethullah. 1997. *Prizma*, vol. I–II. Izmir: Nil Yayıncılık, p. 282.

83. Ibid., p. 285.

84. The project of Akademi has changed from being a research center to a publication center, which works on printing books and volumes of the followers.

85. See Kasaba 1996: 16. Kasaba clearly summarized this historical legacy of the ambivalence: "So prominent and active are [the religious orders] in the peripheries of big cities that some writers have discovered in them the constituents of civil elements of a genuine civil society in Turkey. To the extent to which they are voluntary, perform civic functions and serve as means of political participation,

religious orders can be seen as constituents of civil society. It is obviously the case that, over their long history before and during the single party era, some of these orders have evolved and developed means of not only surviving under restrictive conditions but also broadening their horizons in reaching out to other groups. However, one should also point to the extent to which most of these orders exist not to encourage but to stunt the effective growth of men and women as free-thinking subjects of history."

86. Goffman, Erving. 1959. *The Presentation of the Self in Everyday Life.* Garden City, NY: Doubleday. Goffman's path-breaking work has challenged the idea of the "true self." According to him, the self is nothing more than a series of per-formances that change from context to context. A strong evidence for associating the performances and the self is that the self is performing even when nobody is observing. Hence, self-presentation must not be confused with dissimulation or hiding one's agendas.

87. Zubaida, Sami. "Public Sphere in the Middle East," paper presented at the Center for Middle Eastern Studies at Harvard University, 3 March 2005.

88. Yavuz 2000a; Eickelman, Dale. 2000. "Islam and the Languages of Moder-nity," *Deadalus* 129 (1): 119–135.

89. Here, it is useful to remember Tilly's remark. In contrast to the predomi-nant belief that forms of collective actions emerge from disorganization, chaos and uncertainty, people act collectively as a result of organizational skills and resources of mobilization. Similarly, window sites are exemplary products of neat and re-sourceful organization. See Tilly, Charles. 1978. *From Mobilization to Revolution.* New York: Random House; Hunt, Lynn. 1984. "Charles Tilly's Collective Action" in Skocpol, Theda (ed.) *Vision and Method and Historical Sociology.* New York: Cam-bridge University Press.

90. From author's field notes (2004) on the interfaith dinner organized by the movement in Cambridge, Massachusetts.

91. See Tocqueville 2000: 489.

92. See especially the collection of essays by Hefner 2005.

93. Author's interview, February 2005, Boston, Massachusetts.

94. For example, my interviews with the male followers tended to be more re-vealing and efficient when they were conducted in their households among their family members than when they were in the associations and public sites.

95. See Özyurek 2004 for the increasing use of Atatürk's symbols in the pri-vate sphere by secular actors.

96. One exception to this is the religious text readings in the United States, which, in addition to community building, seek interfaith dialogue. The women's groups in Boston were very open to women from other religious denominations.

97. Mardin 1989: 229.

98. The devout in the service prioritize *hizmet* above anything else in their lives, including family, school and work. I met followers in U.S. graduate schools, including Ivy League universities such as Harvard and MIT, who were devoting a lot of time to *hizmet*.

99. Many teachers, who were appointed to the former Soviet countries ac-

cepted the duty as a service. They reported that they worked for months without any payment. Another follower who I interviewed in Massachusetts referred to his daily religious practice, such as *namaz*, as *hizmet*. When I asked why *namaz* would be a service, he answered that in a non-Muslim context, it is very hard to follow the requirements and daily rituals of Islamic practice. "The only way to facilitate it is to encourage the practice collectively and to create a group spirit. In this sense, *namaz*, like any other practice, becomes a *hizmet* in the international realm. Besides, we also make Americans familiar with true Islam."

100. There is a gap between the original Western notion of "private" and the Muslim ways of collective life in the back stages of the movement.

101. My participation observations in various sites of dormitories and Işık Evleri revealed that close-knit interpersonal relations and a rule-observing attitude to everyday life was parallel to the discipline in the dormitories.

102. Some parents stated that "the people in charge of the dormitories are honest and virtuous Muslim people. We can leave our kids to their trust."

103. In each dormitory there are several *ablas* and *ağabeys*, who are responsible for the students and extracurricular activities. They help them with their homework. They are responsible for discipline and order in everyday life in the dormitory. The *ablas* and *ağabeys* usually are volunteer workers of the Community.

104. Perez Diaz 1993: 7.

105. See Yavuz 2003a: 181, 198–199. He uses the term "nationalist-statist" to describe Gülen's identity and his understanding of Islam.

106. Social actors contest these boundaries between states and societies through a continuum of encounters, ranging from party politics and electoral voting to symbolic politics, civic disobedience, resistance, protest and revolution. For an in-depth account, see Wedeen, Lisa. 1999. *Ambiguities of Domination: Politics, Rhetoric and Symbols in Contemporary Syria*. Chicago: University of Chicago Press.

107. See Yavuz 2003: 204.

108. For a different view, see Yavuz 2003a: 273. He argues: "Pluralism is the major characteristic of Turkish Islam. This pluralism has been the major sustainer and support base for the democratisation movement in Turkey."

109. Zubaida 2003. *Law and Power in the Islamic World*. London, New York: I. B. Taurus, p. 5.

110. al-Azm, Sadik J. 1996. "Is Islam secularizable"? *Jahrbuch fur Philosophie des Forschungsinstituts fur Philosophie*, vol.7; Eickelman 1998: 261.

111. Despite the predominance of secularization in the region, however, the boundaries between Islam and the state are not taken seriously by scholars such as Gellner. See Gellner, Ernest. 1992. *Postmodernism, Reason and Religion*. London, New York: Routledge, p. 5. Gellner argued that the increasing power of Islam in modern times is due to its uniquely secularization-resistant character. While other monotheistic religions declined under secularization, he argued, Islam has risen.

112. White 2002; Aromand 1999; Zubaida 1997. "Religion, the State and Democracy: Contrasting Conceptions of Society in Egypt" in Beinin, J., and Stork, J. (eds.) *Political Islam*. Berkeley, Los Angeles: University of California Press.

Chapter 3: Contestations over Education

1. For a theoretical discussion on civil society, dissent and consent, see Hall 1995: 26.

2. See especially Gellner, Ernest. 1995. *Nations and Nationalism.* Cambridge: Cambridge University Press.

3. High-school-level courses on religion remained as elective courses until Kenan Evren, Turkey's military commander and temporary president during the military rule of 1980–1983, turned them into a required course in 1983.

4. See especially Agai, Bekim. 2003. "The Gülen Movement's Islamic Ethic of Education" in Yavuz and Esposito (eds.) *Turkish Islam and the Secular State.* Syracuse, NY: Syracuse University Press, pp. 48–69. Agai's work shows how the centrality of education has transformed the movement, while its long-term goal is to change the society.

5. Heper 1985: 99–104.

6. See "Islamist Evangelists," *Economist,* 8–14 July 2000: 52.

7. Smith, Adam. 1986 [1776]. *Wealth of Nations.* London: Penguin Books.

8. Gülen, Fethullah. 1996a. *İnancın Gölgesinde,* vol. I. Izmir: Nil Yayınları, pp. 48–51. Fethullah Gülen (1996:49) opposes the idea of equality that communism advocates. According to Gülen, wealth cannot be taken from the rich by force. One can only gain the love and trust of property owners in order to convince them to give to the poor willingly. Equality cannot be attained by doing social injustice to those who earned their wealth by respecting the ethics of trade.

9. Keyder, Çağlar. 1997. "Whither the Project of Modernity" in Bozdogan, Sibel, and Kasaba, Reşat (eds.) *Rethinking Turkish Modernity and National Identity.* Seattle: University of Washington Press, p. 47.

10. See especially Başkan, Filiz. 2004. "The Political Economy of Islamic Finance in Turkey: The Role of Fethullah Gülen and Asya Finans" in Henry, C. M., and Wilson, R. (eds.) *The Politics of Islamic Finance.* Edinburgh: Edinburgh University Press; Yavuz, Hakan. 1999b. "Search for a New Contract: Fethullah Gülen, Virtue Party and the Kurds," *SAIS Review,* 19 (1): 6. In addition to Samanyolu television station and Burç FM radio station, the movement owns the following journals and magazines: *Zaman, Zafer, Sızıntı, Aksiyon, Ekoloji, Yeni Umut, Fountain.*

11. The movements' high schools have displayed enormous success in nationwide exams such as the university entrance exam and international mathematic competitions in Turkey. It is important to note that the schools accept successful students after filtering them by an exam. This must also have an effect on the overall success of the schools.

12. See *Hürriyet,* 8 April 1998; and *Milliyet,* 19 April 1998 for striking examples of Fethullah Gülen's declarations about the schools.

13. Some of the member organizations are the following: Atatürkçü Düşünce Derneği (Atatürkist Thought Association) Altmış Sekizliler Vakfı (Foundation of the Generation of '68), Cumhuriyet Okur Girişimi (Initiative of the Readers of the *Cumhuriyet* Newspaper), Çağdaş Eğitim Vakfı (Foundation of Modern Educa-

tion), Dayanışma Derneği (Mutual Support Association), 55 Sanat Örgütü (55 Art Associations) and Sosyal Demokrasi Vakfı (Social Democracy Foundation).

14. Cited in Kasaba, Reşat. 1997. "Kemalist Certainties and Modern Ambiguities" in Bozdogan, Sibel, and Kasaba, Reşat (eds.) *Rethinking Modernity and National Identity in Turkey*. Seattle: University of Washington Press, pp. 27–28.

15. Ibid., p. 27. Kasaba states, "Certain cultures were judged to be unsuitable to take part in progress unless they abandoned their identity. The progressive tenets of the enlightenment became an excuse for dividing people into rigid groups and categories, . . . a vehicle for describing and justifying the desired and deserved upward movement of their ethnically defined 'solid community' in history."

16. Ilhan, Atilla. 1995. "Fethullah Hoca Bizim Protestanımız," *Yeni Yüzyıl*, 26 August.

17. Gülen 1997: 283.

18. From the author's interviews in 1997–1999, Istanbul.

19. *Takiye* originally meant concealment practiced by Shiites for self-protection and to hide esoteric knowledge from the crude. In contemporary Turkey, it is used as deception and concealment of Islamic agendas from the laicist state.

20. The secularists refer to the followers of the Gülen movement as "Fethullahist." The followers find the term offensive not only because they are against dividing ideologies, but also because they think the name suggests an individual cult.

21. *Hoca Efendi'nin Okulları*. 1998. Istanbul: I.U Basım Evi. The book has is published with the contributions of the civil society organizations listed in note 13.

22. Ibid., p. 20.

23. Ibid., p. 20.

24. Ibid, pp. 20–21.

25. Ibid., p.14; see the interview conducted on 24 August 1997.

26. The purpose was to behave according to what the situation requires, having no true colors but simply adapting to the environment to avoid and manage conflict.

27. *Hoca Efendi'nin Okulları*. 1998, p. 14.

28. The show on 27 February 1998 is discussed in a book by the programmer, Cevizoğlu, H. 1999. *Nuculuk Dünü Bugünü* (Nur Movement, Yesterday, Today). Istanbul: Beyaz Yayınları. The five-hour show is known for hosting very controversial debates and also for accepting calls from the audience.

29. Ibid., pp. 112, 119, 126.

30. Ibid, pp. 113–114.

31. *Zaman*, 19 April 1998.

32. See Nazlı Ilıcak's column in *Akşam*, 27 December 1997.

33. *Zaman*, 27–28 March 1998.

34. Heper and Toktas 2003.

35. I am indebted to Charles Taylor for his questions, which made me think further about this particular event.

36. With regard to the symbolic quality of "Muslim Politics," Eickelman, Dale, and Piscatori, James. 1996. *Muslim Politics*. Princeton, NJ: Princeton University Press.

37. For a theoretical discussion on the discrepancies and overlaps between the state's image and practices, see Migdal 2001: 16–23.

38. Migdal, Joel. 1994. "The State in Society: An Approach to Struggles for Domination" in Migdal, Joel, Kohli, Atul, Shuh, Vivienne (eds.) *State Power and Social Forces*. Cambridge: Cambridge University Press, p. 12.

39. *Zaman*, 19 April 1998.

40. Ibid., p. 9.

41. For the change in Fethullah Gülen's ideas, see Gündem (2005). This change shows the extent to which Gülen is open to reconsider, revise and re-adapt his thoughts in the light of social and political change.

42. "Fethullah Gülen icin Beraat Karari" (Decision to Acquit Fethullah Gülen), *Milliyet*, 6 May 2006.

43. After working in the formation of the sociology department at Boğaziçi University in Istanbul, Mardin continued his career at American University in Washington, D.C., as the chair of Islamic studies. He currently teaches at Sabancı University in Istanbul. He wrote a masterpiece on the Nur movement, *Religion and Social Change in Turkey*, which is a sociological study that attempts to understand the movement.

44. Uluengin, Hadi. "Mardin- i Nursi," *Hürriyet*, 23 December 2004.

45. Ülsever, Cüneyt, "Muazzam bir dönüşüm yaşıyoruz farkında mısınız?" (Are you aware that we are going through an amazing transformation?), *Hürriyet*, 22 December 2004.

46. Migdal 1994: 12.

Chapter 4: The Appeal of Cooperation

1. Greenfeld, Liah. 2001. *The Spirit of Capitalism: Nationalism and Economic Growth*. Cambridge, MA, London: Harvard University Press, p. 2.

2. Although the collaboration between the state and Islam in ethnic politics is specific to the Central Asian context, the affinities between the state and Islamic Turkish actors are manifested in other international contexts, such as in North America and Europe.

3. Mardin, Şerif. 1991b. *Türkiye'de Din ve Laiklik Makaleler 2*. Istanbul: Iletisim Yayınları, pp. 16–17.

4. Landau, Jacob M. 1995. *Pan-Turkism: From Irredentism to Cooperation*. London: Indiana University Press.

5. Hann, Chris. 1997. "The Nation-State, Religion and Uncivil Society: Two Perspectives from the Periphery," *Daedalus*, 126 (2): 27–43.

6. Lewis 1968: 343.

7. Akçura, Yusuf. 1998. *Üç Tarz-ı Siyaset*. Ankara: Türk Tarih Kurumu Basım Evi, pp. 34–35.

8. Ruffin, M. Holt, and Waugh, Daniel. 1999. *Civil Society in Central Asia*. Seat-

tle: University of Washington Press; Tazmini, G. 2001. "The Islamic Revival in Central Asia: A Potent Force or Misconception?," *Central Asia Survey*, 20 (1): 63–83.

9. Ruffin, M. Holt. 1999. "Introduction" in Ruffin, Holt and and Waugh, Daniel (eds.) *Civil Society in Central Asia*. Seattle: University of Washington Press, p. 9.

10. Diamond, Larry. 2002. "Elections without Democracy. Thinking about Hybrid Regimes," *Journal of Democracy* 13 (2): 32.

11. Polonskaya, L., and Malashenko, A. 1994. *Islam in Central Asia*. Ithaca: Ithaca College Press.

12. Ruffin 1999: 13; Zhovtis, E. A. 1999. "Freedom of Association and the Question of Its Realization in Kazakhstan" in H. Ruffin (ed.) *Civil Society in Central Asia*. Seattle: University of Washington Press, pp. 57–70.

13. Brubaker, Rogers. 1996. *Nationalism Reframed: Nationhood and the National Question in the New Europe*. Cambridge: Cambridge University Press.

14. Balcı 2003: 5.

15. There are two high schools for girls, two high schools for boys and a university (coed) in Almati. The basic language of instruction is English, but the schools also teach in Turkish and Kazak and offer courses in the Russian language. The Community organizes an exam at the national level in order to recruit students. The students' success in the international competitions, referred as "Olympics," is strikingly high. Thus, the prestige of Turkish schools in Almati has increased rapidly in the last decade.

16. Ibid., p. 25. Here, note how she challenges the artificial dichotomy between individualism and the collectivist nature of nationalism.

17. Hedetoft, Ulf. 1995. *Signs of Nations: Studies in the Political Semiotic of Self and Other in Contemporary European Nationalism*. Aldershot, UK: Dartmouth, pp. 27–34.

18. Butenschon, Nils. 2000. "State, Power and Citizenship in the Middle East" in Butenschon (ed.) *Citizenship and State in the Middle East*. Syracuse, NY: Syracuse University Press, p. 20.

19. Ibid., p.20.

20. Smith, Anthony. 1999. "Ethnic Election and National Destiny: Some Religious Origins of Nationalist Ideals, Nations and Nationalism," *Nations and Nationalism* 5 (3): 336–337.

21. Smith, Anthony. 1986. *The Ethnic Origins of Nations*. Oxford, New York: Blackwell, p. 32.

22. Yack, Bernard 1999. "The Myth of the Civic Nation" in Beiner, Reinhart (ed.) *Theorizing Nationalism*. Albany: State University of New York Press, pp. 103–106.

23. Taylor, Charles. 1992. *Multi-Culturalism and the Politics of Recognition*. Princeton, NJ: Princeton University Press.

24. See Greenfeld 2001: 2.

25. Quotation in heading from author's interview with a follower, Almati, 1999. Information about KATEV from KATEV's documents: the curriculum, the list of the courses offered and the bulletins on the cultural events and handouts.

26. See Durkheim, Emile. 1961. *Moral Education*. London, New York: Free Press, p. 11.

27. Ibid., p. 5.

28. Hutchinson, John. 1994. *Modern Nationalism*. London: Fontana, p. 41.

29. Greenfeld 2001: 23.

30. See especially Özdalga, Elisabeth. 2003. "Following the Footsteps of Fethullah Gülen: Three Women Teachers Tell Their Stories" in Yavuz and Esposito (eds.) *Turkish Islam and the Secular State*. Syracuse, NY: Syracuse University Press, pp. 85–115. Özdalga's research on the women teachers shows the individual aspect of the education in movement schools by highlighting the emphasis on the formation of self-identity.

31. Quotation in heading from author's interview with a follower, Almati, 1999.

32. See Hedetoft 1995: 20.

33. Ibid., p. 25.

34. Yack 1999: 114.

35. For a broader discussion of this matter, see Turam 2004b: 357.

36. Ibid, p. 357: "The analytical dichotomies between culture/community versus politics/state inhibit our capacities to shift the exclusive focus from confrontation . . . to affinities between Islamic movements and the nation-states."

37. Hedetoft 1995: 20. For discussions of the binary structure of nationalism, see also Ibid., pp. 13–14; and Anderson, Benedict. 1983. *Imagined Communities*. London: Verso.

38. *Yeni Yüzyil*, 27 March 1998.

39. *Zaman*, 27 March 1998.

40. Hall, John A. 1998a. *The State of the Nation*. Cambridge: Cambridge University Press.

41. Brubaker 1996: 21. In his earlier work, Brubaker (1992) made the clear-cut separation between civic and ethnic forms of nationalism. However, his recent work has denounced this dichotomy by introducing new terminology, such as state-framed and counter-state nationalisms. Brubaker, Rogers. 1998. "Myths and Misconceptions in the Study of Nationalism" in Hall, J. A. (ed.) *The State of the Nation*. Cambridge: Cambridge University Press.

42. Author's interview with Fethullah Gülen in Pennsylvania, 26 May 2005.

43. Gülen, Fethullah. 1979. "*Asker Millet*" (Soldier, Nation) *Sızıntı*, no. 5.

44. Beissinger, Mark. 1998. "Nationalisms That Bark and Nationalisms That Bite: Ernest Gellner and the Substantiation of Nations on the State of the Nation" in Hall, John A. (ed.) *The State of the Nation*. Cambridge: Cambridge University Press.

45. Mardin 1991b: 142.

46. Nairn, Tom. 1997. *Faces of Nationalism*. London, New York: Verso, p. 28.

47. Ignatieff, Michael. 1994. *Blood and Belonging: Journeys into the New Nationalism*. New York: Farrar, Straus and Giroux, p. 9. While Ignatieff is right about the attachment of the cosmopolitans to their nation, his endorsement of the dichotomy of ethnic and civic nationalism is misleading. His dislike for the former (the cultural ideal of belonging) and his promotion of the latter (the political doctrine of self-determination) is problematic, as modern nationalism intermingles

cultural and political in complicated ways. Unlike the analytical categories, the everyday practices fuse the forces from below and top-down.

48. Winrow, Gareth M. 1997. "Turkey and the Newly Independent States of Central Asia and the Transcaucasus," *Middle East Review of International Affairs (MERIA)*, 1 (8).

49. Demire, Engin C., Balcı, Ayşe, Akkok, Füsun. 2000. "The Role of Turkish Schools in the Educational System and Social Transformation of Central Asian Countries: The Case of Turkmenistan and Kyrgyzstan," *Central Asian Survey*, 19 (1): 141–155.

50. See especially Jurgensmeyer, Mark. 1993. *The New Cold War: Religious Nationalism Confronts the State*. Berkeley and Los Angeles: University of California Press.

51. Başkan Gülalp, Haldun. 2006. "Introduction: Citizenship versus Nationality?" In Gülalp, Haldun (ed.) Citizenship and Ethnic Conflict: Challenging the Nation-State. London and New York: Routledge, p. 5.

52. For a similar argument, see Başkan 2005: 856. For the opposite view, see Yavuz. 2003a: 198–199. Yavuz sees the movement as "co-opted" by the state. This perspective misses the power of non-confrontation and the agency of the non-defiant Islamic actors. Contrary to the predominant view, challenging and confronting the state does not endow the Islamic actors with power and agency to bring about change.

53. Brubaker, Rogers. 2004. *Ethnicity without Groups*. Cambridge, MA: Harvard University Press.

54. See, for example, Bayar, Sezai. 2005. *Yaşadıklarım Yazmadıklarım*. Ankara: Duman Yayınları, p. 140. Note Bayar's anecdote about Kenan Evren, a military official who served as a temporary President of the country during the military regime in 1980–1983. Bayar asked him why he insisted on making religion a required course in high schools. Evren answered that as religion is extremely important, he personally worked on making the course on religion obligatory by constitution.

55. Bessinger 1998: 176.

56. Ibid., p. 177.

57. Foucault's view of the state as a "mythicized abstraction" has been most influential in anthropology. It has resulted in numerous works that focus on practices that merely reflect and reinforce rather than mold this abstraction, that is the image of the state. The predominance of the Foucault effect deflects attention away from the practices that engage the state and transform both its policies and images.

58. Brubaker 1998.

Chapter 5: Compromising Women's Agency

1. See, for example, Norris, Pippa, and Inglehart, Ronald. 2003. "Islamic Culture of Democracy: Testing the Clash of Civilization Thesis" in Inglehart, Ronald (ed.) *Human Values and Social Change*. Leiden, London: E. J. Brill, pp. 5–33. Gender

issues are argued to be the only exception to the convergence of pro-democratic values between the Muslim and Western worlds.

2. Toprak 2006: 27. She argues, "Take out the issue of gender from the Islamist project, little would remain that might be incompatible with a 'modern way of life' as opposed to an 'Islamic way of life.'"

3. Ibid. p. 27. "Women are especially in peril, under Islamic states whose instruments of repression are mostly used against women."

4. For the complexity of the link between women's mobilization and transition politics, see Waylen, Georgina. 1994. "Women and Democratization: Conceptualizing Gender Relations in Transition Politics," *World Politics*, 46.

5. See especially Waylen, Georgina. 1998. "Gender, Feminism and the State: An Overview," in Randall, Vicky and Waylen, Georgina (eds.) *Gender, Politics and the State*. London and New York: Routledge, p. 5. Marxist and radical feminists disagree with nationalist and liberal feminists on their benign view of the state with regard to gender relations. Radicals see the state as an inherently patriarchal institution, which institutionalizes male domination. For an example of this view, see Mackinnon, Catherine. 1983. "Feminism, Marxism, Method and the State: Towards a Feminist Jurisprudence," *Signs*, 8 (2): 635–658.

6. Alvarez, Sonia. 1990. *Engendering Democracy in Brazil. Women's Movements in Transition Politics*. Princeton, NJ: Princeton University Press, p. 271.

7. Safa, Helen. 1990. "Women's Social Movements in Latin America," *Gender and Society*, 4 (3).

8. Karmi, G. 1996. "Woman, Islam and Patriarchalism" in Yamani, Mai (ed.) *Feminism and Islam*. London: Ithaca Press, p. 81. As the type and intensity of male domination vary widely across the Muslim world, the "social and practical questions [need to be] understood as a specific response to the contemporary sociopolitical situation." Put differently, Karmi argues that patriarchy should not be seen as a correlation of Islam. On the contrary, it is often manifested in the broader social and political conditions. These conditions often intertwine secular and Islamic roots of patriarchal practices.

9. Tekeli, Sirin. 1998. "Türk Aydınlanması Kadınlara Nasıl Baktı?" in Arat, Necla (ed.) *Türkiye'de Aydınlanma*, Istanbul: Adam Yayınları, p. 178–179.

10. Tekeli, Sirin. 1981. "Women in Turkish Politics" in Abadan-Unat (ed.) *Women in Turkish Society*. Leiden: E. J. Brill, p. 297.

11. Cited from Abadan-Unat. 1981. *Atatürk'ün Söylev ve Demeçleri*, 21 January 1923, pp. 147–148.

12. *Atatürk'ün Söylev ve Demeçleri*. 1961: 216.

13. "Our women's movement, even what we might call today a feminist movement, goes back to 1869. . . . It is the oldest in the area. . . . Since the Ottoman Empire extended into Eastern Europe at that time, we were part of those developments—intellectual, social . . . and then of course in the *Tanzimat* Period it took off." Interview with Tekeli, cited in Fernea, W. 1998. *In Search of Islamic Feminism*. New York, London: Doubleday. See also Çakır, Serpil. 1994. *Osmanlı'da Kadın Hareketi*. Istanbul: Metis Yayınları; Berktay, Fatmagül. 2001. "Osmanlı'dan Cumhuriyete Feminizm" in Mehmet, O. Alkan (ed.) *Tanzimat ve Meşrutiyetin Birikimi: Modern Türkiye'de Siyasi Düşünce*, vol. 1. Istanbul: Iletisim Yayınları.

14. Peirce, Leslie. 1993. *The Imperial Harem: Women and Sovereignty in the Ottoman Harem*. New York, Oxford: Oxford University Press, p. vii. Peirce continues, arguing that women in the Imperial harem used to hold power "in creating and manipulating the domestic political factions, in negotiating with foreign powers, and in acting as regents for their sons. Furthermore, they played a central role . . . in public rituals of imperial legitimization and royal patronage of monumental building and artistic production."

15. Arat, Yeşim. 2000a. "Gender and Citizenship in Turkey," in Suad, Joseph (ed.) *Gender and Citizenship in Middle East*. Syracuse, NY: Syracuse University Press, pp. 275–287.

16. Abadan-Unat, Nermin. 1981. *Women in Turkish Society*. Leiden: E. J. Brill, p. 19; Tekeli 1981: 299.

17. Kandiyoti, Deniz. 1991. *Women, Islam and the State*. London: Macmillan.

18. Moghadam, Valentine. 1993. *Modernizing Women in Gender and Society in the Middle East*. Boulder, CO: Lynne Rienne Publishers, p. 81.

19. Arat, Yeşim 1998. "Türkiye'de Modernleşme Projesi ve Kadınlar" in Bozdogan, Sibel and Kasaba, Reşat (eds.) *Türk Modernleşmesi ve Milli Kimlik*. Istanbul: Türk Tarih Vakfı, p. 87.

20. Kandiyoti, Deniz. 1987. "Emancipated but Unliberated? Reflections on the Turkish Case," *Feminist Studies*, 13 (2): 317–338.

21. White, Jenny. 2003. "State Feminism, Modernization and the Turkish Republican Woman," *NWSA Journal*, 15 (3): 145–160.

22. Arat, Yeşim. 1989. *The Patriarchal Paradox*. Rutherford, NJ: Fairleigh Dickinson University Press.

23. Ibid.

24. Ibid., 116–117, 119.

25. Arat, Necla. 1998. *Aydınlanmanın Kadınları*. Istanbul: Cumhuriyet Kitap Klubü.

26. Cited in Arat. 1998: 33, from Abadan-Unat. 1996. *Kum Saatini İzlerken*. Istanbul: İletisim Yayınları.

27. Arat, Necla 1998: 32.

28. Author's interview with a senior secularist feminist, 2004, Istanbul.

29. Arat, Yeşim. 2000b. "From Emancipation to Liberation: The Changing Role of Woman in Turkey's Public Realm," *Journal of International Affairs*, 54 (1).

30. Arat 2000b: 107, 122.

31. Author's interview with Islamic female actors in 2003–2004. Indeed, secular feminism has not only excluded but also confronted Islamic feminism. One of my interviewees was a female activist who had participated in the Beijing conference. As she detailed in our chat, the split between these secular and Islamic Turkish women came to the surface at the women's conference and led to the exclusion of the Islamist group.

32. A colloquial term that implies close-to-familial proximity in terms of trust and protection that men would feel for their sister.

33. A young male Ph.D. student in sociology complained about hostility, barriers of access and limited disclosure of information, especially during his fieldwork in Central Asia. He said that he could not avoid being identified as a journalist searching for "hidden agendas."

34. In the North American context, the patterns and degrees of gender segregation vary widely from extreme rigidity to absolute absence, especially among student followers.

35. For fruitful adoptions of the term *patriarchy*, see especially Walby, Sylvia. 1990. *Theorizing Patriarchy*. Oxford: Blackwell. Walby uses the term *patriarchy* as an important analytical tool to problematize the continuity of organized and structured forms of gender inequality at different levels, such as within the family, in social groups and movements, in religious associations, in voluntary organizations and in the state and other political institutions.

36. Walby 1990: 20. Note that Walby's notion of *patriarchy* rejects "both biological determinism and the notion that every individual man is in a dominant position and every woman in a subordinate one."

37. This particular assumption about femininity facilitated my own multi-sited research and access to various private (domestic) sites in similar ways.

38. For an in-depth study of women's neighborhood activities in Istanbul, activities that expand the private sphere to the streets and the neighborhood, see Mills, Amy. Forthcoming. "Gentrification and Gendering of a *Mahalle* Space in Istanbul," *Gender, Place and Culture*.

39. See Kandiyoti. 1988. "Bargaining with Patriarchy," *Gender and Society*, 2 (3): 280–281. Kandiyoti analyzes how women in "classical" patriarchies participate in the male-dominated culture and social structure that subordinates them.

40. Arat 1998: 87.

41. In this sense, Kemalist women were expected no less than the Islamic women to be homemakers. With regard to the popular image of educated and modern women as mothers and housewives, see Kandiyoti, Deniz. 1998. "Afterword" in Abu-Lughod, Lila (ed.) *Remaking Women: Feminism and Modernity in the Middle East*. Princeton, NJ: Princeton University Press.

42. The gender gap index by the World Economic Forum (2005) listed Turkey as the country that has the second-largest gender inequality after Egypt. While the data and methods of the index can be criticized, the results reveal a remarkable gap between the widely shared perception of gender equality and the actual situation in Turkey. Turkish women's self-perception of their situation as better than the rest of the Muslim world and their comparison of themselves with the West can be explained by the generalization of elite women's status to the female population at large. For the gender gap index, see http://news.bbc.co.uk/1/shared/bsp/hi/pdfs/16_05_05_gender_gap.pdf.

43. See Gülen 1996b: 125, author's translation.

44. Gülen, Fethullah. 1997. *Prizma*, vols. I–II. Izmir: Nil Yayıncılık, p. 25.

45. Ibid., p.26.

46. Gülen 1996b: 124.

47. For a clear analysis of the change in Fethullah Gülen's ideas, see Gündem, Mehmet. 2005. *Fethullah Gülen ile 11 Gün* (Fifteen Days with Fethullah Gülen). Istanbul: Alfa Yayınları.

48. Arat 2000a: 285.

49. Cited in Kuru. Forthcoming. The Council of State's ruling on 13 December 1984; no. 1984/1574.

50. For a different view on veiling in Turkey, see Kalaycıoğlu, Ersin. 2006.

"The Mystery of the Turban: Participation of Revolt?" in Çarkoğlu, Ali, and Rubin, Barry (eds.) *Religion and Politics in Turkey.* New York and London: Routledge, p. 104. Kalaycıoğlu notes that "not all turban wearing women in Turkey share . . . the political message. . . . At the same time, those women who are trying hard to distance themselves from their peasant roots and transform themselves into urban women seem also to don the turban."

51. Karmi 1996: 82–83. Karmi argues that "the actual role of the Qur'an in patriarchalism is of secondary importance, for the real problem for woman is patriarchalism itself," which must be understood separate from Islamism.

52. Lazreg, Marnia. 1994. *The Eloquence of Silence: Algerian Women in Question.* New York: Routledge.

53. Göle, Nilüfer. 1996. *The Forbidden Sacred.* Ann Arbor: University of Michigan Press, p. 21.

54. Ibid., p. 2.

55. Arat 2005: 50.

56. White 2002: 213.

57. Ibid., 215, 226, 220.

58. See, for example, Moghissi, Hiadeh. 1999. *Feminism and Islamic Fundamentalism. The Limits of Postmodern Analysis.* London: Zed Books;

59. See also Çınar, Alev. 2005. *Modernity, Secularism and Islam in Turkey. Bodies, Places and Time.* Minneapolis: University of Minnesota Press, p. 54. Cinar argues that by "rescuing the female body," the males gain agency and legitimate their transformative efforts. Hence, by volunteering for gender reform, they seem to be endowed with power to "liberate" the female body, but they are empowered by taking it "under [their] protection."

60. See, for example, Fox, B. J. 1988. "Conceptualizing Patriarchy," *Canadian Review of Sociology and Anthropology,* 2., p. 165: "Discussions of power or systems of power, must involve an explanation of the source of the power. The arguments that rest on assumptions of innate male desire for power are invalid." The static definition of patriarchy essentializes women as an ultimately oppressed category. See also Arat 1989: 18. "Within this framework, the power of the subjugator is emphasized while the power of the subjugated is underplayed."

61. Arat 2000a: 285.

62. White 2002: 214.

63. For a discussion on the Merve Kavakçı Affair, see Shively, Kim. 2005. "Religious Bodies and the Secular State: The Merve Kavakçı Affair," *Journal of Middle East Women's Studies* 1 (3), pp. 20–45. Currently, Kavakçı resides in the United States.

64. Lerner, G. 1986. *The Creation of Patriarchy.* Oxford: Oxford University Press. Lerner argues that particular manifestations of patriarchy could not have developed without women's systematic consent and conformity.

65. For a similar situation, see Waylen 1994: 339. Waylen analyzes Latin American women, who felt alienated from male-dominated politics. As a result, these women's view of their own activities became apolitical.

66. Waylen 1994: 354.

67. Arat 2000a: 278.

68. Arat 2005: 9. Arat's study is an illuminating example of how Islamist

women of Refah translated their participation in the private sphere into the political realm.

69. Hall, John A. 2006. "Political Questions" in Hall, John A. and Schroeder, Ralph (eds.) *An Anatomy of Power: the Social Theory of Michael Mann*. Cambridge: Cambridge University Press, p.35.

Chapter 6: The AKP Institutionalizes the Engagement

1. Perez-Diaz 1993: 28–29.

2. For exceptions, see Hall, John. 1992. "Trust in Tocqueville," *Policy Organization and Society*, no. 5; Berman 2001.

3. For a remarkable example of how community movements lead to diffuse social and cultural change at large, see Staggenborg, Suzanne. 1995. "Can Feminist Organization Be Effective?" in Ferre, Myra M. (ed.) *Feminist Organization: Harvest of the New Women's Movement*. Philadelphia: Temple University Press.

4. Author's interviews with political leaders, Ministers and proponents and opponents of the party.

5. While the Nur movement was close to the Democrat Party (1946–1960) and the Adalet Party (1961–1981), the Gülen movement is known for its sympathies for recent center-right parties, mainly the Anavatan (Motherland, ANAP) (1983–), and, marginally, Doğru Yol (True Path, DYP) (1983–).

6. Kuru, Ahmet T. Forthcoming. "Reinterpretation of Secularism in Turkey: The Case of the Justice and Development Party" in Yavuz, Hakan (ed.) *Transformation of Turkish Politics: The Justice and Development Party*. Salt Lake City: University of Utah Press.

7. See, for example, Bulaç, Ali. 1995. "Refah'ın Önünü Kesecek misiniz?" (Are You Going to Block Refah?) *Yeni Şafak*, 12 July.

8. Author's interview with Fethullah Gülen, 26 May 2005.

9. Author's interviews, since 2002, with the followers and the leaders of the Gülen movement and interview with Fethullah Gülen in 2005.

10. See *Hürriyet* daily for Erdoğan's talk at Belfer Center on 30 January 2004.

11. Özbudun 1996: 131–132.

12. See especially O'Donnell, Guillermo and Schmitter, Philippe C. 1986. *Transitions from Authoritarian Rule: Tentative Conclusions about Uncertain Democracies*. Baltimore: Johns Hopkins University Press; Weiner, Myron and Özbudun, Ergun. 1987. *Competitive Elections in Developing Societies*. Durham, NC: Duke University Press.

13. Turam, Berna. Forthcoming. "The Power of Nonconfrontation: An Understudied Subject of Islam and Democracy" in Ibrahim, Abu-Rabi (ed.) *Challenges and Responses of Contemporary Islamic Thought: The Contributions of M. Fethullah Gülen*. Albany: SUNY Press.

14. Heper and Toktas 2003.

15. Ibid. Along these lines, Erdoğan defines himself as a democrat. See Turan, Yılmaz. 2001. *Tayyip: Kasımpaşa'dan Siyasetin Olumlu Saflarına*. Ankara: Ümit Yayınları, p.117.

16. Heper and Toktas 2003.

17. Toprak, Binnaz. 1988. "The State, Politics and Religion in Turkey" in

Heper, Metin, and Evin, Ahmet (eds.) *State, Democracy and the Military*. Berlin:, NY: Walter de Gryter, p. 136; Heper 1985.

18. See *Hürriyet*, 28 August 2001. Erdoğan argues that the verses in the Kuran and the Prophet's *hadits* are not about statemaking but are about the ruler's attitudes and actions.

19. Cited in Kuru. Forthcoming. The AKP, Parti Programı [The Party Program], 2002.

20. White 2005.

21. For a fruitful critique of the unresolved conflict between the advocates of community rights and individual liberties, see Taylor, Charles. 1989. "Cross-purposes—the Liberal-Communitarian Debate" in Rosenblum, Nancy (ed.) *Liberalism and the Moral Life*. Cambridge, MA: Harvard University Press. Taylor brilliantly argues against the dichotomy between the individual and the community, which he sees as persisting as the result of the liberals and communitarians *talking past* each other.

22. Yavuz 1999a.

23. Author's interviews, 2003, Ankara.

24. Here, I specifically refer to the cooperation in ethnic politics (discussed in chapter 4) and alliances in gender politics (discussed in chapter 5). These outcomes of the shifts in state-Islam relations would neither be foreseen nor welcome by the EU. Moreover, the EU pressure alone cannot account for the changes in the private sphere, changes such as those that surface in dinner table conversations at home, where people are hardly obliged to follow the impositions of international forces.

25. For a productive debate on the issue, see Alpay, Sahin, "AKP'nin reformcu pili bitti mi?" (Did AKP's Reform-Oriented Energy Come to an End?), *Zaman*, 29 December 2005; Alpay, Sahin, "AB Köstek mi Destek mi?" (Is EU a Support or Impediment?) *Zaman*, 3 January 2006.

26. See Toprak 2006: 33. Toprak rightly argues that the Refah's yearning for democracy was motivated mainly by its needs for religious freedom. However, she saw this as a difference between the pro-democratic AKP and the anti-democratic Refah. My analysis suggests some continuity between the Refah and AKP, as both were motivated by their keen need for religious freedom. However, the latter has had more learning experience in terms of balancing contestation and cooperation with the state. Put differently, it is more careful and successful in limiting its disagreements with the state, while working on consensus on several principles of liberal democracy.

27. For more details, see Tepe 2005: 78.

28. *New York Times*, 6 June 2004.

29. *New York Times*, 5 November 2003.

30. For detailed accounts of these shifts in the military, see Heper, Metin. 2006. "Justice and Development Party Government and the Military in Turkey" in Çarkoğlu, Ali and Rubin, Barry (eds.) *Religion and Politics in Turkey*. London and New York: Routledge.

31. Ibid., p. 75

32. See Heper 1985: 144. In addition to the discrepancy between Atatürk's vision and accomplishment during his life, there was a gap between his thought and the bureaucrats' application of it.

33. Özyürek's in-depth ethnography (2004) shows how Atatürkism has spon-

taneously become not only privatized but also commercialized, as Islam has entered the public sphere.

34. See especially Katouzian, Homa. 2004. "State and Society under Reza Shah" in Atabaki, Touraj and Zurcher, Eric (eds.) *Men of Order: Authoritarian Modernization under Atatürk and Reza Shah*. London: I. B. Tauris, p. 28. He contrasts the illegitimacy of Reza Shah of Iran with Atatürk's large social base.

35. See for example, Yavuz 2000a: 21, 24–26.

36. Hall 2002.

37. I am indebted to John A. Hall for generously sharing his insights on this issue with me.

38. See, for example, Fish, Steven M., and Brooks, Robin S. 2004. "Does Diversity Hurt Democracy?" *Journal of Democracy*, 15 January (1): 154–166. The quantitative study shows that there is no direct link between diversity and failure of democracy. However, the question of the political conditions under which diversity may or may not hurt democracy remains to be explored further.

39. See, for example, Tocqueville's (2000) example of the nineteenth-century United States.

40. Barnett, Rubin. 2004. *The Fragmentation of Afghanistan*. New Haven, CT: Yale University Press; Goodson, Larry. 2003. "Afghanistan's Long Road to Reconstruction," *Journal of Democracy*, 14 (1): 83.

41. Peake, Gordon. 2003. "From Warlords to Peacelords? (The Future of Afghanistan)," *Journal of International Affairs*, 56 (2): 181–192.

42. See for example, Atilla Ilhan's views on the Gülen movement and laicism, *Yeni Yüzyıl*, 26 August 1995; see also the perspective of Atilla Dorsay, a self-defined secularist intellectual in Turkey, *Yeni Yüzyıl,* 12 May 1998.

43. Heper 2006: 73.

44. Heper, Metin. Forthcoming. "The European Union and the Military and Democracy in Turkey," *South European Society and Politics*.

45. Toprak 2006: 41.

46. Cited in Kasaba. Forthcoming. TÜSIAD, *Türkiye ekonomisi, 2004*. Istanbul, 2005.

47. Migdal 1988: 14.

48. Çarkoğlu, Ali. "Conclusion" in Çarkoğlu, Ali and Rubin, Barry (eds.) *Religion and Politics in Turkey*. New York and London: Routledge, p. 169. "All the pillars of the Turkish Republic seemed to be under attack. . . . The nation was threatened by a conflict between Kurds and Turks, . . . conflicts between the secularists and Islamists, Alevis and Sunnis, . . . omnipresent tension in Turkish gender relations."

Conclusion

1. Diamond, Larry, and Plattner, Marc. 2001. "Introduction" in Diamond, Larry, and Plattner, Marc (eds.) *The Global Divergence of Democracies*. Baltimore: Johns Hopkins University Press, p. xvi.

2. Sen, Amartya. 2001. "Democracy as a Universal Value" in Diamond, Larry, and Plattner, Marc (eds.) *The Global Divergence of Democracies*. Baltimore: Johns Hopkins University Press.

3. Norris, Pippa, and Inglehart, Ronald. 2003. "Islamic Culture of Democracy:

Testing the Clash of Civilization Thesis" in Inglehart, Ronald (ed.) *Human Values and Social Change: Findings from the Value Surveys.* Leiden, London: E. J. Brill, pp. 5–33.

4. Ibid., p. 16.

5. Brumberg and Diamond 2003: ix.

6. Ibid, p. x.

7. Diamond Larry, Plattner Marc, Brumberg, Daniel. 2003. *Islam and Democracy in the Middle East.* Baltimore: Johns Hopkins University Press.

8. Lewis, Bernard. 1975. *The Emergence of Modern Turkey.* Oxford: Oxford University Press; Lerner, Daniel. 1964 [1958]. *The Passing of Traditional Society. Modernizing the Middle East.* New York: Free Press; Gellner 1994b. "Kemalism" in his *Encounters with Nationalism.* Oxford: Blackwell; Gellner. 1997. "The Turkish Option in Comparative Perspective" in Bozdogan, Sibel, and Kasaba, Reşat (eds.) *Rethinking Turkish Modernity and National Identity.* Seattle: University of Washington Press.

9. Note especially Heper 1985: 48 for the distinction and discrepancy between Atatürk's Republic that he accomplished "during his life" and the grand design of the state "as it was espoused by him."

10. My critical stance on the idea of "Turkish Islam" has benefited a great deal from my conversations with Elisabeth Özdalga. See especially her recent article. Özdalga. 2006. "The Hidden Arab: A Critical Reading of the Notion of 'Turkish Islam,'" *Middle Eastern Studies,* 42 (4): 547–566.

11. Yavuz 2003a: 273. Yavuz argues "Turkish Islam is a Sufi Islam with dense Sufi networks that transmit the flow of ideas, practices, and leaders, helping to link local and universal versions of Islam."

12. Aras 1998: 29.

13. Bulaç, Ali. "Niçin Orta Doğu değil de Orta Asya?" (Why Not the Middle East but Central Asia?," *Yeni Şafak,* 13 July 1995.

14. Ünal, Ali. 2002. *M. Fethullah Gülen. Bir Portre Denemesi,* Istanbul: Nil Yayınları, pp. 147–152.

15. White 2005: 87.

16. Tezcür, Murat Güneş, Bahar, Mehri, Azddarmaki, Taghi. Forthcoming. "Religious Participation among Muslims: Iranian Exceptionalism," *Critique: Critical Middle Eastern Studies.*

17. Zubaida 2000: 77.

18. Montesquieu. 1909 [1748]. *The Spirit of Laws.* London: George Bell and Sons; 1972 [1743]. *Persian Letters.* New York: Garland Publications.

19. Tamir, Moustafa. 2000. "Conflict and Cooperation between the State and Religious Institutions in Contemporary Egypt," *International Journal of Middle East Studies,* 32, pp. 3–22.

20. See Brumberg, Daniel. 2001. *Reinventing Khomeini.* Chicago: University of Chicago Press, p. 120. "When finally pressed to choose between contending visions of authority, Khomeini chose in favor of the state . . . or the system" (Ibid., p. 150). The revolutionary leader opted for order and stability provided by an Islamic state.

21. Toprak 2006: 42.

22. Turam. Forthcoming.

23. Skocpol, Theda. 1979. "Introduction" to her *States and Social Revolutions: A*

Comparative Analysis of France, Russia, and China. Cambridge, New York: Cambridge University Press. Note her famous structuralist phrase "revolutions are *not made*, they *come*." I argue that engagements *come* independent of social actors' intentions. Yet they are largely shaped by their encounters with illiberal states in the Middle East. Hence, state-Islam links must be prioritized in social research.

24. Heper. 1985: 153. Note Heper's critique that political science has also not systematically incorporated a notion of the state that is autonomous from social forces.

25. Huntington, Samuel. 1968. *Political Order in Changing Societies*. New Haven, CT: Yale University Press.

26. For an exception, see Posusney, Marsha Pripstein, and Angrist, Michele Penner. 2005. *Authoritarianism in the Middle East. Regimes and Resistance*. Boulder, London: Lynne Rienne Publishers.

27. Remmer, Karen L. 1991. "New Wine or Old Bottlenecks? The Study of Latin American Democracy," *Comparative Politics*, July.

28. See, for example, Brumberg. 2003a. "Islamists and Politics of Consensus" in Diamond et al. *Islam and Democracy in the Middle East*. Baltimore: Johns Hopkins University Press.

29. Brumberg 2001: 101.

30. Tocqueville 2000: 274.

31. Ibid, p. 282. "Despotism can do without faith," he argued, "but freedom cannot."

32. Ibid., p. 284.

33. Tocqueville. 1955. *The Old Regime and the French Revolution*, translated by Stuart Gilbert. Garden City, NY: Doubleday.

34. Heper 1985: 99, 108; Özbudun, Ergun. 1976. *Social Change and Political Participation in Turkey*. Princeton, NJ: Princeton University Press.

35. Hall 1995: 12.

36. Rosenblum 1998: 75.

37. For an analysis of the effects of the Shah's despotic rule on the political and counter-elite, see Zonis 1971: 39–45, 330–341.

38. Putnam, Robert. 2001. *Bowling Alone: The Collapse and Revival of American Community*. New York: Simon and Schuster.

39. Cook, Karen S., Hardin, Russek, Levi, Margaret. 2005. *Cooperation without Trust?* New York: Russel Sage Foundation.

40. See especially, Levi, Margaret. 1998. "The State of Trust" in Braithwaite, V., and Levi, M. (eds.) *Trust in Governance*. New York: Russell Sage Foundation, pp. 77–102.

41. Heper, Metin. 1997. "Islam and Democracy in Turkey: Toward Reconciliation?" *Middle East Journal*, 51 (1): 45.

42. Here, a clear-cut analytical differentiation between the secular state and laicist activists is imperative. Due to the strong identification of the latter with the Republic, the distinction has often been obscured.

43. Hall, John A. 2003. "Introduction: Nation-States in History" in Paul, T.V., Ikenberry, G. John, and Hall, John A. (eds.) *The Nation-State in Question*. Princeton, NJ: Princeton University Press, p. 6.

Bibliography

al-Azm, Sadik J. 1996. "Is Islam Secularizable?" in *Jahrbuch für Philosophie des Forschungsinstituts für Philosophie*, vol.7.

Abadan-Unat, Nermin. 1981. *Women in Turkish Society*. Leiden: E. J. Brill.

Abrahamian, Ervand.1988 "Structural Causes of the Iranian Revolution" in Goldstone (ed.) *Revolutions: Theoretical, Comparative and Historical Studies*. New York: Harcourt.

Abu-Rabi, Ibrahim. 2003. *Islam at the Cross-Roads: On the Life and Thoughts of Bediüzzaman Said Nursi*. New York: State University of New York.

Agai, Bekim. 2003. "The Gülen Movement's Islamic Ethic of Education" in Yavuz and Esposito (eds.) *Turkish Islam and the Secular State*. Syracuse, NY: Syracuse University Press, pp. 48–69.

Akçura, Yusuf. 1998. *Üç Tarz-ı Siyaset*. Ankara: Türk Tarih Kurumu Basım Evi.

Altınay, Ayşe Gül. 2004. *The Myth of a Military Nation*. Basingstoke, UK: Palgrave Macmillan.

Alvarez, Sonia. 1990. *Engendering Democracy in Brazil. Women's Movements in Transition Politics*. Princeton, NJ: Princeton University Press.

Anderson, Benedict. 1983. *Imagined Communities*. London: Verso.

Anderson, Lisa. 1997 "Fulfilling Prophecies; State Policy and Islamic Radicalism" in Esposito, John (ed.) *Political Islam: Revolution, Radicalism or Reform*. Boulder, Colorado: Lynne Rienne Publishers, 18–31.

———. 1986. *States and Social Transformations in Tunisia and Libya 1830 to 1980*. Princeton, NJ: Princeton University Press.

Angris, Michele Penner. 1999. "The Expression of Political Dissent in the Middle East: Turkish Democratization and Authoritarian Continuity in Tunisia," *Comparative Studies in Society and History* 41 (4): 730–757.

Aras, Bülent. 1998. "Turkish Islam's Moderate Face," *Middle East Quarterly* 5 (3): 23–29.

Arat, Necla. 1998. *Aydınlanmanın Kadınları*. Istanbul: Cumhuriyet Kitap Klubü.

Arat, Yeşim. 2005. *Rethinking Islam and Liberal Democracy*. Albany: State University of New York.

———. 2004. "Boundaries of the Nation-State and the Lure of the Islamic Community in Turkey" in Migdal, Joel. (ed.) *Boundaries and Belonging*. Cambridge: Cambridge University Press.

———. 2000a. "Gender and Citizenship in Turkey" in Suad, Joseph (ed.) *Gender and*

Citizenship in the Middle East. Syracuse, NY: Syracuse University Press, pp. 275–287.

———. 2000b. "From Emancipation to Liberation: The Changing Role of Woman in Turkey's Public Realm," *Journal of International Affairs,* 54 (1).

———. 1998. "Türkiye'de Modernleşme Projesi ve Kadınlar" in Bozdogan, Sibel, and Kasaba, Reşat (eds.) *Türk Modernleşmesi ve Milli Kimlik.* Istanbul: Türk Tarih Vakfı.

———. 1989. *The Patriarchal Paradox.* Rutherford, NJ: Fairleigh Dickinson University Press.

Arjomand, Said. 2000. "Civil Society and the Rule of Law in the Constitutional Politics of Iran under Khatami," *Social Research* 67 (2): 283–301.

———. 1999. "The Law, Agency, and Policy in Medieval Islamic Society: Development of the Institutions of Learning from the Tenth to Fifteenth Century," *Comparative Studies in Society and History,* 41 (2): 263–293.

———. 1988. The *Turban of the Crown. The Islamic Revolution of Iran.* New York: Oxford University Press.

Asad, Talal. 1996. "The Idea of an Anthropology of Islam" in Hall, J. A., and Jarvie, I. (eds.) *The Philosophy of Ernest Gellner.* Amsterdam, Atlanta: Rodopi.

Atabaki, Touraj. 2004. "The Caliphate, the Clerics and Republicanism in Turkey and Iran: Some Comparative Remarks" in Tabaki and Zurcher (eds.) *Men of Order: Authoritarian Modernization under Ataturk and Reza Shah.* London, New York: I. B. Tauris, pp. 45–65.

Atabaki, Touraj, and Zurcher, Eric. 2004. "Introduction" to Atabaki and Zurcher (eds.) *Men of Order: Authoritarian Modernization under Atatürk and Reza Shah.* London: I. B. Tauris, pp. 1–13.

Atacan, Fulya. 2006. "Explaining Religious Politics at the Cross Road: AKP-SP" in Çarkoğlu, Ali, and Rubin, Barry (eds.) *Religion and Politics in Turkey.* New York and London: Routledge, pp. 45–57.

Atatürk, M. K. 1927 [1962]. *Nutuk* (Speech). Istanbul: Devlet Matbaası.

Avcı, Gamze. 2006. "Religion, Transnationalism, and Turks in Europe?" in Çarkoğlu, Ali, and Rubin, Barry (eds.) *Religion and Politics in Turkey.* New York and London: Routledge, pp. 59–71.

Aytaç, Kemal. 1986. *Din Politikası Üzerine Konusmalar.* Ankara: Ankara Üniversitesi Basımevi.

Ayubi, Nazih. 1991. *Political Islam: Religion and Politics in the Arab World.* London, New York: Routledge.

Bakhash, Shaul. 2003. "Iran's Remarkable Election," in Diamond, Larry et al. *Islam and Democracy in the Middle East.* Baltimore: Johns Hopkins University Press.

Balcı, Bayram. 2003. "Fethullah Gülen's Missionary Schools in Central Asia and Their Role in the Spreading of Turkism and Islam," *Religion, State and Society,* 31 (2): 151–177.

Barnett, Rubin. 2004. *The Fragmentation of Afghanistan.* New Haven, CT: Yale University Press.

Barsalou, Judy. 2005. "Islamists at the Ballot Box: Findings from Egypt, Jordan, Kuwait, and Turkey," *United States Institute of Peace Special Report.*

Başkan, Filiz. 2005. "The Fethullah Gülen Community: Contribution or Barrier to the Consolidation of Democracy in Turkey?" *Middle East Studies,* 41 (6): 849–861.

———. 2004. "The Political Economy of Islamic Finance in Turkey: The Role of Fethullah Gülen and Asya Finans" in Henry, C. M., and Wilson, R. (eds.) *The Politics of Islamic Finance.* Edinburgh: Edinburgh University Press.

Bayar, Sezai. 2005. *Yaşadıklarım Yazmadıklarım.* Ankara: Duman Yayınları, p. 140.

Beinin, Joel and Stock, Joe. 1997. *Political Islam: Essays from Middle East Report.* Berkeley, Los Angeles: University of California Press.

Beissinger, Mark. 1998. "Nationalisms That Bark and Nationalisms That Bite: Ernest Gellner and the Substantiation of Nations on the State of the Nation" in Hall, John A. (ed.) *The State of the Nation.* Cambridge: Cambridge University Press.

Berkes, Niyazi. 1999 [1964]. *Development in Secularism in Turkey.* London, New York: Routledge.

Berktay, Fatmagül. 2001. "Osmanlı'dan Cumhuriyete Feminism" in Alkan, Mehmet O. (ed.) *Tanzimat ve Mesrutiyetin Birikimi: Modern Türkiye'de Siyasi Düsünce,* ed., cilt.1. Istanbul: Iletisim Yayınları.

Berman, Sherry. 2001. "Civil Society and Political Institutionalization" in Edwards, Bob, Foley, Michael W., and Diani, Mario (eds.) *Beyond Tocqueville: Civil Society and the Social Capital Debate.* Hanover, NH: University Press of New England.

Boroumand, Ladan, and Boroumand, Roya. 2000. "Illusion and Reality of Civil Society in Iran: An Ideological Debate," *Social Research* 67 (2): 303–344.

Brownlee, Jason. 2006. "Political Crisis and Restabilization: Iraq, Libya, Syria, Tunisia" in Posusney and Angrist (eds.) *Authoritarianism in the Middle East,* Boulder, London: Lynne Rienne Publishers, pp. 43–63.

Brubaker, Rogers. 2004. *Ethnicity without Groups.* Cambridge, MA: Harvard University Press.

———. 1998. "Myths and Misconceptions in the Study of Nationalism" in Hall, J. A. (ed.) *The State of the Nation.* Cambridge: Cambridge University Press.

———. 1996. *Nationalism Reframed: Nationhood and the National Question in the New Europe.* Cambridge: Cambridge University Press.

———. 1992. *Citizenship and Nationhood in France and Germany.* Cambridge, MA: Harvard University Press.

Brumberg, Daniel. 2003a. "Islamists and Politics of Consensus" in Diamond et al. *Islam and Democracy in the Middle East.* Baltimore: Johns Hopkins University Press.

———. 2003b. "Is Iran Democratizing? A Comparativist's Perspective" in Diamond et al. *Islam and Democracy in the Middle East.* Baltimore: Johns Hopkins University Press.

———. 2001. *Reinventing Khomeini.* Chicago: University of Chicago Press.

Brumberg, Daniel, and Diamond, Larry. 2003. "Introduction" to Diamond et al. *Islam and Democracy in the Middle East.* Baltimore: Johns Hopkins University Press.

Bryant, Christopher. 1992. "Civil Society and Pluralism: A Conceptual Analysis," *Sisyphus,* 1(VIII):103–119.

Butenschon, Nils. 2000. "State, Power and Citizenship in the Middle East" in Butenschon (ed.) *Citizenship and State in the Middle East*. Syracuse, NY: Syracuse University Press.

Çakır, Serpil. 1994. *Osmanlı'da Kadıin Hareketi*. Istanbul: Metis Yayınları.

Can, Eyüp. 1996. *Fethullah Gülen Hocaefendi ile Ufuk Turu* (A Tour with Fethullah Gülen Hocaefendi to the Horizon). Istanbul: A. D. Yayınları.

Çarkoğlu, Ali, and Binnaz Toprak. 1999. *Turkiye'de Din, Toplum ve Siyaset*. Istanbul: Turkish Economic and Social Studies Foundation, TESEV.

Çarkoğlu, Ali, and Rubin, Barry. 2006. *Religion and Politics in Turkey*. London and New York: Routledge.

Casanova, Jose. 2001. "Civil Society and Religion: Retrospective Reflections on Catholicism and Prospective Reflections on Islam," *Social Research* 68 (4): 1041–1081.

———. 1994. *Public Religions in the Modern World*. Chicago and London: University of Chicago Press.

Cevizoğlu, H. 1999. *Nuculuk Dünü Bugünü* (Nur Movement, Yesterday, Today). Istanbul: Beyaz Yayınları.

Chaichian, Mohammed. 2003. "Structural Impediments of the Civil Society Project in Iran: National and Global Dimensions," *International Journal of Comparative Sociology* 44 (1): 19–50.

Çınar, Alev. 2005. *Modernity, Secularism and Islam in Turkey: Bodies, Places and Time*. Minneapolis: University of Minnesota Press.

Cook, Karen S., Hardin, Russek, Levi, Margaret. 2005. *Cooperation without Trust?* New York: Russell Sage Foundation.

Delaney, Carol. 1991. *The Seed and Soil: Gender and Cosmology in Turkish Village Society*. Berkeley: University of California Press.

Demire, Engin C., Balcı, Ayşe, Akkok, Füsun. 2000. "The Role of Turkish Schools in the Educational System and Social Transformation of Central Asian Countries: The Case of Turkmenistan and Kyrgyzstan," *Central Asian Survey*, 19 (1): 141–155.

Diamond, Larry. 2002. "Elections without Democracy. Thinking about Hybrid Regimes," *Journal of Democracy* 13 (2): 21–35.

Diamond Larry, Plattner, Marc, Brumberg, Daniel. 2003. *Islam and Democracy in the Middle East*. Baltimore: Johns Hopkins University Press.

Diamond, Larry, and Plattner, Marc. 2001. "Introduction" in Diamond and Plattner (eds.) *The Global Divergence of Democracies*. Baltimore: Johns Hopkins University Press.

Durkheim, Emile. 1961. *Moral Education*. London, New York: Free Press.

Edwards Bob, Foley, Michael W., Mario, Diani. 2001. *Beyond Tocqueville. Civil Society and the Social Capital Debate in Comparative Perspective*. Hanover, NH: University Press of New England.

Eickelman, Dale. 2005. "New Media in the Arab Middle East and the Emergence of Open Societies" in Hefner (ed.) *Remaking Muslim Politics: Pluralism, Contestation Democratization*. Princeton, NJ: Princeton University Press.

———. 2000. "Islam and the Languages of Modernity," *Deadalus* 129 (1): 119–135.

———. 1998. "From Here to Modernity: Ernest Gellner on Nationalism and

Islamic Fundamentalism" in Hall, J. A. (ed.) *The State of the Nation*. Cambridge: Cambridge University Press.

———. 1995. "Forward," in Norton, R. A. (ed.) *Civil Society in the Middle East*. Leiden: E.J. Brill, pp. ix–xv.

Eickelman, Dale, and Piscatori, James. 1996. *Muslim Politics*. Princeton, NJ: Princeton University Press.

Eisenstadt, Shmuel N. 2002. "Concluding Remarks. Public Sphere, Civil Society and Political Dynamics in Islamic Societies" in Hoexter, Miriam, Eisenstadt, Shmuel N., Levtzion, Nehemia (eds.) *The Public Sphere in Muslim Societies*. Albany: State University of New York Press.

Emirbayer, Mustafa, and Sheller, Mimi. 1999. "Publics in History.," *Theory and Society* 28 (1): 145–197.

Entelis, John P. 1996. "Civil Society and Authoritarian Temptation in Algerian Politics: Islamic Democracy vs. Centralized State" in Norton, A. R. (ed.) *Civil Society in the Middle East*. London, New York, Koln: E. J Brill.

Erdoğan, Latif. 1995. *Fethullah Gülen Hocaefendi: Küçük Dünyam* (Fethullah Gülen's Biography). Istanbul: Doğan Kitapçılık.

Esposito, John, and Piscatori, James. 1991. "Democratization and Islam," *Middle East Journal*, 45 (3).

Esposito, John, and Voll, John. 1996. *Islam and Democracy*. Oxford: Oxford University Press.

Evans, Peter. 1995. *Embedded Autonomy*. Princeton, NJ: Princeton University Press.

Evans, Peter, Rueschemeyer, Dietrich, Skocpol, Theda. 1985. *Bringing the State Back In*. Cambridge, New York: Cambridge University Press.

Fernea, W. 1998. *In Search of Islamic Feminism*. New York, London: Doubleday.

Fish, Steven M., and Brooks, Robin S. 2004. "Does Diversity Hurt Democracy?," *Journal of Democracy*, 15 January (1): 154–166.

Fox, B. J. 1988. "Conceptualizing Patriarchy," *Canadian Review of Sociology and Anthropology*, vol 2.

Geertz, Clifford. 1973. *Interpretation of Cultures*. New York: Basic Books.

Gellner, Ernest. 1997. "The Turkish Option in Comparative Perspective" in Kasaba, R., and Bozdogan, S. (eds.) *Rethinking Turkish Modernity and National Identity*. Seattle: University of Washington Press.

———. 1995. *Nations and Nationalism*. Cambridge: Cambridge University Press.

———. 1994a. *The Conditions of Liberty: Civil Society and Its Rivals*. London: Hamish Hamilton.

———. 1994b. "Kemalism," in his *Encounters with Nationalism*. Oxford: Blackwell.

———. 1992. *Postmodernism, Reason and Religion*. London, New York: Routledge.

———. 1981. *Muslim Society*. Cambridge: Cambridge University Press.

Gencel Sezgin, Ipek. 2005. "Islamists during the Early Years of Multi-party Politics in Turkey," 1945–1960." Paper presented at MESA conference, Washington, D.C.

Goffman, Erving. 1959. *The Presentation of the Self in Everyday Life*. Garden City, NY: Doubleday.

Goodson, Larry. 2003. "Afghanistan's Long Road to Reconstruction," *Journal of Democracy*, 14 (1): 82–99.

Göle, Nilüfer. 2000a. *Islamin Kamusal Yüzleri*. Istanbul: Metis Yayınları.

———. 2000b. "Snapshots in Islamic Modernities," *Deadalus*, 129 (1), pp. 91–119.

———. 1997. "Secularism and Islamism in Turkey: The Making of Elites and Counter-elites," *Middle East Journal*, 51 (winter).

———. 1996a. "Authoritarian Secularism and Islamist Politics: The Case of Turkey" in Norton (ed.) *Civil Society in the Middle East*. Leiden: E. J. Brill.

———. 1996b. *The Forbidden Sacred*. Michigan: University of Michigan Press.

Greenfeld, Liah. 2001. *The Spirit of Capitalism: Nationalism and Economic Growth*. Cambridge, London: Harvard University Press.

Guha, R. and Spivak, G., (eds.) 1988. *Selected Subaltern Studies*. Oxford: Oxford University Press.

Gülalp, Haldun. 2006. "Introduction: Citizenship versus Nationality?" in Gülalp (ed.) *Citizenship and Ethnic Conflict: Challenging the Nation-State*. London and New York: Routledge, pp. 1–19.

———. 2005. "Enlightenment by Fiat: Secularization and Democracy in Turkey," *Middle Eastern Studies*, 41 (3): 351–352.

———. 2003. "Whatever Happened to Secularization? Multiple Islams in Turkey," *South Atlantic Quarterly*, 102 (2/3): 382.

———. 1997. "Political Islam in Turkey: The Rise and Fall of the Refah Party," *The Muslim World* 89 (1): 22–41.

———. 1995. "Islamist Party Poised for National Power in Turkey," *Middle East Report*, May/June–July/August, pp. 54–56.

Gülen, Fethullah. 1997. *Prizma*, vol. I–II. Izmir: Nil Yayıncılık.

———. 1996a. *Inancin Gölgesinde*, vol. I. Izmir: Nil Yayınları.

———. 1996b. *Asrın Getirdiği Tereddütler*, vol. 3. Izmir: T.O.V. Yayınları.

———. 1979. "Asker Millet," *Sızıntı*, no. 5.

Gündem, Mehmet. 2005. *Fethullah Gülen ile 11 Gün* (Fifteen Days with Fethullah Gülen). Istanbul: Alfa Yayınları.

Hall, John A. 2006. "Political Questions" in Hall, John A., and Shroeder, Ralph (eds.). *The Anatomy of Power: The Social Theory of Michael Mann*. Cambridge: Cambridge University Press.

———. 2003. "Introduction: Nation-States in History" in Paul, T. V., Ikenberry, G. John, and Hall, John A. (eds.) *The Nation-State in Question*. Princeton, NJ: Princeton University Press.

———. 2002. "Disagreement about Difference" in Malesevic, Simisa, and Haugaard, Mark (eds.) *Making Sense of Collectivity Ethnicity, Nationalism and Globalization*. London, Sterling, VA: Pluto Press.

———. 2000. "Reflections on the Making of Civility in Society" in Trentman, F. (ed.) *Paradoxes of Civil Society*. New York: Berghahn Books.

———. 1998a. *The State of the Nation*. Cambridge: Cambridge University Press.

———. 1998b. "The Genealogies of Civility" in Hefner, R.W. (ed.) *Democratic Civility: The History and Cross-Cultural Possibility of a Modern Political Ideal*. New Brunswick, NJ, London: Transaction Publishers.

———. 1995. *Civil Society. Theory, History and Comparison*. London: Polity Press.

———. 1992. "Trust in Tocqueville," *Policy Organization and Society*, no. 5.

———. 1986. *Powers and Liberties: The Causes and Consequences of the Rise of the West*. London: Penguin Books.

Hann, Chris. 1997. "The Nation-State, Religion and Uncivil Society: Two Per-spectives from the Periphery," *Daedalus*, 126 (2): 27–43.

Hann, Chris, and Dunn, Elisabeth. 1996. *Civil Society: Challenging Western Models*. London and New York: Routledge.

Hattox, Ralph S. 2002 [1985]. *Coffee and Coffeehouses: The Origins of a Social Bever-age in the Medieval Near East*. Seattle and London: University of Washington Press.

Hedetoft, Ulf. 1995. *Signs of Nations: Studies in the Political Semiotic of Self and Other in Contemporary European Nationalism*. Aldershot, Brookfield, VT: Dartmouth Publishing.

Hefner, Robert. 2005. *Remaking Muslim Politics: Pluralism, Contestation, Democrati-zation*. Princeton, NJ: Princeton University Press.

———. 2000. *Civil Islam: Muslims and Democratization in Indonesia*. Princeton, NJ: Princeton University Press.

———. 1998. "A Muslim Civil Society? Reflections on the Conditions of Possibil-ity" in Hefner, Robert (ed.) *Democratic Civility: History and Cross-Cultural Possi-bility of a Modern Political Idea*. New Brunswick, NJ: Trescoton Publishers, pp. 285–323.

Hefner, Robert, and Horvatich, Patricia. 1997. *Islam in an Era of Nation-States*. Hono-lulu: University of Hawaii Press.

Heper, Metin. Forthcoming. "The European Union and the Military and Democ-racy in Turkey," *South European Society and Politics*.

———. 2006. "Justice and Development Party Government and the Military in Turkey" in Çarkoğlu, Ali, and Rubin, Barry (eds.) *Religion and Politics in Turkey*. London and New York: Routledge.

———. 1997. "Islam and Democracy in Turkey: Toward Reconciliation?" *Middle East Journal*, 51 (1).

———. 1985. *The State Tradition in Turkey*. Beverly, UK: Eothen Press.

Heper, Metin, and Evin, Ahmet (eds.) 1988. *State, Democracy and the Military: Turkey in the 1980s*. Berlin, NY: W. de Gruyter.

Heper, Metin, and Toktas, Şule. 2003. "Islam, Modernity, and Democracy in Con-temporary Turkey: The Case of Recep Tayyip Erdoğan," *Muslim World*, 93 (2).

Hoca Efendi'nin Okulları. 1998. Istanbul: I.U Basım Evi.

Hoexter, Miriam, Eisenstadt, Shmuel N., Levtzion, Nehemia (eds.) *The Public Sphere in Muslim Societies*. Albany: State University of New York Press.

Hunt, Lynn. 1984. "Charles Tilly's Collective Action" in Skocpol, Theda (ed.) *Vision and Method and Historical Sociology*. New York: Cambridge University Press.

Huntington, Samuel P. 1996. *The Clash of Civilizations: Remaking of the World Order*. New York: Simon and Schuster.

———. 1968. *Political Order in Changing Societies*. New Haven, CT: Yale University Press.

Hutchinson, John. 1994. *Modern Nationalism*. London: Fontana.

Ignatieff, Michael. 1994. *Blood and Belonging: Journeys into the New Nationalism*. New York: Farrar, Straus and Giroux.

Ismail, Salwa. 2003. *Rethinking Islamist Politics: Culture, the State and Islamism*. Lon-don, New York: I. B. Taurus.

Jamal, Amaney, and Heydeman, Steven. 2004. "Social Capital: Rise and Decline in the Immediate Post 9/11 Environment," Paper for SSRC project.

Jurgensmeyer, Mark. 1993. *The New Cold War: Religious Nationalism Confronts the State*. Berkeley and Los Angeles: University of California Press.

Kalaycıoğlu, Ersin. 2006. "The Mystery of the *Turban*: Participation or Revolt?" in Çarkoğlu, Ali, and Rubin, Barry (eds.) *Religion and Politics in Turkey*. New York and London: Routledge, pp. 91–111.

Kandiyoti, Deniz. 1998. "Afterword," to Abu-Lughod, Lila (ed.) *Remaking Women: Feminism and Modernity in the Middle East*. Princeton, NJ: Princeton University Press.

——. 1991. *Women, Islam and the State*. London: Macmillan.

——. 1988. "Bargaining with Patriarchy," *Gender and Society*, 2 (3): 274–287.

——. 1987. "Emancipated but Unliberated? Reflections on the Turkish Case," *Feminist Studies*, 13 (2): 317–338.

Karal, Ziya. 1981. "The Principles of Kemalism" in Kazancıgil, Ali and Özbudun, Ergun (eds.) *Atatürk, Founder of a Modern State*. Hamden, CT: Archon Books, pp. 11–35.

Karmi, G. 1996. "Woman, Islam and Patriarchialism," in Yamani, Mai (ed.) *Feminism and Islam*. London: Ithaca Press.

Karmon, Ely. 2003. "Radical Islamist Movements in Turkey" in Rubin, Barry (ed.) *Revolutionaries and Reformers*. Albany: State University of New York Press.

Kasaba, Reşat. Forthcoming. "Modern Turkey" in Robinson, Francis (ed.) *The Islamic World in the Age of Western Dominance*. Cambridge: Cambridge University Press.

——. 1998. "Co-habitation of Differences," in Hefner, Robert (ed.) *Democratic Civility: The History and Cross-Cultural Possibility of a Modern Political Ideal*. New Brunswick, NJ, London: Transaction Publishers.

——. 1997. "Kemalist Certainties and Modern Ambiguities" in Bozdogan, Sibel, and Kasaba, Reşat (eds.) *Rethinking Modernity and National Identity in Turkey*. Seattle: University of Washington Press.

——. 1994. "A Time and Place for the Non-state: Social Change in the Ottoman Empire during the "Long Nineteenth Century" in Migdal, Joel et al. (ed.) *State Power and Social Forces*. Cambridge: Cambridge University Press.

Katouzian, Homa. 2004. "State and Society under Reza Shah" in Atabaki, Touraj, and Zurcher, Eric (eds.) *Men of Order: Authoritarian Modernization under Atatürk and Reza Shah*. London: I. B. Tauris.

——. 2003. "The Theory of Arbitrary Rule" in his *Iranian History and Politics*. London: Routledge Curzon.

Kazancıgil, Ali and Özbudun, Ergun. 1981. *Atatürk, the Founder of a Modern State*. Hamden, CT: Archon Books.

Kazemi, Farhad. 1995. "Civil Society and Iranian Politics" in Norton, A. R. (ed.) *Civil Society in the Middle East*. Leiden: E. J Brill, pp. 119–153.

Keane, John. 1988. *Civil Society and the State: New European Perspectives*. London: Verso.

Keyder, Çağlar. 1997. "Whither the Project of Modernity" in Bozdogan, Sibel, and Kasaba, Reşat *Rethinking Turkish Modernity and National Identity*. Seattle: University of Washington Press.

Koğacıoğlu, Dicle. 2004. "Progress, Unity, and Democracy: Dissolving Political Parties in Turkey," *Law & Society Review* 38 (3), 433–462.

Kuru, Ahmet T. Forthcoming. "Reinterpretation of Secularism in Turkey: The Case of the Justice and Development Party," in Yavuz, Hakan (ed.) *Transformation of Turkish Politics: The Justice and Development Party*. Salt Lake City: University of Utah Press.

Landau, Jacob M. 1995. *Pan-Turkism: From Irredentism to Cooperation*. London: Indiana University Press.

Lazreg, Marnia. 1994. *The Eloquence of Silence: Algerian Women in Question*. New York: Routledge.

Lerner, Daniel. 1964 [1958] *The Passing of Traditional Society. Modernizing the Middle East*. New York: Free Press.

Lerner, G. 1986. *The Creation of Patriarchy*. Oxford: Oxford University Press.

Levi, Margaret. 1998. "The State of Trust" in Braithwaite, V., and Levi, M. (eds.) *Trust in Governance*. New York: Russell Sage Foundation, pp. 77–102.

———. 1996. "Social and Unsocial Capital. A Review Essay of Robert Putnam's *Making Democracy Work*," *Politics and Society*, 24.

Lewis, Bernard. 2003. "A Historical Overview" in Diamond, Larry et al. *Islam and Democracy in the Middle East*. Baltimore: Johns Hopkins University Press.

———. 2002. *What Went Wrong? Western Impact and Middle Eastern Response*. Oxford, New York: Oxford University Press.

———. 1993. *Islam and the West*. Oxford, New York: Oxford University Press.

———. 1975 [1968]. *The Emergence of Modern Turkey*. Oxford: Oxford University Press.

Lindholm, Charles. 1996. *The History of the Islamic Middle East*. London: Blackwell.

Longhor, Vickie. 2005. "Too Much Civil Society, Too Little Politics? Egypt and Other Liberalizing Arab Regimes" in Posusney and Angrist (eds.) *Authoritarianism in the Middle East*. Boulder, London: Lynne Rienne Publishers, 193–218.

Mackinnon, Catherine. 1983. "Feminism, Marxism, Method and the State: Towards a Feminist Jurisprudence" *Signs* 8 (2):635–658.

Mandaville, Peter. 2005. "Sufis and Salavis: The Political Discourse of Transnational" in Hefner, Robert (ed.) *Remaking Muslim Politics*. Princeton, NJ: Princeton University Press.

Mann, Michael. 1993. *Social Sources of Power*, vol. 2. Cambridge: Cambridge University Press.

Mardin, Şerif. 2006. "Turkish Islamic Exceptionalism Yesterday and Today: Continuity, Rupture and Reconstruction in Operational Codes" in Çarkoğlu, Ali, and Rubin, Barry (eds.) *Religion and Politics in Turkey*. London and New York: Routledge, pp. 3–25.

———. 2000. *Türkiye'de Din ve Siyaset Makaleler 3*. Istanbul: Iletisim Yayınları.

———. 1994. "'Kontrol Felsefesi' ve Geleceğimiz," in his *Siyasal ve Sosyal Bilimler Makaleler 2*. Istanbul: Iletisim Yayınları.

———. 1991a. "The Nakshibendi Order in Turkish History" in Tapper, Richard (ed.) *Islam in Modern Turkey*. London, New York: I. B. Tauris.

———. 1991b. *Türkiye'de Din ve Laiklik Makaleler 2*. Istanbul: Iletisim Yayınları.

———. 1989. *Religion and Social Change in Modern Turkey: The Case of Bediüzzaman Said Nursi*. Albany: State University of New York.

———. 1983. "Religion and Politics in Modern Turkey," in Piscatori, James (ed.) *Islam in the Political Process*. Cambridge: Cambridge University Press.

———. 1973. "Center Periphery Relations: A Key to Turkish Politics," *Daedalus*, 102.

Migdal, Joel. 2004. *Boundaries and Belonging*. Cambridge: Cambridge University Press.

———. 2001. *The State in Society. Studying How States and Societies Transform and Constitute One Another*. Cambridge: Cambridge University Press.

———. 1997. "Finding the Meeting Ground of Fact and Fiction: Some Reflections on Turkish Modernization" in Bozdogan, Sibel, and Kasaba, Reşat (eds.) *Rethinking Turkish Modernity and National Identity*. Seattle: University of Washington Press.

———. 1994. "The State in Society: An Approach to Struggles for Domination" in Migdal, Joel, Kohli, Atul, and Shuh, Vivienne (eds.) *State Power and Social Forces*. Cambridge: Cambridge University Press.

———. 1988. *Strong Societies, Weak States: State-Society Relations and State Capabilities in the Third World*. Princeton, NJ: Princeton University Press.

Migdal, Joel, Kohli, Atul, and Shuh, Vivienne. 1994. *State Power and Social Forces*. Cambridge: Cambridge University Press.

Mills, Amy. Forthcoming. "Gentrification and Gendering of a *Mahalle* Space in Istanbul," *Gender, Place and Culture*.

Mirsepassi, Ali. 2000. *Intellectual Discourse and the Politics of Modernization*. New York, Oxford: Oxford University Press.

Moghadam, Valentine. 1993. *Modernizing Women in Gender and Society in Middle East*. Boulder, CO: Lynne Rienne Publishers.

Moghissi, Hiadeh. 1999. *Feminism and Islamic Fundamentalism. The Limits of Postmodern Analysis*. London, New York: Zed Books.

Montesquieu. 1909 [1748]. *The Spirit of Laws*. London: George Bell and Sons.

———. 1972 [1743]. *Persian Letters*. New York: Garland Publication.

Mozaffari, Mehdi. 1988. "Islam and Civil Society" in Ferdinand, Klaus, and Mozaffari, Mehdi (eds.) *Islam; State and Society*. London: Curzon Press.

Nairn, Tom. 1997. *Faces of Nationalism*. London, New York: Verso.

Navaro-Yashin, Yael. 2002. *Faces of the State: Secularism and Public Life in Turkey*. Princeton, NJ: Princeton University Press.

Norris, Pippa, and Inglehart, Ronald. 2003. "Islamic Culture of Democracy: Testing the Clash of Civilization Thesis" in Inglehart, Ronald (ed.) *Human Values and Social Change: Findings from the Value Surveys*. Leiden, London: E. J. Brill, pp. 5–33.

Norton, R.A. 1996. *Civil Society in the Middle East*. Leiden: E. J. Brill.

O'Donnell, Guillermo, and Schmitter, Philippe C. 1986. *Transitions from Authoritarian Rule: Tentative Conclusions about Uncertain Democracies*. Baltimore: Johns Hopkins University Press.

Öncü, Ayşe. 1995. "Packaging Islam: Cultural Politics on the Landscape of Commercial Television, *Public Culture* 8 (1): 51–71.

Özbudun, Ergun. 1996. "Turkey: How Far from Consolidation?," *Journal of Democracy*, 7: 131.

————. 1976. *Social Change and Political Participation in Turkey*. Princeton, NJ: Princeton University Press.

Özdalga, Elisabeth. 2006. "The Hidden Arab: The Critical Reading of the Notion of Turkish Islam," *Middle Eastern Studies*, 42 (4): 547–566.

————.2005. "Redeemer or Outsider? The Gülen Community in the Civilizing Process," *Muslim World* 95 (3): 429–446.

————. 2003a. "Secularizing Trends in Fethullah Gülen's Movement: Impasse or Opportunity for Further Renewal?" *Critique: Critical Middle Eastern Studies* 12 (1): 61–73.

————. 2003b. "Following the Footsteps of Fethullah Gülen: Three Women Teachers Tell Their Stories" in Yavuz and Esposito (eds.) *Turkish Islam and the Secular State*. Syracuse, NY: Syracuse University Press, pp. 85–115.

————. 2000. "Worldly Asceticism in Islamic Casting: Fethullah Gülen's Inspired Piety and Activism," *Critique : Critical Middle Eastern Studies*, 17, fall: 83–104.

————. 1998. *The Veiling Issue, Official Secularism and Popular Islam in Modern Turkey*. Richmond, UK: Curzon Press.

Özdalga, Elisabeth, and Persson, S. 1998. *Civil Society, Democracy and the Muslim World*. Istanbul: Türk Tarih Vakfı Yayınları.

Özyürek, Esra. 2004. "Miniaturizing Atatürk: Privatization of State Imagery and Ideology in Turkey.," *American Ethnologist*, 31 (3).

Parla, Taha. 1991. *Siyasi Kültürün Resmi Kaynakları*, vols. I and II. Istanbul: Iletisim Yayınları.

Peake, Gordon. 2003. "From Warlords to Peacelords? (The Future of Afghanistan)," *Journal of International Affairs*, 56 (2): 181–192.

Peirce, Leslie 1993. *The Imperial Harem: Women and Sovereignty in the Ottoman Harem*. New York, Oxford: Oxford University Press.

Perez-Diaz, Victor. 1993. *The Return of Civil Society*. Cambridge, MA: Harvard University Press.

Piscatori, James. 1986. *Islam in a World of Nation-States*. Cambridge: Cambridge University Press.

Polat, Abdumannob. 1999. "Can Uzbekstan Build Democracy and Civil Society?" in Ruffin, Holt, and Waugh, Daniel. (eds.) *Civil Society in Central Asia*. Seattle: University of Washington Press.

Polonskaya, L., and Malashenko, A. 1994. *Islam in Central Asia*. Ithaca: Ithaca Press.

Posusney, Marsha Pripstein. 2006. "The Middle East's Democracy Deficit in Contemporary Perspective" in Posusney, M., and Angristm, M. (eds.) *Authoritarianism in the Middle East*. Boulder, London: Lynne Rienne Publishers, pp. 1–21.

Posusney, Marsha Pripstein, and Penner, Angrist Michele. 2005. *Authoritarianism in the Middle East. Regimes and Resistance*. Boulder, London: Lynne Rienne Publishers.

Putnam, Robert. 2001. *Bowling Alone: The Collapse and Revival of American Community*. New York: Simon and Schuster.

————. 1994. *Making Democracy Work: Civic Traditions in Modern Italy*. Princeton, NJ: Princeton University Press.

Remmer, Karen L. 1991. "New Wine or Old Bottlenecks? The Study of Latin American Democracy," *Comparative Politics*, July.

Rosenblum, Nancy. 1998. *Membership and Morals. The Personal Uses of Pluralism in America*. Princeton, NJ: Princeton University Press.

Roy, Oliver. 1994. *The Failure of Political Islam*. Cambridge, MA: Harvard University Press.

Rubin, Barry. 2003. *Revolutionaries and Reformers. Contemporary Islamic Movements in the Middle East*. Albany: State University of New York Press.

Rubin, Michael. "Talking Turkey. She Is a Democracy," *National Review Online*, 6 August 2004, http://www.meforum.org/article/624/.

Ruffin, M. Holt. 1999. "Introduction" in Ruffin, Holt, and Waugh, Daniel (eds.) *Civil Society in Central Asia*. Seattle: University of Washington Press, pp. 3–27.

Ruffin, M. Holt, and Waugh, Daniel. 1999. *Civil Society in Central Asia*. Seattle: University of Washington Press.

Sachedina, Abdulaziz. 2001. *The Islamic Roots of Democratic Pluralism*. Oxford: Oxford University Press.

Safa, Helen. 1990. "Women's Social Movements in Latin America," *Gender and Society*, 4: (3).

Şahiner, N. 1996. *Bilinmeyen Taraflariyle Said Nursi*. Istanbul: Yeni Asya Yayınları.

Sakallıoğlu, Ümit-Cizre. 1996. "Parameters and Strategies of Islam-State Interaction in Republican Turkey," *International Journal of Middle East Studies*, 28: 231–251.

Saktanber, Ayşe. 2002. *Living Islam: Women, Religion and Politicization of Islam in Turkey*. London: I. B. Tauris.

Salame, Ghassan. 1994. "Introduction: Where Are the Democrats?" in Salame, Ghassan (ed.) *Democracy without Democrats: The Renewal of the Politics in the Muslim World*. London, New York: I. B. Tauris, pp. 1–23.

Schmitter, Philipp. 1997. "Civil Society East and West" in Diamond, Larry et al. *Consolidating the Third World Democracies: Themes and Perspectives*. Baltimore: Johns Hoplkins University Press.

Schwedler, Jillian. 2004. "The Islah Party in Yemen: Political Opportunities and Coalition Building in Transitional Polity" in Wiktorowicz, Quintan (ed.) *Islamic Activism: A Social Movement Theory Approach*. Bloomington: Indiana University Press.

Sen, Amartya. 2001. "Democracy as a Universal Value" in Diamond and Plattner (eds.) *The Global Divergence of Democracies*. Baltimore: Johns Hopkins University Press.

Shively, Kim. 2005. "Religious Bodies and the Secular State: The Merve Kavakçı Affair," *Journal of Middle East Women's Studies* 1 (3), pp. 20–45.

Singerman, Diane. 2005. "Rewriting Divorce in Egypt: Reclaiming Islam, Legal Activism, and Coalition Politics" in Hefner, Robert (ed.) *Remaking Muslim Politics*. Princeton, NJ: Princeton University.

———. 1995. *Avenues of Participation: Family Politics and Networks in Urban Quarters of Cairo*. Princeton, NJ: Princeton University Press.

Sivan, Emanuel. 2003. "Why Radical Muslims Are Not Taking Over Governments?" in Rubin, Barry (ed.) *Revolutionaries and Reformers. Contemporary Islamic Movements in the Middle East*. Albany: State University of New York Press.

Skocpol, Theda. 1999. "Between State and Society: Roots of American Civic Engagement. How America Became Civic" in Skocpol, Theda, and Fiorina, Morris P. (eds.) *Civic Engagement in American Democracy.* New York : Russell Sage Foundation.

———. 1996. "Unraveling from Above," *American Prospect,* 24 (March/April), pp. 20–25, cited in Hall, John A., and Trentman, Frank (eds.) 2005. *Civil Society: A Reader in History, Theory and Global Politics.* Basingstoke, UK: Palgrave Macmillan.

———. 1979. "Introduction" to her *States and Social Revolutions: A Comparative Analysis of France, Russia, and China.* Cambridge, New York: Cambridge University Press.

Smith, Adam. 1986 [1776]. *Wealth of Nations.* London: Penguin Books.

Smith, Anthony. 1999. "Ethnic Election and National Destiny: Some Religious Origins of Nationalist Ideals, Nations and Nationalism," *Nations and Nationalism* 5 (3): 331–355.

———. 1986. *The Ethnic Origins of Nations.* Oxford, New York: Blackwell.

Staggenborg, Suzanne. 1995. "Can Feminist Organization Be Effective?," in Ferre, Myra M. (ed.) *Feminist Organization: Harvest of the New Women's Movement.* Philadelphia; Temple University Press.

Stepan, Alfred. 2000. "Religion, Democracy the 'Twin Tolerations'" in *Journal of Democracy,* 11 (4): 37–58.

Stolle, Dietland. 2003 "The Source of Social Capital" in Hooghe and Stolle (eds.) *Generating Social Capital.* New York: Palgrave Macmillan.

Tamir, Moustafa. 2000. "Conflict and Cooperation between the State and Religious Institutions in Contemporary Egypt," *International Journal of Middle East Studies,* 32, p.3–22.

Taussig, Michael T. 1997. *The Magic of the State.* New York: Routledge.

Taylor, Charles. 1992. *Multi-culturalism and the Politics of Recognition.* Princeton, NJ: Princeton University Press.

———. 1989. "Cross-Purposes—the Liberal-Communitarian Debate" in Rosenblum, Nancy (ed.) *Liberalism and the Moral Life.* Cambridge, MA: Harvard University Press.

Tazmini, G. 2001. "The Islamic Revival in Central Asia: A Potent Force or Misconception?," *Central Asia Survey,* 20 (1): 63–83.

Tekeli, Sirin. 1998. "Türk Aydınlanması Kadınlara Nasıl Baktı?" (How did the Turkish Enlightenment Regard Women) in Arat, Necla (ed.) *Türkiye'de Aydınlanma.* Istanbul: Adam Yayınları.

———. 1981. "Women in Turkish Politics" in Abadan-Unat (ed.) *Women in Turkish Society.* Leiden: E. J. Brill.

Tezcür, Murat Güneş. Bahar, Mehri, Azadarmaki, Taghi. Forthcoming. "Religious Participation among Muslims: Iranian Exceptionalism," *Critique: Critical Middle Eastern Studies.*

Tepe Sultan. 2005. "Turkey's AKP: A Model 'Muslim-Democratic Party'?" *Journal of Democracy,* 16 (3): 69–82.

Tilly, Charles. 2004. "Trust and Rule," *Theory and Society* 33 (1): 1–30.

———. 1978. *From Mobilization to Revolution.* New York: Random House.

Tocqueville, Alexis. 2000 [1835–1840]. *Democracy in America.* Chicago: University of Chicago Press.

———. 1955. *The Old Regime and the French Revolution*, translated by Stuart Gilbert. Garden City, NY: Doubleday.

Toprak, Binnaz. 2006. "Islam and Democracy in Turkey" in Çarkoğlu, Ali, and Rubin, Barry (eds.) *Religion and Politics in Turkey.* London, New York: Routledge.

———. 1996. "Civil Society in Turkey." in Norton, R. A. (ed.) *Civil Society in the Middle East*. Leiden: E. J. Brill.

———. 1988. "The State, Politics and Religion in Turkey" in Heper, Metin, and Evin, Ahmet (eds.) *State, Democracy and the Military*. Berlin, NY: Walter de Gryter.

———. 1984. "Politicization of Islam in a Secular State: The National Salvation Party in Turkey" in Arjamond, S. A. (ed.) *From Nationalism to Revolutionary Islam*. Albany: State University of New York Press.

———. 1981. *Islam and Political Development in Turkey*. Leiden: Brill.

Tugal, Cihan. Forthcoming. "The Appeal of Islamic Politics: The Ritual and Dialogue in a Poor District of Turkey," *Sociological Quarterly*.

Turam, Berna. Forthcoming. "The Power of Nonconfrontation: An Understudied Subject of Islam and Democracy" in Ibrahim, Abu-Rabi (ed.) *Challenges and Responses of Contemporary Islamic Thought: The Contributions of M. Fethullah Gülen*. Albany: SUNY Press.

———. 2006. "What Has the Secular State to Do with Islamic Revival?" in Rabo, Annika and Utas, Bo (eds.) *The Role of the State in West Asia*. Swedish Research Institute.

———. 2004a. "The Politics of Engagement between Islam and the State: Ambivalences of Civil Society," *British Journal of Sociology*, 55 (2).

———. 2004b. "A Bargain between the Secular state and Turkish Islam: Politics of Ethnicity in Kazakstan," *Nations and Nationalism*, 10 (3).

Turan, Yılmaz. 2001. *Tayyip: Kasımpaşa'dan Siyasetin Olumlu Saflarına*. Ankara: Ümit Yayınları.

Ünal, Ali. 2002. *M. Fethullah Gülen. Bir Portre Denemesi*. Istanbul: Nil Yayınları.

Voll, John O. 2003. "Fethullah Gülen: Transcending Modernity in the New Islamic Discourse" in Yavuz and Esposito (eds.) *Turkish Islam and the Secular State*. Syracuse, NY: Syracuse University Press, pp. 238–251.

Walby, Sylvia. 1996. "The 'Declining Significance' or 'Changing Forms' of Patriarchy?" in Moghadam, Valentine (ed.) *Patriarchy and Development*. Oxford: Clarendon Press.

———. 1990. *Theorizing Patriarchy*. Oxford: Blackwell.

Walzer, Michael. 1995. *Toward a Global Civil Society*. Oxford and New York: Berghahn Books.

Waylen, Georgina. 1998. "Gender, Feminism and the State: An Overview," in Randall, Vicky, and Waylen, Georgina (eds.) *Gender, Politics and the State*. London and New York: Routledge.

———. 1994. "Women and Democratization: Conceptualizing Gender Relations in Transition Politics," *World Politics*, 46.

Wedeen, Lisa. 2003. "Seeing Like a Citizen, Acting Like a State: Exemplary Events in Unified Yemen," *Comparative Studies in Society and History*, 45 (4): 680–713.

———. 1999. *Ambiguities of Domination: Politics, Rhetoric and Symbols in Contemporary Syria*. Chicago: University of Chicago Press.

Weiner, Myron, and Özbudun, Ergun. 1987. *Competetive Elections in Developing Societies*. Durham, NC: Duke University Press.

White, Jenny. 2005. "The End of Islamism? Turkey's Muslimhood Model" in Hefner (ed.) *Rethinking Muslim Politics*. Princeton, NJ: Princeton University Press.

———. 2003. "State Feminism, Modernization and the Turkish Republican Woman." *NWSA Journal*, 15 (3): 145–160.

———. 2002. *Islamist Mobilization in Turkey. A Study in Vernacular Politics*. Seattle: University of Washington Press.

———. 1996. "Civic Culture and Islam in Urban Turkey," in Hann, Chris, and Dunn, Elisabeth (eds.) *Civil Society: Challenging Western Models*. London and New York: Routledge.

Winrow, Gareth M. 1997. "Turkey and the Newly Independent States of Central Asia and the Transcaucasus," *Middle East Review of International Affairs, MERIA*, 1 (8).

Wood, Richard L. 2002. *Faith in Action: Religion, Race and Democratic Organizing in America*. Chicago: University of Chicago Press.

Yack, Bernard. 2000. "Popular Sovereignty, Nationalism and the Liberal Democratic State," presented in the workshop What Can States Do Now? at McGill University, Montreal.

———. 1999. "The Myth of the Civic Nation" in Beiner, Reinhart (ed.) *Theorizing Nationalism*. Albany: State University of New York Press.

Yavuz, Hakan. 2003a. *Islamic Political Identity in Turkey,* Oxford: Oxford University Press.

———. 2003b. "The Case of the Nur Movement" in Yavuz, Hakan, and Esposito, John (eds.) *Turkish Islam and the Secular State: The Gülen Movement*. Syracuse, NY: Syracuse University Press.

———. 2000a. "Cleansing Islam from the Public Sphere," *Journal of International Affairs*, 54 (1).

———. 2000b. "Being Modern in the Nurist Way," *ISIM Newsletter*, October, pp. 14–15.

———. 1999a. "Towards an Islamic Liberalism: The Nurist Movement and Fethullah Gülen," *Middle East Journal*, 53 (4).

———. 1999b. "Search for a New Contract: Fethullah Gülen, Virtue Party and the Kurds," *SAIS Review*, 19 (1).

———. 1996. "Yayına Dayalı Islami Söylem ve Modernlik: Nur Hareketi" (Publication-Based Islamic Discouse and Modernity) in *Uluslarası Bediüzzaman Sempozyumu* (International Symposium of Bediüzzaman). Istanbul: Yeni Asya Yayınları, pp. 641–667.

Zhovtis, E.A. 1999. "Freedom of Association and the Question of its Realization in Kazakhstan," in Ruffin, H. (ed.) *Civil Society in Central Asia*. Seattle: University of Washington Press, pp. 57–70.

Zonis, Marvin. 1971. *The Political Elite of Iran*. Princeton, NJ: Princeton University Press.

Zubaida, Sami, 2005. "Public Sphere in the Middle East," paper presented at the Center for Middle Eastern Studies at Harvard University, 3 March.

———. 2003. *Law and Power in the Islamic World.* London, New York: I. B. Taurus.

———. 2000. "Trajectories of Political Islam: Egypt, Iran and Turkey," *Political Quarterly,* 71: 60–78.

———. 1997. "Religion, the State and Democracy: Contrasting Conceptions of Society in Egypt" in Beinin, J., and Stork, J. (eds.) *Political Islam.* Berkeley, Los Angeles: University of California Press.

———. 1996. "Turkish Islam and National Identity," *Middle East Report,* April–June, pp. 10–15.

———. 1995. "Is There a Muslim Society? Ernest Gellner's Sociology of Islam," *Economy and Society,* 24 (2): 151–188.

———. 1993. *Islam, the People and the State.* London: I. B. Tauris.